HETHERINGTON, Penelope. **British paternalism and Africa, 1920–1940.** Frank Cass (dist. by Biblio Dist. Center, 81 Adams Dr., Totowa, NJ 07512), 1978. 196p bibl index. 22.50 ISBN 0-7146-3051-9

Hetherington, the author of this short and most useful study, is a member of the staff of the history department at the University of Western Australia. Her object is to lay out the beliefs and assumptions that lay behind informed opinion from far left to far right. Her sources are journals and books published in Britain between 1920 and 1940 on African affairs. After discussing the nature of these sources, the ideas are set forth under categories such as "trusteeship," social change, theories of race, development and research, education and administration. This book may well become a standard work on the topic, useful not only to those interested in the period, but also to those who would acquire an adequate background for the study of decolonization and independent Africa. Written with considerable grace the book pulls together a number of themes hitherto scattered about in the literature. The bibliography, though not exhaustive, is extensive and useful.

BRITISH PATERNALISM
AND AFRICA 1920–1940

British Paternalism and Africa

1920–1940

Penelope Hetherington

FRANK CASS

First published 1978 in Great Britain by
FRANK CASS AND COMPANY LIMITED
Gainsborough House, Gainsborough Road,
London E11 1RS, England

and in the United States of America by
FRANK CASS AND COMPANY LIMITED
c/o Biblio Distribution Centre,
81 Adams Drive, P.O. Box 327, Totowa, N.J. 07511

Copyright © 1978 Penelope Hetherington

ISBN 0 7146 3051 9

Printed in Great Britain by
Chapel River Press, Andover, Hants

For Kay Fitzgerald,
with gratitude

CONTENTS

	Page
Acknowledgements	ix
Abbreviations	xi
Introduction	xiii

PART 1

| Chapter 1 | THE WRITERS | 3 |
| Chapter 2 | THE JOURNALS | 28 |

PART 2

Chapter 3	THE MEANING OF COLONIAL TRUSTEESHIP	45
Chapter 4	THE PROBLEMS OF SOCIAL CHANGE	61
Chapter 5	THEORIES ABOUT RACE	76
Chapter 6	DEVELOPMENT AND RESEARCH	90
Chapter 7	EDUCATION	110
Chapter 8	ADMINISTRATION	131

Conclusion	154
Bibliography	159
Index	193

ACKNOWLEDGEMENTS

Most of the research for this book was done in Western Australia. Many of the books and journals were not available in Western Australian libraries so that the assistance of the Reid librarians was indispensable. I would like to acknowledge their unfailing help and advice. It was Professor Geoffrey Bolton, now of Murdoch University, Western Australia, who encouraged me to pursue my special interest. I am also indebted to Dr. David Goldsworthy of Monash University for encouragement and advice. Dr. W. Johnson of Magdalen College, Oxford, read the original manuscript and made many helpful suggestions. Lastly I would like to thank Miss Lee Carter for her work in typing and correcting the final manuscript.

ABBREVIATIONS USED IN THE
TEXT AND BIBLIOGRAPHY

J.A.S.	Journal of the African Society
J.R.A.S.	Journal of the Royal African Society
J.R.A.I.	Journal of the Royal Anthropological Institute
I.R.M.	International Review of Missions
N.S.	New Statesman
N.S. and N.	New Statesman and Nation
R.I.I.A.	Royal Institute of International Affairs

INTRODUCTION

This is a study of the beliefs and assumptions of members of the British intelligentsia who concerned themselves with British-African politics in the period between the wars. The journals and books published in Britain during this period were used as source material to discover the attitudes of politicians, missionaries, administrators and others concerning 'African' issues.

In the two decades before the Second World War the debate about the future of the African colonies still seemed to be the preserve of Europeans, anxious to influence British politics according to their own particular brand of paternalism. Some writers still used arguments about Britain's civilizing mission, familiar since the nineteenth century, while others emphasized the need for a period of reconstruction of African society, to be carried out before independence could be granted. Only the Marxist-Leninist writers, and a few of their fellow travellers, rejected doctrines which implied the necessity for continued European presence in Africa.

Nearly all the participants in this discussion wrote as though Britain had unlimited time as arbiter in the affairs of African people. For, in spite of the new emphasis on the doctrine of trusteeship after the First World War, and although Britain now controlled much more African territory, African problems did not loom large in Britain. The involvement of African forces in the war, although vitally affecting African society, had impinged very little on British society at home. There were no African troops in England, nor were there any African centres of general military importance. The post First World War period saw the growth of the West African National Congress, a middle class political protest movement, but it was not until the 1940s that African political movements began to grow on a mass basis, and undertake the kind of propaganda which would seriously influence British opinion. There was undoubtedly an upsurge of interest in African colonies after the First World War, as places offering scope for white settlement, for increased commercial activities, for investment. Yet a variety of problems confronting settlers in East Africa and capitalists in West Africa discouraged interest and enthusiasm. Except in Northern Rhodesia where large-scale copper mining began in the late 1920s there was no significant industrial development in this period. The debate about the African colonies remained on the fringes of political and intellectual life, seldom engaging attention for long. The perfunctory attention devoted to African affairs at imperial conferences underlined the fact that the bonds of Empire were those between Great Britain and her Dominions. African colonies were too undifferentiated, too little understood, too barbaric, to be embraced in quite the same way.

This study of the views of those British intellectuals who wrote about the role of the British in Africa will seek to uncover the convictions and uncertainties which lay behind the views they held. It was recognised that the adventurous days were over and that the period of administrative consolidation was well advanced. In what new roles did the British now cast themselves in Africa? How prevalent were racist views in this period and what form did they take? Were social evolutionary theories, which confidently placed Western Europe at the pinnacle of the development hierarchy, still current among educated laymen? Were nineteenth century theories of Social Darwinism eclipsed by a new twentieth century faith in social engineering? Answers to these questions will be sought in order to throw light on the over-riding paternalist faith of this inter-war period.

It seems clear that many of the attitudes and beliefs common in nineteenth century Britain survived well into the twentieth century. This study avoids all but essential references to earlier periods and concentrates on an analysis of the attitudes of that section of the intelligentsia which concerned itself with questions of politics, race and social change in Africa in the period between the two World Wars. It is not a study of what are sometimes called 'the official classes' and it makes no claims about what ideas lay behind policy decisions. Consequently, the material has not been read with a view to estimating the level of support for particular colonial policies at any given time, but rather to examine the underlying assumptions and beliefs revealed in contemporary books and articles. But because Colonial Office policy statements and Commission Reports often provoked widespread journal debate, these reports and statements were examined and are occasionally mentioned. They provided some idea of the collective wisdom of the time or the direction of thought on particular issues, whatever the original purpose or the outcome of the report might have been.

The Commission reports of this period belong in three main

groups. There were those which concerned political issues, mainly in East Africa, which held the centre of the stage in the 1920s, and had an echo in the Commission set up in 1939 to enquire into closer cooperation or association between the two Rhodesias and Nyasaland.[1] The second group were those which concerned administration rather than policy and which were appointed to enquire into or to justify administrative action in a particular colony, for which the imperial government was ultimately responsible.[2] The third group were those which concerned general developmental issues, in particular education[3] and economic growth.[4] The education issue received occasional attention throughout this period, but the interest in economic issues belonged more clearly to the 1930s. An appreciation of the economic difficulties faced by the colonies was part of the explanation for the change of policy towards colonial development which was reflected in the important Government policy statement of 1940.[5]

The inter-war period was not one of spectacular action by the Colonial Office, nor by individual colonial governments. This may be partly explained by the slow recovery of Great Britain after World War I and her economic depression of the 1930s. More important perhaps, although the period opened with public declarations about trusteeship in Africa, the full implications of this policy were only slowly recognized. During this period many old shibboleths were being discarded and new justifications found for British presence in Africa.

But already, too, Leninist supporters writing in the *Labour Monthly* were discussing the possibility of viable states being created in Africa, as a result of the unifying struggle of the so-called African colonial proletariat against their imperial oppressors. The African nationalists of the post Second World War period, whether Leninist or not, also stressed the primacy of political independence and rejected paternalism of all kinds. Part of the explanation for this unequivocal attitude may be discovered in a closer analysis of various paternalist views, whether they were preservationist or developmental in their implications.

The first section contains a broad survey of both the relevant literature and of the people who concerned themselves with 'African' questions. The second section attempts an analysis of prevailing beliefs about the questions of race; social evolution; the new emphasis on social engineering; the supposed role of education; and the current views about the role of the British administrator.

NOTES

1. *The Rhodesia-Nyasaland Royal Commission Report,* Cmd 5949, (1939).
2. For example, *The Report of the Commission into the Disturbances on the Copper Belt,* Cmd 5009, (1936).
3. These included the two Phelps-Stokes Commissions of 1921 and 1925.
4. For example, the three Pim Commission Reports on the economic situation in the High Commission Territories. See bibliography.
5. *Statement of Policy on Colonial Development and Welfare,* Cmd 6175, (1940).

PART I

CHAPTER 1

THE WRITERS

At the end of the first World War Germany's colonies in Africa were handed over to Britain, France and Belgium as mandated territories.[1] The Permanent Mandates Commission was empowered to receive regular reports concerning these (and other) mandated territories and, if necessary, to call responsible administrative officials for interrogation leading to a report to the Council and Assembly of the League of Nations. In the next twenty years the mandates system came under frequent review by those interested in the operations of the League and in international politics. The introduction of this system, according to which these European powers held the former German colonies 'in trust' for an indefinite period, also provoked a new interest in the methods and purpose of administration in Africa.[2] In Britain comparisons were now made between the administrative methods used by the British and those formerly used by Germany. Writers also began to ask what 'trusteeship' really meant and whether it was a term which could properly be used to describe British policies in all her African territories.

It was part of the European liberal tradition that every society had the right to govern itself and great emphasis was placed on this right of self-determination by Woodrow Wilson at the time of the Peace Settlement. The growing agitation for political independence in India after the war received increasing support from radical groups in Britain who were prepared to see the dismemberment of the Empire. But there were difficulties about applying this notion to the so-called 'primitive' societies of Africa, where there had been no recent history of centralized states, and whose people had been arbitrarily incorporated into a number of European colonies in the last quarter of the nineteenth century. In British territories no Africans participated directly in the administration of their people and the colonies lacked the kind of internal cohesion which seemed to be a necessary basis for self-government.

None of the writers in this period confidently expected an early end to colonial rule and the creation of independent states in Africa. A small group of Marxists who argued, like Lenin, that imperialism was the final stage of capitalism, supported the idea of a revolutionary stance by Africans. They were the fore-runners of those African nationalist leaders who would later argue that political independence was the necessary prerequisite for the economic and social development of Africa. But almost all British writers in this period believed that social and economic advance must precede political independence. There were a variety of conflicting opinions about what policies should be pursued in Africa but only the Marxists thought of involving the Africans in a consideration of their future. For this reason British attitudes in this period must be seen as overwhelmingly paternalist.

Those who wrote about African colonial issues belonged to a number of different professional groups. They included administrators, missionaries, anthropologists, writers, politicians and academics. Some had spent a large part of their working lives in Africa while others had lived and worked almost entirely in England. Some writers devoted themselves almost entirely to one particular question, such as educational policy, while others concerned themselves with a wide variety of colonial issues.

Among those administrators whose work had kept them in Africa before 1920 were Sir Harry Johnston[3] and Sir Frederick Lugard.[4] Johnston, who had been closely involved in British expansionist activity in the late nineteenth century, impinged briefly on the scene in Britain after 1920. But, in spite of his experiences as an adventurer, administrator, artist and scholar, he died in comparative obscurity in 1927. His was a remarkable career which could, perhaps, only be paralleled by that of Lugard, born in the same year and retired to England in 1920, but not to a life of obscurity. Already author of *The Rise of our East African Empire*[5] and a *Report on the Amalgamation of Northern and Southern Nigeria,* which was published as a Colonial Office report in 1920,[6] Lugard now had published what was probably the most influential book on colonial affairs in the whole inter-war period. This was *The Dual Mandate in British Tropical Africa* which ran into four editions and became 'the staple diet of reading in colonial administration for young cadet officers.'[7] Books and articles about Africa frequently contained references to the wisdom and expertise of Lord Lugard, not only on matters concerning colonial administration but on what were often referred to, more generally, as 'African questions'.[8] He was a kind of elder statesman whose approval and support was required for any new project concerning

Africa. Nor did his fame rest solely on his past record and his important book, for he wrote widely on Africa for a number of journals published during this period.

Lugard served in the Afghan war in 1879–80 and later in the Sudan and Burma campaigns of the 1880s. From 1888, when he commanded an expedition against slave traders on Lake Nyasa, until 1920, Lugard was active in military and administrative work in Africa, except for the period of five years between 1907 and 1912 when he was Governor of Hong Kong. His career in Africa ended with his position as Governor General of Nigeria from 1914 to 1919.[9]

During the period between 1920 and 1945 Lugard involved himself in British and international activities concerning Africa,[10] as well as speaking in the House of Lords on colonial issues. He also began revising his *Dual Mandate,* an activity he finally abandoned.[11] He was the British member of the Permanent Mandates Commission for the League of Nations from 1922 to 1936 and also a member of the Colonial Office Advisory Committee on Native Education in British Tropical Africa, a committee set up in 1923.[12]

Lugard stands out as one of the most remarkable men of this period, not only for his wide experience and ability, but because he provided a bridge between the nineteenth and twentieth centuries. At the beginning of the post-war period his book provided a theoretical framework for the spread of administration which, from then on, would be the main task of the British in Africa. At the same time he began a new career in British-African politics, this time from home base and free of the opposition he had encountered from the Colonial Office during his administrative career. He was the expert on African affairs, but with a faith in British paternalism, and with theories of race differences and social evolution which had their origins in the second half of the nineteenth century. He helped to bolster the conservative prejudices of administrative personnel and, by his exposition of the theory of the dual mandate, according to which British and African interests were compatible, he provided a new ideology which justified British presence in Africa.

The period under review allows for no more than a mention of Sir Charles Temple,[13] who was Lieutenant Governor of Nigeria from 1914 to 1917, and the author of the perceptive and entertaining book *Native Races and Their Rulers.*[14] Temple's work suggests a man of unorthodox views and a keen sense of humour.

Most of the governors, who were still on active service in Africa, confined themselves to superficial and often platitudinous articles which appeared in the *Journal of the African Society*. The emphasis in these articles tended to be on the 'progress' of various colonies and suggested both that the articles were solicited and that the writers felt themselves disqualified by their offical positions from taking part in any controversial debate. Some of these men subsequently wrote about this period in their autobiographical works, mostly published after 1940.[15] Some of them wrote histories or ethnological accounts of the places and peoples[16] they knew or accounts of their experiences in areas other than Africa.[17]

But not all the governors on active service were inhibited by their position from engaging in controversy. Sir Donald Cameron,[18] who entered the Civil Service of Nigeria in 1908 and rose to be Governor of Tanganyika from 1924 to 1931 and of Nigeria from 1931 to 1935, took a lively interest in the theory and practice of indirect rule. He supported indirect rule policies on the grounds that this system provided the only firm basis for education and change. Cameron was violently opposed to the scheme for Closer Union in East Africa which had the strong support of the white settlers.

In taking this stand Cameron found himself in opposition to Sir Edward Grigg[19] who had left a political career in England in 1925 to become Governor of Kenya for six years. Grigg was an enthusiastic supporter of Closer Union in East Africa and was responsible for the building of a new Government House at Nairobi which he envisaged as the future capital city of this proposed union of British territories. His views were widely publicised in conservative journals while he held the position of Governor of Kenya.

The creation in 1926 of the International Institute of African Languages and Cultures reflected the growing interest in promoting closer contacts between missionaries, administrators and anthropologists. A particularly interesting exchange concerning applied anthropology was published in the journal *Africa* in 1930. This was between Sir Philip Mitchell[20] and Bronislaw Malinowski, who was then Professor of Anthropology at London University.[21] Mitchell, who worked in various capacities in East Africa, and was Governor of Uganda from 1935 to 1940, was convinced that the anthropologist should provide the kind of information about African societies which was needed for more effective administration.[22] The administrators who wanted the help of the anthropologists were interested in maintaining political stability in societies which had been radically changed as a result of

European influences. Mitchell, for example, talked about the practical tasks in African administration, but did not question the ultimate purpose of British rule or whether it was being carried out in the interests of the Europeans or Africans. For many administrators Lugard's theory of the dual mandate had satisfactorily answered this question.

In West Africa, where there were no white settlers, British administrators were in a better position to demonstrate their commitment to the future independence of the Africans. Sir Gordon Guggisberg,[23] Governor of the Gold Coast from 1919 to 1927, was convinced that economic and social development, accompanied by the provision of Western education, would make it possible for the African people to govern themselves within the framework of Western institutions.

Next to Lugard the most influential administrator who joined the debate about African colonial policies was Lord Hailey[24] whose career had originally centred on the Indian Civil Service. Hailey joined this service in 1895 and rose to be Governor of the Punjab from 1924 to 1925 and of the United Provinces from 1925 to 1934, by which time he had spent nearly forty years in India. He then returned to England to direct the African Survey which had originated in a suggestion of General Smuts and which was financed by the Rockefeller Foundation.[25]

In the last few years of the 1930s Hailey wrote a number of journal articles, recorded talks for the B.B.C. and in 1940 toured East, West and Central Africa to study native administration. In 1936 Hailey had succeeded Lord Lugard as the British permanent member of the Mandates Commission of the League of Nations. His involvement in British-African colonial affairs in the late 1930s and early 1940s offered a curious parallel with that of Lugard in the 1920s. The publication of *An African Survey* meant that he had, in a sense, usurped Lugard's position as author of the most influential book on colonial administration. At a joint meeting of the Royal African Society and the Royal Empire Society in December 1938, the Chairman, Sir Frederick Sykes, said, referring to the survey

This monumental work places him in the foremost rank alongside Lord Lugard, Sir Harry Johnston and other students of the African problem, and it will remain for a long time the bible of colonial administrators.[26]

The survey was, in fact, widely distributed to the metropolitan and territorial personnel concerned with administration in Africa.

Like Lugard, Hailey had returned from a prolonged period in the overseas service to begin a new career in British-African politics at home.[27] Unlike Lugard he could envisage the end of British rule in Africa and was, in fact, critical of the kind of indirect rule policies which Lugard had been responsible for both introducing and defending. Hailey wanted to see a greater participation by Africans in political life. But he also advocated intervention by Britain to speed up the process of economic and social change in Africa. For him, too, the paternalist framework had to remain for the present.

Many men who had worked in the lower echelons of the African colonial service wrote books and articles about colonial issues. Administration and education policies received the greatest attention, usually from men who had retired from the service to live in England.

The administrative device of indirect rule, which was applied earlier and more completely in Nigeria than elsewhere, was celebrated by many writers in this period as though it was some kind of special art to be applied to the governing of 'backward' people. By the end of the 1930s there were critics who had begun to see that the system had inhibited the growth of African participation in central government and had perpetuated local loyalties which belonged to the pre-colonial era. One of the earliest critics of the system was J. F. J. Fitzpatrick[28] who had joined the Nigerian service in 1913, served in the Nigerian Regiment during the war, and rejoined the Nigerian service in 1919. One of his colleagues in Nigeria was the novelist, Joyce Cary[29] who left the service as a result of ill-health in 1920. Also critical of the system was G. C. B. Cotterell[30] who had served in the Royal Naval Air Service during the war and gone to Nigeria in 1920. The criticisms of W. R. Crocker[31] applied not so much to the system of indirect rule as to the colonial service as a whole. He was critical of the Colonial Office bureaucracy which, he believed, had great power and no responsibility; and he complained of the 'undistinguished' nature of much administrative practice. Crocker spent the period from 1930 to 1934 in Nigeria after which he joined the International Labour Office.

The establishment of the Colonial Office Advisory Committee on Education in British Tropical Africa in 1923 reflected an official recognition of the growing importance of this issue. Apart from Lord Lugard other members of this committee contributed to the literature about educational policies, usually in the *Journal of the African Society.* Sir James Currie,[32] one of the original members of the committee, had been Director of Education in the Sudan and Principal of Gordon College, Khartoum. Also at some time members of this committee were H. S. Scott[33] and E. R. J.

Hussey.[34] Scott had been Director of Education in the Transvaal and in Kenya before his return to England in 1935, while Hussey had worked in the Sudan, Somaliland and Uganda before becoming Director of Education in Nigeria from 1927 to 1936. After his return to England, Hussey was active as an educational adviser, lecturer and author. Also concerned with education in Africa was Dr W. Bryant Mumford[35] who had worked for the Education Department in Tanganyika in the 1920s and with the Colonial Department of the Institute of Education, University of London from 1933 to 1941. Mumford collaborated with G. St. J. Orde-Browne in the writing of *Africans Learn to be French*,[36] a survey of French colonial education policies. Orde-Browne had spent the first two decades of the century in military and administrative service and from 1926 to 1931 was Labour Commissioner in Tanganyika. He subsequently undertook special investigations into labour problems in several parts of the Empire.[37] His writings appeared throughout the 1920s and 1930s.

Undoubtedly some of the most conservative views about British policies were expressed by men who had worked in East or Central Africa from the 1890s onwards. This group included H. M. Hole,[38] R. C. F. Maugham[39] and C. W. Hobley[40] all of whom returned to England during or after the first World War. They wrote histories of Rhodesia, Nyasaland and Kenya and contributed occasionally to conservative journals. However there were men who had worked in East and Central Africa who were highly critical of British rule. The most remarkable of them was Dr Norman Leys[41] who was first employed as a medical officer with the African Lakes Company. He later worked for the medical service in Kenya and Nyasaland. After his retirement to England in 1918 he began an attack on land policies and racial discrimination in East Africa in a series of books and articles. Leys dealt most specifically with Colonial Office policies in Kenya but also mounted a wide ranging attack on the underlying assumptions of colonial rule. On the occasion of his death he was described in an obituary in the Anti-Slavery Reporter as 'one of a generation now vanishing; deeply religious, resolutely democratic, regardless of odds when right was to be defended, a friend of all down trodden folk.'[42] The pre-occupation of Leys with the issue of justice for the Africans in Kenya was shared by his friend William McGregor Ross[43] who worked for twenty three years as an engineer in the East African Protectorate (later Kenya). After his retirement he used his diaries as the basis for a book about Kenya which was critical of British colonial policies. Further criticism came from F. H. Melland[44] who went to Northern Rhodesia as a servant of the B.S.A. Company in 1901. He later served in the administrative service when Northern Rhodesia was declared a colony. Melland was a devout Christian who believed firmly in Britain's mission to bring civilization and Christianity to Africa. But like many Christians he was disturbed by the materialism of Western industrial life and admired many features of African communal society. In 1918 he had written a book attacking Germany's administrative policies in Africa implying the superiority of British methods.[45] But many articles written between the wars demonstrate that he was not uncritical of British policies and in 1931 he collaborated with T. Cullen Young to produce *African Dilemma*. This book brought together a number of articles written earlier and was published in the hope that it would lead 'to pressure by the electorate on government so that action be taken.' Melland believed that Britain could only continue to hold so much of Africa if she carried out genuine trusteeship policies. Melland began writing for British journals after his retirement in 1927 and was still contributing to several journals in the late 1930s, both under his own name and using the pseudonym 'Africanus'.

After 1920 Protestant missionary bodies, which were entrenched in many different parts of colonial Africa, faced a number of new and apparently urgent problems. The growing number of settlers in East Africa had led to a deterioration in race relations which seemed likely to affect the future of missionary activity. Many missionaries were caught up in the growing confrontation between Africans and Europeans over questions of land and labour, and the claims by white settlers for greater political autonomy. Increased European activity had also speeded up the rate of change in African societies. Many missionaries believed that the future stability of these societies, and the ultimate success of their work of evangelization, depended on more positive action by the British Government to prevent exploitation in Africa.

The missionaries in Africa could not afford to reach a position of open confrontation with the various colonial administrations and some of them may have identified more readily with their European counterparts than with the Africans. But, again, the situation in East Africa produced men who championed the cause of the African. One such was W. E. Owen[46] who had worked in Uganda for the Church Missionary Society for fourteen years before he was transferred to Kenya in 1918, where he held the post of Archdeacon of Kavirondo from 1918 to 1945. Owen encouraged the development of organs of African opinion[47] and represented the Africans in the Kenya Legislative Council. He was a republican who wanted to see the end of this system of indirect representation and the introduction of the principle of no taxation without representation. Another missionary who identified strongly with the African people was Arthur Shearly Cripps,[48] an Anglican priest and poet who spent almost all his adult life in the service of the Society for the Propagation of the Gospel in Rhodesia.

Two men who were particularly interested in education were A. G. Fraser[49] and J. W. C. Dougall.[50] Fraser collaborated with Sir Gordon Guggisberg in writing the book *The Future of the Negro* which reflected their shared view that the African people should be educated in preparation for the exercise of self-government. Dougall was the first principal of the Jeanes School at Kabete, Kenya, which trained young men and women to supervise the work of village schools in East Africa and to try to relate the work of the school to the African community.[51]

A number of missionaries who had spent many years in Africa, but had returned to England to retire, continued to interest themselves in Africa. They included Dr. Robert Laws,[52] one of the founders of the Livingstonia Mission in Nyasaland, and the Very Reverend Donald Fraser[53] who had worked at Livingstonia from 1896 to 1925. One of the earliest missionaries in Central Africa for the London Missionary Society was W. C. Willoughby[54]. In 1898 he accompanied the three African chiefs, Sebele, Bathoen and Khama on a visit to England to make a personal petition to Queen Victoria against the surrender of the Bechuanaland Protectorate to the British South Africa Company. He was responsible for the establishment of the Tiger Kloof Training Institution in Bechuanaland.

But some of the most prolific writers about Africa were men who had worked in an administrative capacity for missionary bodies, or for other organizations connected with missionary work. They included Handley D. Hooper,[55] A. M. Chirgwin[56] and Basil Mathews.[57] But, undoubtedly, the outstanding figure connected with missionary work in this period was J. H. Oldham[58] who might be more accurately called a Christian statesman. He spent a brief period working for the Y.M.C.A. in India and first became well known in England as a result of his work as one of the organizing secretaries of the World Missionary Conference held at Edinburgh in 1910. He became full time secretary of the Continuation Committee set up after this Conference and then of the International Missionary Council, into which the Committee was transformed in 1921. He was the first editor of the *International Review of Missions,* a position he held from 1912 until 1927, and was closely connected with the work of the International Institute of African Languages and Cultures, of which organization he was administrative director from 1931 until 1938. Other activities included membership of the Colonial Office Advisory Committee on Native Education from 1925 to 1931 and of the East African Commission on Closer Union which reported in 1929.

On the occasion of his retirement from the International Missionary Council in 1939, the Committee of the Council passed a resolution recording Oldham's great contribution to African affairs.[59] In particular they referred to his close cooperation with the Government and his deep and lasting influence on Colonial Office policy. Oldham took an active interest in the affairs of East Africa in the early 1920s[60] and was especially concerned over the problems of the relationship between Church and State which grew out of the issue of educational policies in Africa.[61] Oldham contributed to many journals in this period and wrote a number of books, most of them emphasizing his vital interest in the success of missionary work in Africa.

Almost equally important for his contribution to the literature of this period was Edwin W. Smith.[62] A member of the Primitive Methodist Mission, Smith worked in Northern Rhodesia for seventeen years during which time he translated the New Testament into the Ila language and built the Kasenga mission. He subsequently entered the service of the British and Foreign Bible Society for which he worked until 1939. During this period he wrote a number of books on Africa some of which were studies of African societies. His books and articles reflected his belief that the missionary and anthropologist had a great deal to learn from one another, a belief which led to his support for the establishment of the International Institute of African Languages and Cultures in 1926.

The founding of this Institute, and the publication of the journal *Africa*, provided a forum for some of the professional anthropologists of the 1930s who were interested in the effects of European influence on African societies and in the relationship between anthropologists and administrators. But much anthropological and ethnological work had already been done in Africa by both missionaries and administrators some of whom had had no formal training in this discipline. As well as Edwin Smith, who was President of the Anthropological Institute from 1933 to 1935, the missionaries in this group included John Roscoe,[63] T. Cullen Young[64] and Diedrich Westermann.[65] Westermann had worked in West Africa as a missionary from 1901 to 1908 and was later Professor of African Languages at the University of Berlin. He was also one of the two first directors of the International Institute of African Languages and Cultures. Those administrators who made remarkable contributions to the anthropological literature of this period included R. S. Rattray,[66] C. K. Meek[67] and J. H. Driberg.[68] All these men were also interested in some aspects of colonial policy in Africa.[69]

The period between the wars was remarkable for an upsurge of interest in anthropological studies. The social evolutionary theories of the earlier period were under attack at this time by the new functionalist school of anthropologists led by A. R. Radcliffe-Brown[70] and Bronislaw Malinowski[71] who began teaching at the London School of Economics in 1927. The first studies of Africa by people trained by Malinowski were those of E. E. Evans Pritchard in the Sudan and of Audrey Richards in Northern Rhodesia.[72]

Some of this group, including Malinowski himself, were caught up in a debate in the 1930s about the relationship between anthropology and administration. Malinowski obviously thought that anthropology could be of great practical value although he was reluctant to see the independence of the anthropologist compromised. On the other hand Lucy Mair[73] wrote a number of articles in which she argued for the development of a close relationship so that administration could be founded on a more 'scientific basis'.

In practice the professional anthropologists could not divorce themselves from the colonial situation in Africa. Some of them were commissioned to write reports about African societies[74] and even their independent research work provided the kind of information which was likely to be useful to the administrator.[75] The attempt to introduce the system of indirect rule, according to which administrators would operate through tribal institutions, compelled administrators to admit that they needed the help of the anthropologists. On the other hand they were not always prepared to grant them a free hand in research. The symbiotic relationship between the two groups was illustrated by the events which led to the resignation of Godfrey Wilson[76] from the position of Director of the Rhodes-Livingstone Institute in Northern Rhodesia in 1941.[77] Wilson was interested in the underlying conflicts in Northern Rhodesia society and wanted to make a close investigation of the situation which had developed on the Copper Belt. He found his research there, and at Broken Hill, inhibited by local administrators and European managers of the mining companies.[78]

This survey of administrators, missionaries and anthropologists, who interested themselves in colonial issues, illustrates certain differences between these professional groups. It is apparent that very few men at any level in the Colonial Service took an active part in writing about colonial issues until they had retired. When they did so after retirement it was generally in their capacity as 'experts', or as mild reformers rather than as serious critics. In this respect Norman Leys was the outstanding exception. There was a more critical spirit among the missionaries some of whom were moved to write articles for British journals from their posts in Africa. Their criticisms and suggestions for reforms were aimed at ending the exploitation of Africans by Europeans. Because of the importance they attached to the work of evangelization they wanted to see a more rigorous application of trusteeship principles and the maintenance of political stability. But both the missionaries and anthropologists needed to work in harmony with the British administrators in Africa because, for both professional groups, the success of their work depended on this.

Some of those already mentioned (including Lord Lugard, Lord Hailey, J. H. Oldham and Norman Leys) were deeply involved in political activities in England after 1920, either in Parliament or in pressure group activities. They now worked with other men whose careers were more clearly centred in politics or political journalism.

Some writers still justified the retention of African colonies—and even supported dreams of imperial federation[79]—on the grounds of Britain's requirements as a world power and because of the supposed superiority of her administrative methods. These were the assumptions implicit in the articles in the Round Table. They were also to be found in the writings of L. S. Amery[80] and W. G. A. Ormsby-Gore,[81] two Conservative politicians, who both held the post of Colonial Secretary at some time between the wars. Amery was Under-Secretary of State for the Colonies while Lord Milner was at the Colonial Office. During his own period as Colonial Secretary he attempted to bring about the federation of East African territories. Amery was an admirer of Joseph Chamberlain and a supporter of the ideals of the Round Table group. Ormsby-Gore was Under-Secretary of State during Amery's period at the Colonial Office and gradually moved to a pro-settler position on East Africa during his chairmanship of the Commission on Closer Union in East Africa. These were the only two men holding the position of Colonial Secretary during the inter-war period who wrote about Africa.

A tradition of critical analysis of European activities in Africa had been established by the Anti-Slavery Society in the nineteenth century and later by E. D. Morel who was responsible for a crusade against Belgian atrocities in the Congo in the first two decades of the twentieth century.[82] The colonial settlement at the Peace Conference had brought into focus the notion of trusteeship and those of liberal persuasion now wrote at length on Britain's obligations in Africa and on the role of administration.

It was Sir John Harris,[83] one of the most prolific writers on Africa, who expressed most clearly the dilemma of these liberal reformers. European impact on Africa had seriously disrupted African social systems, and grave injustices had been inflicted on many Africans by European settlers or traders over whom the administrators apparently did not wish to exercise any real control. Yet these liberal-humanitarians were convinced that Christianity and Western civilization must be brought to Africa. In his books and articles Harris argued that the situation was one which challenged the European, as a Christian, to deal justly with his fellow man. Harris had been a missionary in the Congo and had worked with Morel in the Congo Reform movement. For many years he held the position of Parliamentary Secretary for the Anti-Slavery and Aborigines Protection Society.

Harris had much in common with Charles Roden Buxton[84] who was the great grand-son of the famous Thomas Fowell Buxton. A member of the Labour Party and for some time Chairman of the Labour Party's Imperial Advisory Committee, Buxton was largely responsible for directing the attention of the Party to racial problems in East Africa.[85] During this period the *New Statesman* and *Contemporary Review* also carried a number of hard hitting articles written by Lord Olivier who had retired from the Colonial Service in 1920 but continued to be active in Labour Party politics. According to George Bernard Shaw, he, Olivier and Sidney Webb, all members of the Fabian Society, had not given much thought to the future of the colonies before 1914.[87] But the introduction of the Mandates System after the war seemed to Olivier to challenge the earlier notion of the colonies as imperial estates to be exploited by the white man. Olivier argued that this system of trusteeship, which contained only an ill-defined notion of good-will towards the African, should be backed up by responsible policies on the part of the British Government.

The Labour Party harboured people with widely differing opinions about colonial issues in this period. Some members of Parliament who took an interest in Africa, including Major A. G. Church,[88] Dr Haden-Guest[89] and Dr Drummond Shiels,[90] held fairly conservative views. But the work of J. A. Hobson in 1902,[91] and of his friend H. L. Brailsford,[92] laid the basis for a radical critique of colonial rule after the first World War. Brailsford was the author of *The War of Steel and Gold,* which was published in 1914, and was associated with the founding of the Union of Democratic Control which aimed at bringing an end to secret diplomacy. It was Leonard Woolf,[93] who joined the Labour Party and the Fabian Society during the war, who applied the ideas of these men to the colonial Empire in Africa. Woolf was the secretary of the Labour Party's Imperial Advisory Committee from 1918 to 1939[94] and he and Roden Buxton were responsible for the pamphlet *The Empire in Africa: Labour's Policy* published in 1920[95] but not adopted by the party until 1926.[96] This programme argued for an extension of the Mandates System to the whole of Africa, for an open-door policy in the African colonies and for the recognition that self-government for the Africans was the ultimate aim of the Labour Party. Woolf pointed out that two contradictory policies were being pursued in East and West Africa and emphasized the importance of land rights and education.

Throughout the 1920s and 1930s Norman Leys, also a member of the Labour Party's Imperial Advisory Committee, kept up his attack on settler policies in East Africa. In the 1930s two men whose experiences had mostly been in South Africa joined in the debate. Leonard Barnes[97] lived in South Africa from 1925 to 1932 partly as a settler and partly as a journalist. Several of his books concerned his experiences in South Africa but in 1935 he wrote *Duty of Empire* which established him as a strong supporter of radical changes in colonial office policy. In this book Barnes spoke of the "astonishing contrast between West Africa on the one hand and South and East Africa on the other"[98] and argued that the difference lay in the alienation of African land and the political ascendancy of the white settlers. Both he and W. M. Macmillan[99] hoped to persuade the Colonial Office that serious injustices were being inflicted on the native population of East Africa; that the future political development of independent African states depended on the educated Africans rather than on tribal chiefs; and that the future independence of the colonies should be accepted as the basis for Colonial Office policy.

W. M. Macmillan returned to England in 1933 after a long period as Professor of History at Witwatersrand University in South Africa. During the 1930s he travelled in Africa and also enquired into the disturbances in the West Indies, which became the basis for his book *Warning from the West Indies: A Tract for Africa and the Empire.* In this book Macmillan emphasized the importance of developing the colonies in readiness for independence, a theme which he further elaborated in a pamphlet called *Democratise the Empire! a policy for Colonial change* which was published in 1941.[100] Macmillan believed that the prevailing *laissez-faire* policy which was supported by those who opposed industrialization, was at the root of the trouble in Africa. He referred to the 'anaemic' doctrine of trusteeship and demanded a clear statement that self-government was the eventual goal in Africa.

The late 1930s also saw the development of a new interest in the African colonies amongst members of the Fabian Society. The South African born economist, Rita Hinden,[101] had worked in Palestine during the 1930s but in 1940 she was largely responsible for the formation of the Fabian Colonial Bureau. She became the Secretary of the organization while A. Creech-Jones,[102] a Labour M.P. who was later to become Secretary of State for the Colonies, became the Chairman.

There were, in Britain, a few close followers of Lenin whose work on imperialism had added a new dimension to Marxist theory. The publication of the *Labour Monthly* from 1921 onwards gave several members of the Communist Party an opportunity to write on colonial issues. The journal was edited by Palme Dutt[103] and in the 1930s contained articles written by the West Indian George Padmore[104] and by Jomo Kenyatta.[105] Padmore was critical of white controlled bodies which pontificated about Africa and wanted to see the African people consulted about their future.[106] Kenyatta came to England to represent the Kikuyu Central Association and while there made contact with the League Against Imperialism, an international communist organization set up in Brussels in 1928.[107] The first chairman was A. Fenner Brockway,[108] later an important figure in British-African politics, but at this time particularly interested in Indian politics.

Some of the most prolific writers on Africa in this period were academics who wrote scholarly books about Africa and also contributed to well-known journals. Two important British Empire historians were Sir Charles Lucas[109] and Reginald Coupland.[110] Lucas served the Royal Colonial Institute (later the Royal Empire Society) in a number of capacities from 1907 onwards and promoted his conservative views in the journal *United Empire*. Coupland was Beit Professor of Colonial History at Oxford from 1920 to 1948. His was an important influence on African colonial affairs because he was largely responsible for the special courses for future colonial administrators which were begun at Oxford in 1926.[111]

Also involved in the teaching programme of the colonial civil service was Margery Perham[112] who became a don at Oxford in 1924. By 1940 she was regarded as the 'recognised academic authority on colonial problems',[113] a reputation she built up through her teaching, her writing and her travels in Africa.

There were two other academics who were particularly interested in the African colonies but who were not historians. Julian Huxley,[114] British biologist and writer, undertook a tour of the African colonies on behalf of the Colonial Office Advisory Committee on Native Education, at the completion of which he wrote *African View* and a variety of journal articles on colonial issues. The particular interest of A. Victor Murray[115] was African education. His teaching posts were in England but he held a travelling research fellowship in 1927 which took him to Africa. He was educational advisor to the Christian Council of Nigeria in 1932 and lectured in South Africa in 1934.

A number of men who had served in the Indian Civil Service or who had had long experience in India exercised an important influence on British attitudes to Africa between the wars. Lord Hailey is the most outstanding example but Sir Alan Pim,[116] who had had a distinguished career in the Indian Civil Service from 1894 to 1930, also turned his attention to Africa after his retirement. There were three men whose views on education were important. Sir Valentine Chirol[117] did not write about Africa, but his books on India influenced those who were trying to reshape the education system in Africa. Arthur Mayhew[118] who had worked in the Indian educational service from 1903–1922 was joint secretary of the Advisory Committee on Education in the Colonies from 1929–1939. William Jesse,[119] who had spent 20 years as Headmaster of Meerut College in India and published pamphlets on Indian education, was Headmaster of Kenton College in Kenya from 1924–1929 and in the 1930s wrote several articles on colonial affairs in Africa.

Two other men whose experiences were primarily in India also took an interest in special aspects of life in Africa. C. F. Strickland,[120] whose special interest lay in promoting cooperative enterprises, had worked in the Indian Civil Service for 25 years and after his retirement turned his attention to Africa. Charles F. Andrews[121] was a missionary who had gone to Delhi in 1904 as a member of the Cambridge Brotherhood. He was primarily interested in Indian nationalism and lived in India, but he also visited Kenya on two occasions and was highly critical of colonial policies as they affected Indians in Kenya.

Although this study concentrates on writers who were born in

Britain and who either worked there or served in some capacity in the British Empire, it is important to recognise that there were several outsiders whose books were published in the period between the wars and whose work was well known in England. The study of colonial affairs prepared by George Louis Beer[122] for the Colonial Section of the American Commission to Negotiate Peace, was published in 1923[123] and in 1928 the massive study of Raymond Buell[124] appeared. This two-volume report called *The Native Problem in Africa* attempted

> to set forth the problems which have arisen out of the impact of primitive people with an industrial civilization, and to show how and to what extent these problems are being solved by the governments concerned.[125]

This vast and detailed work, which included many useful appendices and a valuable bibliography for each territory, covered the British, French and Belgian territories as well as South Africa and Liberia. The book was presented as a Report to the Committee of International Research of Harvard University and Radcliffe College which had provided the grant for Buell's fifteen months investigation abroad.

Two other Americans are important for their interest and involvement in British-African affairs. Thomas Jesse Jones[126] was the Educational Director of the Phelps Stokes Fund from 1913 to 1946[127] and in the 1920s was Chairman of the Phelps Stokes Education Commission which investigated education in Africa.[128] John Merle Davis[129] was the editor and part author of the book *Modern Industry and the African* published under the auspices of the Department of Social and Industrial Research of the International Missionary Council.[131] This work was the result of an investigation by a group of six people[132] into the effects of the Copper Mines of Central Africa 'upon Native Society and the work of Christian Missions'.

It is apparent that investigations and surveys about what were often called African 'problems' were becoming fashionable in the 1930s. The most famous survey was that carried out by Lord Hailey and is generally regarded as having originated in a suggestion made by General Smuts,[133] who delivered the Rhodes Memorial Lectures at Oxford in 1929. These lectures were published in *Africa and Some World Problems* in 1930.

The writers of the 1920s were still bemused by notions of Britain's civilizing mission and the small voice of criticism was stilled by the authoritative tones of Lord Lugard. But by the late 1930s the volume of criticism had swelled to a chorus. The theory of the dual mandate, which had earlier been surrounded by an aura of respectability, was now widely regarded with suspicion while the policy of indirect rule was under attack for a variety of reasons. It was now recognised that there were two conflicting policies being pursued in East and West Africa and that Colonial Office policy lacked clear direction. Many well meaning people believed that future policies must be based on knowledge and research.

A new form of paternalism was now apparent. This time it was led by the reformers who stressed the importance of education, development and preparation for eventual independence. It was Lord Hailey who distilled these views into respectable form and provided a new orthodoxy which would justify British presence in Africa.

NOTES

1. Article 22 of the Covenant of the League of Nations dealt with the status of dependencies which had formerly belonged to Germany and Turkey. Togoland was divided between Britain and France, most of the Cameroons went to France but a strip adjoining Nigeria went to Britain while German East Africa was divided between Britain (Tanganyika) and Belgium (Ruanda-Urundi).
2. See bibliography for the work of Alfred Zimmern, Norman Angell, Norman Bentwich and L. S. Amery.
3. Harry Hamilton Johnston (1858–1927). G.C.M.G. cr. 1901. King's College, London Royal Academy of Arts 1876–80. See R. A. Oliver, *Harry Johnston and the Scramble for Africa* (London, 1957) and Alex Johnston, 'Sir Harry Johnston', *J.A.S.* XXVII (1927–1928), pp. 1–6.
4. Frederick Dealtry Lugard (1858–1945). First Baron Abinger.
5. Published in 1893 by Blackwood.
6. Cmd. 468, 1920. This report has since been published as a book. See A. H. M. Kirk-Greene (Ed.), *Lugard and the Amalgamation of Nigeria* (London, 1961).
7. See J. M. Lee, *Colonial Development and Good Government* (London, 1967), p. 43, for the view that Lugard's book had wide influence in this period.
8. See I. F. Nicolson, *The Administration of Nigeria, 1900–1960* (London, 1969), for an account of how Lord and Lady Lugard promoted this notion.
9. For a detailed account of Lugard's life see Margery Perham, *The Life of Frederick Dealtry Lugard*, 2 vols. (London, 1956, 1960).
10. See Margery Perham, 'Lord Lugard: a preliminary evaluation', *Africa,* 20 (1950), pp. 228–293, for a brief and useful survey of this involvement.
11. See J. M. Lee, *Colonial Government,* p. 45, for an account of the revision he had done and of his decision to abandon it as an 'anachronism'.
12. This committee was established partly as a result of the findings of the Phelps-Stokes Commission on Education. It was later called the Advisory Committee on Education in the Colonies.
13. Charles Lindsay Temple (1871–1929). C.M.G. 1910.
14. This book was published in Cape Town in 1918 and republished by Cass in 1968, with an introduction by M. Hiskett.

15. See Sir Henry Heskeith Bell, *Glimpses of a Governor's Life* (London, 1946); Sir Alan Burns, *Colonial Civil Servant* (London, 1949); Sir Philip Mitchell, *African Afterthoughts* (London, 1954); Sir Charles Dundas, *African Crossroads* (London, 1955). The exception was the work of Sir Donald Cameron, *My Tanganyika Service and Some Nigeria* (London, 1939).

16. Sir Herbert R. Palmer, *Sudanese Memoirs* (Lagos, 1928), *A Sudanese Kingdom* (London, 1931), *The Bornu of the Sahara and Sudan* (London, 1936); Sir Alan Burns, *A History of Nigeria* (London, 1929) and *A History of the British West Indies* (London, 1954).

17. Sir Hugh Clifford wrote several books based on his experiences in Malaya, as well as *German Colonies* (London, 1918) and *The Gold Coast Regiment in the East African Campaign* (London, 1920).

18. Donald Charles Cameron (1872–1948). G.C.M.G. cr. 1932. Educated at Rathmines School, Dublin. Entered the West Indian Civil Service, British Guiana 1890–1904. Mauritius 1904–7. Transferred to the Nigerian Colonial Service, 1908.

19. Edward William Macleay Grigg (1879–1955). First Baron Altrincham. New College, Oxford. Journalist 1903–1913. Grenadier Guards 1914–1918. Military Secretary to Prince of Wales, 1919. Private Secretary to Lloyd George 1921–22. M.P. (Liberal), 1922–25. Governor of Kenya, 1925–31. M.P. (Conservative) 1933–45.

20. Philip Euen Mitchell (1890–1964). G.C.M.G. cr. 1947. Trinity College, Oxford. Assistant Resident, Nyasaland 1912. K.A.R. 1915. A.D.C. and Private Secretary to Acting Governor, Nyasaland 1918–19. Administrative posts in Uganda and Tanganyika 1919–1935. Governor of Uganda 1935–1940.

21. See this chapter, footnote 71.

22. For an analysis of the views expressed by Mitchell and Malinowski, see Wendy James, 'The Anthropologist as Reluctant Imperialist' in Talal Asad (Ed.), *Anthropology and the Colonial Encounter* (London, 1973).

23. Gordon Guggisberg (1869–1930). K.C.M.G. cr. 1922. Royal Military Academy, Woolwich. R.E. 1889. Special employment by the Colonial Office as a surveyor in West Africa. Surveyor General in Nigeria 1910–1914. Governor of the Gold Coast 1919–1927. See R. A. Wraith, *Guggisberg* (London, 1967).

24. William Malcolm Hailey (1872–1969). First Baron cr. 1947. Corpus Christi College, Cambridge. Indian Civil Service 1895–1934.

25. See ch. 6 for further details about this Survey. The book *An African Survey* was published in London in 1938, and excited considerable comment.

26. Reported in *United Empire*, new series, XXX (1939), p. xi.

27. Lord Hailey continued to play an important part in the early 1940s. He toured East, West and Central Africa to study native administration in 1940. Chief of Economic Mission to the Belgian Congo in 1940. Chairman of the School of Oriental and African Studies, 1941. Chairman of the Colonial Research Advisory Committee, 1942.

28. Joseph Frederick John Fitzpatrick (1882–   ). Educated at Ratcliff's College, Leicester. Served in Boer War. Passed in all Tropical African Service Courses in 1913.

29. Joyce Cary (1888–1957). Trinity College, Oxford. Wrote a number of novels with an African setting. Wrote a political tract about Africa in 1941. See M. Mahood, *Joyce Cary's Africa* (London, 1964).

30. George Cecil Blencowe Cotterell (1897–   ). Educated at Shrewsbury School. Royal Naval Air Service 1916–1919. Nigerian Service 1920.

31. Walter Russell Crocker (1902–   ). Balliol College, Oxford and Stanford University, U.S.A. Nigerian Service 1930–34. I.L.O. 1935.
32. James Currie (1868–1937). K.C.M.G. cr. 1933. After 1922 Director of the Empire Cotton Growing Corporation.
33. Herbert Septimus Scott (1873–1952). Kt. cr. 1948. Hertford College, Oxford. Inspector of Schools, Transvaal, 1902. Secretary Transvaal Education Department 1911. Director of Education, Transvaal 1924. Director of Education, Kenya 1928.
34. Eric Robert James Hussey (1885–1958). C.M.G. cr. 1933. Hertford College, Oxford. Heath Clark Lecturer (joint), University of London 1939. Member of governing body of School of Oriental and African Studies, 1939.
35. William Bryant Mumford (1899–1951). Attended Royal Naval College, Dartmouth and St. John's College, Cambridge. Education Department, Tanganyika, 1923. Worked at this time for a doctorate at Toronto University. Carnegie Research Fellow at Yale. Lecturer and Professor, Colonial Department of Institute of Education, London University, 1933–1941. Secretary General of the U.N. Information Organization 1941–1951.
36. Granville St. John Orde-Browne (1883–1947), Kt. cr. 1947. Attended Royal Military Academy Woolwich. R.A. 1902. Adviser on colonial labour to Secretary of State 1938.
37. In Northern Rhodesia, 1937. In the West Indies, 1938. In West Africa, 1939. In the Far East, 1941.
38. Hugh Marshall Hole (1865–1941). Balliol College, Oxford. Entered B.S.A. Co. 1890. Various civil service posts in Southern Rhodesia and Northern Rhodesia, 1891–1914. Rejoined B.S.A. Co. in London 1914.
39. Reginald Charles Fulke Maugham (1866–1956). Educated privately. Secretary to Nyasaland Administration 1894. Consular posts in various parts of Africa 1896–1928.
40. Charles William Hobley (1867–1947). C.M.G. cr. 1904. Educated Birmingham University. B.S.A. Co. 1890. Various administrative positions in East African Protectorate 1894–1921.
41. Norman MacLean Leys (1875–1944). A medical graduate of Glasgow University 1900.
42. Obituary. *Anti-Slavery Reporter and Aborigines Friend*, October, 1944.
43. William McGregor Ross (1878–1940). University College, Liverpool. Director of Public Works, East African Protectorate (later Kenya) 1905–1923.
44. Frank Hulme Melland (1879–1939). Merton College, Oxford. Went to Africa in 1901 with the B.S.A. Co. Later a magistrate in the Colony of Northern Rhodesia. Spent 26 years in Africa.
45. *The Prussian Lash in Africa*, (London, 1918).
46. Walter Edwin Owen (1879–1945). Attended Islington Theological College. Ordained 1904. Worked in Uganda 1904–18 and in Kenya 1918–1945.
47. He founded and led the Kavirondo Tax Payers' Association.
48. Arthur Shearly Cripps (1869–1952). Trinity College, Oxford. Anglican missionary priest in Rhodesia, 1901–1953. See Douglas V. Steere, *God's Irregular: Arthur Shearly Cripps* (London, 1973).
49. Alexander Gordon Fraser (1873–1962). Trinity College, Oxford. Ordained 1914. Worked for Church Missionary Society in Uganda 1900–1903. Principal Trinity College, Kandy, Ceylon 1904–24. Principal Achimota College, Gold Coast 1924–35. Chairman of the C.M.S. Commission on Village Education, 1919, which reported to C.M.S. 1920.
50. James Watson Cunningham Dougall. Church of Scotland Mission. First Principal of Jeanes School, Kabete, Kenya.

51. The Anna T. Jeanes Foundation was established in 1907 by an American Quaker woman of that name to assist elementary schools for Negroes in the Southern States of U.S.A. Some of the money was later used for establishing schools in Africa. See C. P. Groves, *The Planting of Christianity in Africa 1914–54*, vol. IV (London, 1958).

52. Robert Laws (1851–1934). Aberdeen University, Anderson's University, Glasgow. Edinburgh Theological College. A medical missionary who went to Nyasaland with the Free Church Mission in 1875.

53. Donald Fraser (1870–1933). Glasgow Free Church Theological College. Livingstonia Free Church Mission 1896–1925. Moderator of the Free Church of Scotland 1922–33. See Agnes R. Fraser, *Donald Fraser of Livingstonia* (London, 1934).

54. William Charles Willoughby (1857–1938). In South Africa and Bechuanaland for L.M.S. from 1882–1883 and from 1892–1917. Professor of African Missions at Hartford Seminary, Connecticut 1919–1931.

55. Handley D. Hooper (1891–1966). Queen's College Cambridge. Church Missionary Society, Kaluhia, 1916–1926. Africa Secretary for C.M.S. 1926–1949.

56. Arthur Mitchell Chirgwin (1885–1966). University College, London University. Richmond Theological College 1907–1910. Pastoral work 1910–1920. Assistant Home Secretary, London Missionary Society, 1920. Foreign Secretary L.M.S., 1929. General Secretary L.M.S., 1932–50.

57. Basil Mathews (1879–1951). Mansfield College, Oxford. Editorial Secretary, L.M.S. 1910–1919. Subsequently journalist and writer.

58. Joseph Houldsworth Oldham (1874–1969) C.B.E. 1941. Trinity College, Oxford. Secretary of Student Christian Movement 1896–1897. Secretary Y.M.C.A., Lahore, India 1897–1900.

59. See *International Review of Missions*, XXVIII (1939) in Quarterly notes at the end of the volume.

60. See Roland Oliver, *The Missionary Factor in East Africa* (London, 1952), p. 250 f.

61. *Ibid.*, p. 266 f. for an account of the invitation to Oldham to submit suggestions for a modus vivendi between Government and missions on education. For further details of Oldham's career see George Bennett, "Paramountcy to Partnership: J. H. Oldham and Africa", *Africa*, 30 (1960), pp. 356–60.

62. Edwin W. Smith (1876–1957). Educated Enfield College, York. Primitive Methodist Mission, Rhodesia, 1898–1915. Rome Secretary for British and Foreign Bible Society 1916. Later Secretary for Western Europe and Editorial Secretary, British and Foreign Bible Soceity.

63. John Roscoe (1861–1932). Attended C.M.S. Theological College, Islington. Missionary in Uganda for C.M.S., 1884. Retired from Africa in 1909. Honorary degree from Cambridge, 1910.

64. T. Cullen Young (1880–1955). Attended Glasgow Academy. Theological Studies at Glasgow and New College, Edinburgh. Livingstonia Mission, 1905–1931. Deputy Secretary and Home Superintendent of Missionary Tract Society 1931–40. General Secretary for the United Society for Christian Literature 1940–46. See the introduction by Ian Nance to the 1970 Cass edition of *Notes on the History of the Tumbuka-Kamanga Peoples* written by T. Cullen Young.

65. Diedrich Westermann (1875–1956). Educated at Basel and Tübingen. Missionary in West Africa 1900–08. Lecturer in African Languages, Univer-

sity of Berlin, 1909. Professor of African Languages, University of Berlin from 1920. Travelled extensively in Africa.

66. Robert Sutherland Rattray (1881–1938). Exeter College, Oxford. Barrister at Law. D. Anth. (Oxon.). Service with African Lakes Company, British Central Africa 1902–7. Entered colonial service 1907. Seconded for anthropological work 1921.

67. Charles Kingsley Meek (1885–1965). Brasenose College, Oxford. Joined Nigerian colonial service 1912. Anthropological officer for Northern Provinces 1924. Retired 1933. Heath Clark Lecturer, London University, 1939. Senior Research Fellow, Oxford, 1943. Lecturer in Anthropology, Oxford, 1947.

68. Jack Herbert Driberg. Colonial Servant and trained ethnologist. Worked in Uganda and Sudan Political Service. Later lecturer in Ethnology at Cambridge.

69. See *An African Survey*, p. 50 ff., for details of the appointment of government ethnologists and anthropologists to various colonial services in Africa.

70. A. R. Radcliffe-Brown (1881–1955).

71. Bronislaw Malinowski (1884–1942). Educated Polish University, Cracow. Fieldwork in Australia and New Guinea, 1914–1918. Professor of Anthropology, University of London, 1927 (tenable at the London School of Economics). See R. Firth (Ed.), *Man and Culture: An Evaluation of the work of Bronislaw Malinowski* (London, 1957).

72. See A. I. Richards, "Practical Anthropology in the Lifetime of the International African Institute", *Africa,* XIV (1944), p. 290–300.

73. Lucy Philip Mair (1901–   ). Newnham College, Cambridge. Worked as lecturer, reader and professor of anthropology at the London School of Economics, 1927–1963.

74. The anthropologists I. Schapera, M. Read, A. I. Richards and P. J. Peristiany were commissioned to prepare reports for the African Survey.

75. During the earlier period the administrators had got into difficulties because of misconceptions about the nature of African political systems and land tenure.

76. Godfrey Baldwin Wilson (1908–1944). Educated Oxford. Attended Malinowski's seminars at L.S.E. Fieldwork in Rhodesia. Director of Rhodes-Livingstone Institute 1937–41.

77. Established in 1937.

78. See Richard Brown, 'Godfrey Wilson and the Rhodes-Livingstone Institute' in Talal Asad (Ed.), *Anthropology and the Colonial Encounter.*

79. See Edward Grierson, *The Imperial Dream: the British commonwealth and Empire, 1775–1969,* (London, 1972), Ch. 11, p. 152–158.

80. Leopold Stennet Amery (1873–1955). Balliol College, Oxford, Times Correspondent during Boer War. M.P. (Cons.), 1911–1945. Under Secretary of State for the Colonies, 1919–1921. First Lord of the Admiralty, 1922–24. Secretary of State for the Colonies, 1924–29.

81. William George Arthur Ormsby-Gore (1885–1964). 4th Earl of Harlech. New College, Oxford. M.P. (Cons.), 1910–1938. First British representative on the Permanent Mandates Commission. Under Secretary of State for the Colonies 1922–24 and 1924–29. Post Master General 1931. First Commissioner of Works 1931–6. Secretary of State for the Colonies 1936–38. High Commissioner for the U.K. in South Africa, 1941–44.

82. E. D. Morel (1873–1924). See W. R. Louis and J. Stengers, *E. D. Morel's History of the Congo Reform Movement* (Oxford, 1968).

83. John Hobbis Harris (1874–1940). Kt. cr. 1933. Missionary in the Congo early

in 20th Century. Associated with Congo Reform Movement. M.P. (Lib.) 1923–24. Secretary to the Anti-Slavery and Aborigines Protection Society.

84. Charles Roden Buxton (1875–1942). Trinity College, Oxford. Treasurer of the I.L.P. 1924–27. Principal of Morley College for Working People. See Victoria de Bunsen, *Charles Roden Buxton: A Memoir* (London, 1947).

85. See R. G. Gregory, *Sidney Webb and East Africa*, (Berkeley, 1962), p. 84.

86. Sydney Olivier (1859–1943). First Baron cr. 1924. Corpus Christi College, Oxford. Entered Colonial Office, 1882. A wide variety of posts including Governor of Jamaica, 1907–13. Retired from Colonial Service, 1920. Secretary to Fabian Society, 1886–90. M.P. (Lab.). Secretary of State for India 1924–25.

87. See M. Olivier (Ed.), *Sydney Olivier. Letters and Selected Writings* (London, 1948) which includes an introduction by George Bernard Shaw.

88. Archibald George Church (1886–1954). University College, London. M.P. (Lab.) 1923–24 and 1929–31. Labour member of the East African Commission of 1924. A member of the Colonial Office Advisory Committee on Education in the Colonies 1925–1942.

89. L. Haden-Guest (1877–1960). First Baron cr. 1950. Owen's College, Manchester and London Hospital. M.P. (Lab.) 1923–27, 1937–45 and 1945–50.

90. Drummond Shiels (1881–1953). Edinburgh University. M.P. (Lab.) 1924–31. Under Secretary of State for India Office 1929. Under Secretary of State for Colonial Office 1929–31.

91. John Atkinson Hobson (1858–1940). Lincoln College, Oxford. Author of *Imperialism: a Study* published in 1902.

92. Henry Noel Brailsford (1873–1958). Glasgow University. Wrote regularly for the *Nation* from 1907. Editor of *New Leader,* 1922–1926. Joined staff of *New Statesman and Nation* in the 1930s and remained chief leader writer until 1946.

93. Leonard Woolf (1880–1969). Trinity College, Cambridge. Ceylon Civil Service 1904–11. Founded Hogarth Press, 1917. Editor of *International Review,* 1919. Editor of the International Section of *Contemporary Review,* 1920–21. Literary Editor, the *Nation,* 1923–1930. Joint Editor, *Political Quarterly,* 1931–59. See Leonard Woolf, *Downhill All the Way* (London, 1967).

94. Nine committees were set up after 1918 to advise the Labour Party on policy. Woolf was Secretary of the Advisory Committee on International Questions and of the Imperial Advisory Committee.

95. See Leonard Woolf, *Downhill All the Way,* p. 233.

96. Then called *Labour and the Empire: Africa.*

97. Leonard Barnes (1895–   ). University College, Oxford. Entered Colonial Office, 1921. Lived in South Africa 1925–32. Worked for the *Natal Witness, Cape Times* and *Johannesburg Star.* Investigated social conditions in the High Commission Territories of Basutoland, Swaziland and Bechuanaland, 1930–31.

98. See *Duty of Empire,* p. 141.

99. William Miller Macmillan (1885–   ). Merton College, Oxford. Lecturer, Rhodes University College, 1911. Professor of History, University of Witwatersrand, 1917–1933. Sometime research fellow at All Souls College, Oxford. Heath Clark Lecturer, University of London, 1939. A member of the Labour Party's Imperial Advisory Committee. See L. C. Sutherland, 'William Miller Macmillan, an Appreciation' in K. Kirkwood (Ed.), *St. Antony's Papers,* No. 21 (London, 1969).

100. This was one of a number of pamphlets in a series called *The Democratic Order*, which was edited by Francis Williams and published by Kegan Paul.
101. Rita Hinden (1909–1972). Born South Africa. Attended Cape Town University, Liverpool University and L.S.E. Lived in Palestine during part of the 1930s. Full-time Secretary of the Fabian Colonial Bureau 1940–50. Editor of *Socialist Commentary*, 1950–72.
102. Arthur Creech-Jones (1891–1964). National Secretary, Transport and General Workers' Union, 1919–1929. Organizing Secretary, Workers' Travel Association, 1929–1939. M.P. (Lab.) 1935–64. Secretary of State for the Colonies, 1946–50.
103. Rajani Palme Dutt (1896–1974). Balliol College, Oxford. Expelled from Oxford, 1917, a fortnight before the Bolshevik Revolution for conducting Marxist propaganda against 'imperialist wars'. Editor *Labour Monthly* 1921–74; *Workers' Weekly*, 1922–24; *Daily Worker*, 1936–38.
104. George Padmore (1902–1959). Real name Malcolm Ivan Meredith Nurse. Born Trinidad. Educated in America. Active in Communist Party in America and Europe. Moved to London, 1935. Later an advisor to Nkrumah in Ghana. See *Black Revolutionary* (London, 1967).
105. Jomo Kenyatta (1890–   ). First went to England as Secretary of the Kikuyu Central Association. Spent most of the 1930s in England and Europe. First Prime Minister of Kenya. See J. Murray Brown, *Kenyatta* (London, 1972), especially chapters 10–15.
106. See *Black Revolutionary*, p. 84.
107. This organization was established in 1928 and collapsed in 1935 with the creation of the Popular Front in Europe.
108. Archibald Fenner Brockway (1888–   ). Baron cr. 1964. Politician, Pacifist, Internationalist. M.P. (I.L.P. and later Labour Party) from 1929. Chairman, League against Imperialism, for short period in 1928. Chairman British Centre for Colonial Freedom, 1942–47. First Chairman of Congress of Peoples Against Imperialism, 1948–
109. Charles Prestwood Lucas (1853–1931). K.C.B. cr. 1912. Balliol College, Oxford. Historian of the British Empire.
110. Reginald Coupland (1884–1952). Trinity College, Oxford. Held various posts at Oxford from 1907–1948. Member of the Royal Commission on the Superior Civil Services of India, 1923. Advisor, Burma Round Table Conference 1931. Member of the Palestine Royal Commission 1936–37. Member of Stafford Cripps Mission to India 1942.
111. Called the Tropical African Service Courses—set up at both Oxford and Cambridge in 1926. See R. Furse, *Aucuparius: Recollections of a Recruiting Officer* (London, 1962).
112. Margery Perham (1895–   ). St. Hugh's College, Oxford. First visited Africa in 1923.
113. See R. Heussler, *Yesterday's Rulers*, p. 134–5.
114. Julian Huxley (1887–1974). Lecturer in Zoology at King's College, London, 1923–35. A prolific writer on the biological sciences.
115. Albert Victor Murray (1887–1967). Magdalen College, Oxford. Secretary of S.C.M., 1913–22. Lecturer in education at Birmingham (Selly Oak Colleges), 1922–33. Professor of Education, University College Hull, 1933–45.
116. Alan William Pim (1870–1958). Headed the Economic Commission investigating Swaziland and Zanzibar 1932, Bechuanaland 1933, British Honduras 1934, Basutoland 1935, Kenya 1936, Northern Rhodesia 1937.
117. Valentine Chirol (1852–1929). Kt. cr. 1912. Clerk in the Foreign Office

1872–76. Travelled extensively in India. Director of Foreign Department of the *Times,* 1899–1912. Author of *Indian Unrest* (London, 1926), *India, Old and New* (London, 1921) and *India* (London, 1926).

118. Arthur Innes Mayhew (1878–1948). C.M.G. cr. 1936. New College, Oxford. Indian Educational Services, 1903–22. Master of Eton College 1922–28, Secretary of Colonial Office Advisory Committee on Education in the Colonies 1929–39.

119. William Jesse (1870–1945). Selwyn College, Cambridge. Headmaster Meerut College 1903–23. Kenton College, Kenya 1924–29.

120. C. F. Strickland (1881–1962). New College, Oxford. Indian Civil Service 1905–1930.

121. Charles F. Andrews (1871–1940). Pembroke College, Cambridge. Lived in India. Supporter of Gandhi and author of books about Gandhi.

122. George Louis Beer (1872–1920). Born and educated in America. Historian. Chief of Colonial Division of American Commission to Negotiate Peace, Paris, 1918–19.

123. George Louis Beer, *African Questions at the Peace Conference,* Edited by Louis Herbert Gray (New York, Macmillan, 1923).

124. Raymond Leslie Buell (1896–1946). Educated at University of Grenoble, France and at Princeton and Miami Universities. Held a variety of academic posts in America on international affairs, about which he wrote widely.

125. See the Preface of *The Native Problem in Africa.*

126. Thomas Jesse Jones (1873–   ). Born in Wales. Went to America in 1884. Studied at Washington and Lee University, the Union Theological Seminary, New York and Columbia University. Joined the Hampton Institute.

127. For information concerning this fund see Ch. 7.

128. See ch. 7.

129. John Merle Davis (1875–1960). Educated Oberlin College, Hartford Theological Seminary and in Europe. Director of Department of Social and Economic Research and Counsel, International Missionary Council 1930–1946.

130. Published in London by Macmillan, 1933.

131. This organization was set up to provide information about nature of social and economic change affecting Christian mission work.

132. J. Merle Davis; Charles W. Coulter (Professor of Sociology, Ohio Wesleyan University); Leo Marquard (History Master, Gray College School, Johannesberg); Ray E. Phillips (missionary and welfare worker, Johannesberg); E. A. G. Robinson (Lecturer in Economics at the University of Cambridge); Mabel Shaw (Principal, Livingstonia Girls' School, Mbereshi).

133. Jan Christian Smuts (1870–1950). Field Marshall. Educated at Stellenbosch. P.M. of South Africa 1919–24 and 1939–48. South African representative in the Imperial War Cabinet 1917–18. Plenipotentiary with General Botha for South Africa at the Peace Conference in Paris 1919.

CHAPTER 2

THE JOURNALS

The journals which published articles about Africa in this period were of several different kinds. Some journals catered for British settlers, administrators, traders and commercial agents and the articles they contained were written by people who identified with one or other of these groups. Some were written by and for missionaries at home and in the field, usually covering Africa as part of the wider picture of missionary activity, while some dealt almost solely with the interests of the commercial world. Some journals claimed to be making an objective analysis of African problems with articles by people with first-hand and expert knowledge. A great variety of journals dealt with African questions only occasionally as part of their general coverage of international affairs.

The *Journal of the African Society* was the organ of the African Society founded in 1901 in honour of Mary Kingsley.[1] Sir H. H. Johnston, who retired from the presidency of the Society in 1920, gave an address on the occasion of his retirement,[2] in the course of which he outlined the origin and purpose of the Society, and lamented the financial difficulties which made it seem likely that the organization would have to cease operating. He recorded that three quarters of the members of the Society either lived in Africa permanently or had been employed there for a large part of their lives. He said that the society

> had been from its first inception, and has remained, purely a scientific society, aiming at the quite impartial scientific study of Africa. It was never intended that the African Society should usurp the functions of the Royal Colonial Institute, the Aborigines Protection Society, the Congo Reform Association, or any society for the attacking or defending of Alcohol or Free Trade.

The same insistence on the Society's freedom from involvement in political issues was made by the new president, Lord Buxton,[3] in his first presidential address.[4]

Its main object is the philosophic and scientific study of African subjects, races, customs, history and languages. Politics, Commerce and Propaganda are outside its scope. It forms a Central Institution, which through its meetings, lectures, dinners, luncheons and quarterly journal, brings together those interested in African questions.

In spite of Johnston's gloomy prognostications, the Society began to thrive again under Buxton's presidency. Buxton encouraged participation by individuals whose membership brought prestige to the Society so that by 1922 the membership had increased,[5] and the debt which had worried Johnston was wiped out. From the time of Buxton's first presidency onwards, the social prestige of the membership was noticeable and in 1933 H.R.H. the Prince of Wales agreed to become the patron of the African Society, now to be called the Royal African Society. Buxton stressed that the value of the Society lay very largely in the close contact which the journal provided between those in the field and those interested in Africa at home.[6] An account of Buxton's contribution on the occasion of his retirement in 1933, after twelve years as president, makes clear the purpose and direction which he gave to the Society in this period.

Imbued with the evident desirability of bringing together those connected with African administration in friendly and sociable discussion, and at the same time making them and their work known to important personages, Secretaries of State and other authorities, Lord Buxton, by a series of public lectures and social entertainments ... succeeded in most happily bringing together Governors and Administrators from Africa, the principal officers and officials of the Government, the Colonies and Dominions, and where possible, a member of the Royal Family as principal guest.[7]

The journal of the Society stated quite plainly at the beginning of each number that it dealt with various subjects 'about which information is imperfect and opinion divided', so that each writer was held responsible for his own views. Apart from ethnographic material, the journal increasingly concerned itself with questions of administration, African education, land and labour issues and occasionally an article arising out of current political issues such as the crisis in Bechuanaland in 1933 or Germany's colonial claims. There were also regular gubernatorial contributions about progress in particular colonies and the great tasks ahead. While the general tone of the contributions was conservative, many were from people with wide experience in a particular area of African administration,[8] who were critical of government policies, and able to offer constructive alternatives. An occasional contribution came from well known critics of conservative policies and supporters of the Labour Party.[9] The contents of the journal in the 1930s reflected the growing interest in the question of European impact on African society, particularly in its implications for administration. This interest was reflected in the publication in 1939 of an eighty page supplement providing a wide ranging commentary on Lord Hailey's *African Survey.*

In spite of Buxton's claims about 'the scientific study of African subjects', the bias in the *Journal of the African Society* was clearly towards the observations of laymen, with wide administrative experience in Africa. The journal *Africa,* on the other hand, was supposed to provide objective observations from people who were experts in the fields of anthropology, linguistics and education so that they could be applied by the administration or used as the basis for making policy decisions. The International Institute of African Languages and Cultures,[10] which published the journal *Africa,* also stressed the importance of liaison between those at home and those in administration in Africa, but this time it was not the administrator who could inform the policy makers, but rather the social scientist who could inform both. Diedrich Westermann, a German missionary and linguist involved in the work of the Institute, argued that the International Institute aimed to provide 'a clearing house of information and to bring about a closer relationship between scientific research and practical tasks in Africa.'[11] The international aspect of this organization and the greater emphasis on publications of scientific objectivity and the financial support which it enjoyed[12] suggests an organization both more ambitious and more professional than the African Society. These factors may have helped to conceal from those working within the Institute the fact that they too were prone to share the assumptions and commitments of their society about Africa. They believed that there was room for debate about the possible effects of the application of particular educational or administrative policies; that there was an urgent need to examine the effects of European impact on African societies so that such policies could be improved. But the writers in *Africa* did not question the long-term presence of Britain in Africa, nor did they find it necessary or desirable to involve Africans directly in any debate about African politics. *They* were the interpreters of African opinion.

The founding of the International Institute of African Languages and Cultures, followed by the publication of *Africa* from 1928, provided a vehicle for those who were interested in fostering a close relationship between anthropology and administration, and also provided professional anthropologists with a journal in which they could discuss the problems of applied anthropology and the methodology required to study societies in a state of rapid social change.

Edwin W. Smith states that the idea of founding the Institute first 'crystallized' at a meeting including missionaries and others in 1924.[13] According to Smith

> dissatisfaction with the prevailing order of things occupied the minds of all who were faced with the burning problems of Africa at the time. They were not content to allow a negative policy of drift to continue. They realized that they were confronted with one of the major problems of our age. They saw the need for the application of scientific method to the solution of the questions arising generally from the contact of Western civilization and African culture and particularly from the attempt to educate Africans on modern lines.

In this article the author describes in detail the events which led to the foundation of the Institute in June 1926, including reference to the work of international liaison done by J. H. Oldham[14] and Mr. Hanns Vischer,[15] and the election of Sir Frederick Lugard as the Chairman of the Executive Council.[16]

The objects of the Institute were sufficiently wide-ranging to cover a variety of activities. The Institute was to act as a clearing house of information and as a body publishing material in African languages and cultures, both in the journal *Africa* and in book form. Smith's article makes clear that the early emphasis on language and literature rapidly admitted a study of problems of culture contact, until finally it became clear that the study of the European impact on African society, hitherto neglected, had become the special interest of the Institute. In the past the *Journal of the African Society* had been the only journal in which short accounts of African social systems had been regularly published. The new journal, *Africa,* emphasized the contact of cultures, rather than more orthodox ethnographic accounts, and the problems of applied anthropology. Smith remarks that

> perhaps it is going too far to say that the Council cherished the ambition of creating a new branch of anthropology, but it was along these lines that they determined to proceed.[17]

The *United Empire*[18] was originally the journal of the Royal Colonial Institute and then of the Royal Empire Society as it was called after 1933, when it could claim a membership of 17,000 fellows.[19] The Royal Colonial Institute was formed in 1868 by a group which wished to promote imperial ideas at a time when there was a wide-spread support for the 'Little Englander' position.[20] The conservative nature of the Institute and of its journal appeared clearly in an editorial comment in 1922 on the work of the Institute which said, inter alia,

> It is impossible to look at the state of the world, to note the disintegrating forces which were released during years of bitter warfare, without realising that at no time in the last half century was there more urgent need of those patriotic, unifying, and educative energies which draw inspiration from the motto of the Institute 'King and United Empire'.[21]

The Institute had branches and membership all over the Empire and the journal reflected the emphasis on Dominion interests, rather than the colonies. The journal contained frequent photographs of war memorials and of Empire stalwarts who had done good service for King and country. The annual general meeting, attended always by a high percentage of people with honours of various kinds, seemed frequently to begin with a depressing account from the Chairman of the troubled state of the world!

The journal contained a variety of articles about Africa sometimes couched in general terms viewing Africa as part of the Empire, and sometimes concerning the problems of particular colonies. These articles were almost always published from talks given at the central branch of the Institute, with some resumés of talks at other branches. The contributors to this journal, and therefore those addressing Colonial Institute gatherings, included F. D. Lugard, L. S. Amery, W. G. A. Ormsby-Gore, Sir Edward Grigg and other conservative figures. Towards the end of the 1930s, Lord Hailey was represented by two articles. The emphasis of much of the material about Africa in this journal was on Britain's civilizing mission, but more realistic discussion came occasionally from the Education Circle, a group set up within the Colonial Institute in 1932 to discuss the problems of education in Africa.

Although the tone of the articles was often similar, the *United Empire* should not be confused with the *Empire Review* (*and Journal of British Trade*) which was founded in 1901 by a group of people, including Cecil Rhodes,[22] who were concerned with fostering what they called common bonds of loyalty and the integrity of the Empire. In an editorial statement in 1928, the ideology of this journal[23] was clearly explained.

> The British Empire extends to all parts of the Globe; it embraces every kind of climate and produces every sort of commodity. Millions of square miles, at one time untilled and without population, have been brought under cultivation and are inhabited by the British race;

and millions of natives once subject to barbarian rule now enjoy the benefits of British administration. Yet how few of us recognize the responsibilities which the possession of this grand inheritance entails, responsibilities vividly brought home to us by H.M. King George when, as heir apparent, he exhorted the Old Country to 'wake up' in order that we may maintain our supremacy against the ever widening inroads of foreign competition and to remember that it is a matter of primary importance to develop the outlying portions of our great estate by a business-like method of migration . . . we must appreciate to the full the living realities of these places, great and small, painted red on the map. To aid in the attainment of this knowledge, to awaken the feeling of appreciation and to preach the ethics of Empire, this Review was founded.[24]

A great majority of the articles which concerned Africa in this journal were written by Europeans in Africa, particularly settlers. They were, however, partly directed towards readership at home, as well as catering for fellow settlers and traders. Accounts of customs and happenings in Africa were generally superficial and unscientific and often padded out with details of a comparatively lurid nature.[25] There were frequent articles concerning trading and mineral prospects in Africa: R. C. F. Maugham provided a regular article for the big game hunter; and A. H. Bridgeman and others filled in details of domestic arrangements in Africa, entertainments and sports, presumably aimed at the potential settler or administrator. The two themes of loyalty to the Empire and respect and affection for Royalty were common to every volume, but the discussion of actual political problems received comparatively scant attention. Some articles, however, were clearly designed to redress the balance at home by providing the settlers' or administrators' view of current issues.[26] This journal, in particular, provided Britain with a feed-back of ideas from the settler and trader frontier in Africa, as the *Journal of the African Society* provided the administrators' view point. Some journals, such as those of the Association of Civil Servants in various colonies,[27] aimed at limited circulation in Africa, but the *Empire Review* aimed at a wider circulation.

Another most important European 'frontier' in Africa was that of the missionary bodies and individually and collectively they published a great variety of journal material,[28] some of it aimed at the British public and telling the sort of tales of missionary endeavour and missionary success which might encourage financial assistance. Two more substantial reviews, the *Church Missionary Review*[29] and the *East and the West*[30] united in 1927 to form the *Church Overseas,* which was subtitled 'a quarterly review of the missionary work of the Church of England'. This journal and its predecessors contained articles indicating general agreement that Africans had suffered exploitation at the hands of Europeans, and that the missions, and Christians generally, were bound to support the cause of the African whose interests must remain paramount. In general the British government was seen as the agent for protection as against the predatory activities of other groups and individuals.

The two most important missionary publications of the period were the *International Review of Missions* and *World Dominion*. Both contained articles written by missionaries and others in the field as well as by contributors living in Britain. The articles in both journals debated major issues faced by the Church in the mission field, as it sought to bring Christian teachings to societies in a state of increasingly rapid change. The *International Review of Missions* was first published in 1912 by the International Missionary Council, a body set up to continue the ecumenical work of the World Missionary Conference held at Edinburgh in 1910. Its first editor was the secretary of this Council, J. H. Oldham.[31] The journal *World Dominion*[32] was the organ of the World Dominion Movement. It was first published in 1926 advocating 'informed, continuous, co-ordinated evangelism to reach everyone at home and abroad.'

The particular interests of the commercial world were reflected in a number of journals published during part or all of this period. The illustrated monthly, the *African World,* established in 1902, covered the whole continent, and dealt briefly with those aspects of African commercial, agricultural and industrial life which might interest Europeans living and working in Africa. In 1931 the Tothill Press launched the *Crown Colonist,*[33] which aimed at a wide cross section of readers both in Great Britain and in the colonies in the areas of government and administration as well as commerce, industry and agriculture. This proved to be a conservative journal publishing only short articles on political issues. The short-lived *Imperial Commerce and Affairs,*[34] and the *Imperial Review,*[35] first published in 1934, were both dominated by British and Dominion interests. Both dealt only occasionally with African questions, usually in articles which concerned wider imperial issues.

It could be argued that none of the journals examined so far were primarily concerned with politics, if that word is defined fairly narrowly. They all provided the British audience at home with views and information interpreted by people who had first hand experience of life in Africa. The journal, the *Round Table*[36] was of a different kind. The authors of the articles in this journal were never disclosed but the devotion of the journal to overt political questions and the purpose of the journal were made clear in its first issue in 1910. An introductory article explained that ignorance about the empire had led to misgivings about it.

Many associate imperialism with the projects of jingoes and capitalists, and object to it, just because they admire the ideals of liberty, and justice, and personal responsibility upon which the Empire rests . . .[37]

The promoters of the journal were that group of young men known as Milner's Kindergarten,[38] who had worked with Milner in South Africa after the Boer War. They were anxious to provide a journal which would lead to information and sound judgment about the Empire, since

all who have grown up under the Union Jack are in their hearts devoted to it, for it stands to them for a great tradition in the past, a great inspiration in the present . . . and a still greater promise in the future.[39]

This journal devoted only about one article a year to African colonial questions, sometimes covering a particular colony, sometimes debating broader imperial issues concerning Africa. It avoided articles written in the interests of any local political conflict, and claimed that all articles were written by people with first hand knowledge.

The eulogy written at the time of Milner's death[40] and the account of Kipling after his death,[41] revealed the underlying *Round Table* convictions that good government was better than self government and that the justification for the British Empire was duty and service by the ruling race which had a particular genius for governing backward people. A trenchant criticism of their neglect of the African subjects of the Empire was made by W. M. Macmillan, who said 'the pity is that they were so much of one political complexion, and their South African experience so exclusively gained at a time when the quarrels of British and Dutch crowded out of sight the affairs of the black majority of the population.'[42]

Much of the journal material was oriented differently, although the contributors had often had first hand and long experience in Africa.[43] The difference lay in the fact that many journals dealt only incidentally with imperial issues and African politics as part of a much wider coverage of domestic and international affairs. Those which gave least coverage of African affairs were the famous quarterlies which survived from the early 19th century,[44] although the *Edinburgh Review* published a number of important reviews of books on African questions in this period. The conservative periodicals, the *National Review*[45] and the *English Review,* which merged in 1937, published occasional articles.[46]

The journals published monthly or weekly, some of them survivals from the nineteenth century, gave a varying amount of space to African issues. The supposedly impartial *Fortnightly Review*[47] dealt only occasionally with African questions, whereas the *Contemporary Review*[48] and *Nineteenth Century and After*[49] published regular and valuable articles on African questions in this period 1920 to 1940. The writers whose work appeared in the *Contemporary Review* maintained a steady Left-Liberal position,[50] whereas the contributors to the *Nineteenth Century and After* were a very disparate group.[51]

The *Spectator,*[52] an 'independent' weekly review, showed the same absence of commitment to a particular view in this period.[53] Much of the debate about African questions appeared in the correspondence columns and through book review articles in this weekly, as also in the *Nation and Atheneum*[54] and in the *New Statesman,* which after 1930 was called the *New Statesman and Nation.*[55] In this inter-war period African problems received less weekly coverage, over all, than did questions concerning India, and there were comparatively few major articles or editorials on African questions. However, the correspondence columns of the *New Statesman and Nation* provided lively debate in the 1930s with contributions from several of the best known critics of colonial policy,[56] whose views coincided with those of the new editor, Kingsley Martin.[57]

The disaster of the first World War gave impetus to the study of international political questions. In 1920 the Royal Institute of International Affairs was founded, 'to encourage and facilitate the scientific study of international questions',[58] and in 1922 the journal *International Affairs* was first published by the Institute to secure a wider audience for their debates. The Institute claimed to have no particular bias but on African questions the contributors to this journal and to its counterpart in America, *Foreign Affairs,*[59] were all supporters of what might be called a policy of enlightened paternalism.

Other important journals published during this period, and supporting a particular political viewpoint, included the *Political Quarterly,* the *Socialist Review* and the *Labour Monthly.* The first, established in 1930 for the expression of left-wing views on international questions, contained contributions from intellectuals known for their involvement with the British Labour Party, some of whom were the architects of Labour Party colonial policy in the post-war period.[60] The political commitment of the *Political Quarterly* places it clearly with the Party journals, especially as the *Labour Magazine,* the official journal of the T.U.C. and Labour Party, first published in 1922, contained no lengthy articles concerning international issues.[61] On the other hand the *Socialist Review,* published by the Independent Labour Party, concentrated attention on international politics. However, almost all articles concerning Africa were Europe-centric, couched in general argument about imperialism, and apparently written by people with no special knowledge of African conditions.[62]

Until the 1930s, the same could be said of the *Labour Monthly,* first published by International Labour in 1921 and edited by Palme Dutt.[63] Although this was an important journal of the extreme left in Britain,[64] representing international communism, it gave only minor coverage to African questions from 1920 to 1940. In the 1920s the paper concentrated on Leninist versions of imperialism in various parts of the world, including Africa. During the 1930s George Padmore and Jomo Kenyatta contributed to this journal on several occasions, but from 1935 onwards it was pre-occupied with the question of Abyssinia and German colonial claims. These issues provided the opportunity for propaganda about 'imperialist struggles' and a clear statement in 1936 of the communist version of the way independence would be achieved in Africa.[65]

The importance of the members of the Fabian Colonial Bureau[66] as the architects of the British Labour Party's post-war colonial policy invites examination of the Fabian contribution in the inter-war period. This was a period of stagnation for the Fabian Society[67] but the New Fabian Research Bureau was founded in 1931.[68] It published a series of pamphlets, of which only one concerned the African colonies,[69] as well as a quarterly journal which contained occasional articles about colonial affairs. This *New Fabian Research Bureau Quarterly* became the *Fabian Quarterly* in 1939 when the New Fabian Research Bureau amalgamated with the Fabian Society.

There were two other journals which deserve particular mention. One was the *Anti-Slavery Reporter and Aborigines' Friend,* published by the Anti-Slavery and Aborigines' Protection Society.[70] This journal regularly published an account of the debate on the occasion of the Colonial Office vote in the House of Commons and reported verbatim relevant sections of question time in the two Houses. Part of each edition was devoted to recording correspondence between the Society and Colonial

Office officials on crucial questions of government policy in Africa. This journal reflected the views and reported the activities of many responsible citizens with strong liberal-humanitarian convictions.

The other journal of importance was *Oversea Education,* subtitled 'A journal of Educational Experiment and Research in Tropical and Sub-tropical Areas', which was published from 1929 onwards for the Secretary of State for the Colonies. This journal contained regular reports of the proceedings of the Advisory Committee on Education in the Colonies as well as a variety of articles concerning educational problems in colonial areas. Some concerned the problems of teaching particular subjects in an alien environment while many more general articles contributed valuable material to the debate about the nature and purpose of colonial educational policy.

This broad coverage of the journals which were either regularly or occasionally concerned with British-African issues suggests, perhaps, a wider interest in Africa than was in fact the case. Those journals of the first group, which were most closely concerned with African issues, were clearly directed very largely towards a limited and specific audience, many of whom spent most of their lives in Africa. The regular quarterlies, monthlies and weeklies sometimes gave regular coverage to African affairs but the emphasis was on regularity rather than frequency. Neither these serious journals, nor those which advocated a particular party ideology, provoked or reflected a wide interest in African questions, whereas Indian politics were debated frequently.

It is possible to see the first ten years of this period as a time when the only end to Colonial Office control, which could really be envisaged by anyone, was that which might occur as a result of yielding to settler demands in East Africa. In the 1930s, there was a growing body of radical opinion, which emphasized the need to think in terms of ultimate independence for black Africans, and which therefore urged interventionist policies in Africa to prepare for this day. According to these writers, trusteeship involved a great deal more than the protection and preservation of African societies. It involved the acceptance of the need for change and actual preparation for independence. Nor were these ideas confined to radicals. The setting up of the machinery for the African Survey,[71] carried out under the direction of Lord Hailey, reflected a desire to discover 'the facts' about African colonies, so that this information could be made the basis for new policy decisions.

There were several reasons why the urgency apparent in the public debates of the time was not also reflected in changes in colonial policy. One was the economic depression in Britain and elsewhere in the early 1930s, which made debate about developmental work in African colonies seem rather utopian.[72] After 1935 two other outside issues intervened. First the Abyssinian War engaged the attention of many writers and from that time on interest shifted to German colonial claims, which raised the wider question of ultimate political control over these areas. By the year 1938, most journals neglected colonial issues, except where they impinged on international questions. Nevertheless the British colonial policies carried out during and after World War II reflected the new ideas current in the 1930s.[73]

NOTES

1. Mary Kingsley (1862–1900). An English woman who made journeys to West Africa 1894–1895. Lectured on West Africa all over England 1896–9. Author of several books on West Africa.

2. Sir H. H. Johnston, Address on Retirement from the Presidency. See *J.A.S.*, XX (1920–21), p. 83.

3. Sydney Charles Buxton, 1st Earl cr. 1920 (1853–1934), Liberal M.P. 1883–85 and 1886–1914, Governor General of South Africa 1914–1920.

4. Lord Buxton's Presidential Address. See the report of the General Meeting, *J.A.S.*, Volume XX.

5. The membership stood at 700 in the 1922–23 year. See the remarks by Sir Henry Galway on the occasion of the re-election of Lord Buxton to the Presidency, *J.A.S.*, XXII (1922–23), p. 140.

6. Lord Buxton's address to the Annual General Meeting in 1924.

7. From a speech by General Sir Reginald Wingate (Bart.) on the retirement of Lord Buxton. See *J.A.S.*, XXXII (1934), p. 113.

8. For example G. St. J. Orde-Browne who spent most of his adult life in Africa, including six years as Labour Commissioner in Tanganyika, and later investigated labour conditions in several territories. He wrote several books about African problems.

9. E.g. W. M. Macmillan who contributed articles in the mid '30s and Leonard Barnes. Barnes was a member of the African Society which he joined in 1932.

10. Later called the International African Institute.

11. D. Westermann, 'The Work of the International Institute of African Languages and Cultures', *I.R.M.*, XXVI (1937), pp. 493–9.

12. It received financial support from the Rockefeller Foundation, the Carnegie Trust, most of the colonial governments in Africa, and the Union of South Africa.

13. Edwin W. Smith, 'The Story of the Institute: A Survey of Seven Years', *Africa*, 7 (1934), pp. 1–27.

14. J. H. Oldham was administrative director of the Institute from 1931–1938.

15. Hanns Vischer (1876–1945), at that time general Colonial Office supervisor of educational departments of the various African dependencies.

16. For further accounts of the origin and work of the Institute see F. D. Lugard, 'The International Institute of African Languages and Cultures', *Africa,* I (1928), pp. 1–12 and 'The Human Side of African Development', *United Empire,* New Series, XIX (1928), pp. 415–18.
17. Edwin W. Smith, 'The Story of the Institute . . .', p. 20.
18. The name was changed to the *Journal of the Royal Commonwealth Society* in 1958.
19. In various parts of the Empire.
20. For a history of this organization, see A. Folsom, *The Royal Empire Society* (London, 1933).
21. Editorial notes and comments, *United Empire,* New Series, XIII (1922), p. 194.
22. See 'The Vision of Cecil Rhodes', *Empire Review,* LVIII (1933), p. 14.
23. This journal became the *Commonwealth and Empire Review* in 1944, vol. 78.
24. Editorial introduction entitled 'The Empire Review', *Empire Review,* XLVIII (1928).
25. See, for example, the two articles entitled 'African Drug Addicts' and 'East African Exorcism' in *Empire Review,* LX (1934).
26. For example the article by Lord Cranworth, 'Kenya and her critics', *Empire Review,* XLIII (1925), pp. 327–35 and Sir Edward Grigg, 'The East African Report', *Empire Review,* LIV (1931), pp. 370–77.
27. *The Nigerian Journal* (the official organ of the Association of European Civil Servants), published in Lagos from 1920 and *The Gold Coast Journal* (the official organ . . .), published in Accra from 1931.
28. See for example:—*Inland Africa,* the organ of the Africa Inland Mission, first published in 1920; *Africa's Silent Messenger,* the organ of the International Holiness Mission, first published in 1934; *The African Missions of the White Fathers,* a bi-monthly magazine first published in 1927 by the Society of Missionaries of Africa; *Outward Bound,* a monthly edited by Basil Mathews, and published from 1920–1924.
29. Published by the Church Missionary Society.
30. First published by the Society for Propagation of the Gospel in Foreign Parts in 1902.
31. J. H. Oldham was Editor from 1912 to 1927.
32. A quarterly international review of missionary activities. Subsequently incorporated in the quarterly *Frontier.*
33. Called the *New Commonwealth* after 1950.
34. Published 1920–1925 by the Imperial Commercial Association.
35. Published under the auspices of the Empire Trade League. It incorporated the *Empire Mail* after 1935.
36. Subtitled 'A Quarterly Review of the Politics of the British Empire'.
37. *Round Table,* 1 (1910), p. 1.
38. Philip Kerr (1882–1940), later Lord Lothian, was responsible for founding the *Round Table.* For an account of the aims of this group, see D. C. Watt, *Personalities and Policies,* (London, 1965). They aimed at 'the creation of a super state, in which all the races of the Empire were to be penetrated by British traditions and British purposes.' See also Walter Nimocks, *Milner's Young Men,* (Durham, 1968) especially Ch. 11, for an account of the founding of this journal.
39. *Round Table,* 1 (1910), p. 1.
40. *Round Table,* 15 (1924–25), pp. 427–30.
41. *Round Table,* 26 (1935–36), pp. 330–34.

42. W. M. Macmillan, 'Colour and the Commonwealth', *New Statesman and Nation,* 1 June, 1935.

43. A number of journals have been ignored because the material was too brief or ephemeral, e.g. *West Africa* first published in 1917. On the other hand some of the journals which contained occasional articles of interest are not referred to in this survey. These include *World Review,* the *World Today,* the *Geographical Magazine,* and the *Listener.*

44. These included the *Edinburgh Review,* the *Quarterly Review* and *Black-wood's Magazine.* For an account of their origins see G. Hagberg-Wright, 'The Evolution of the Periodical', *19th Century and After,* 101 (1927), pp. 320–29.

45. First published in 1883.

46. They contained occasional articles reflecting the claim made by the editor of the *English Review* that they stood for 'England, and for the interests of England, which include in their embrace the Empire of which she is still the heart and core.' See the editorial article 'The English Review', Vol. 36 (1923).

47. At this time published monthly. For details concerning this journal see Arthur Waugh, 'The Biography of a Periodical', *Fortnightly Review,* 132 (1929), pp. 512–24.

48. A liberal journal, first published in 1866. In this period Sir John (J. H.) Harris and Sydney Olivier were its regular contributors.

49. Called the *Twentieth Century* after 1950. For an account of this journal's origins see D. Tribe, 'In the beginning'. *Twentieth Century,* 175 (1967), pp. 4–6.

50. J. H. Harris, Sydney Olivier and Charles Roden Buxton.

51. Both Lord Lugard and Leonard Barnes, for example, appeared among contributors in the 1930s.

52. For details about the origins and history of this weekly see A. Strachey, *St. Loe Strachey: His Life and His Paper, the Spectator,* (London, 1930).

53. The contributors in this period included F. D. Lugard, Margery Perham, Donald Cameron, J. H. Harris, C. R. Buxton, J. H. Driberg, and F. H. Melland.

54. The *Nation* 'swallowed' the great Victorian literary weekly, the *Atheneum,* in 1921.

55. In 1930 the *National and Atheneum* was bought by the *New Statesman.* For details of the history of these papers see Edward Hyams, *The. New Statesman, 1913–1963* (London, 1963).

56. These included Sydney Olivier, Norman Leys, W. M. Macmillan, H. N. Brailsford and Jomo Kenyatta.

57. See Edward Hyams, *The New Statesman: 1913–1963,* for an account of the views. on imperial questions of the Webbs (the founders of the New Statesman), Clifford Sharp (the editor in the 1920s) and Kingsley Martin (the editor in the 1930s).

58. Quoted from the frontispiece of the R.I.I.A. publication *The British Empire* (London, 1937). For a history of the R.I.I.A. see Stephen King-Hall, *Chatham House,* (London, 1937).

59. Published in New York from 1922 onwards, and designed to provide a forum for discussion of international politics. Apart from the contributions of Raymond Buell, the author of *The Native Problem in Africa,* (New York, 1928), all the contributions about Africa in this period were provided by British writers including Philip Kerr, H. H. Johnston, Evans Lewin and F. D. Lugard.

60. These contributors included Dr. Drummond Shiels, W. M. Macmillan, C. R. Buxton, Leonard Barnes, Harold Laski and A. Creech Jones. For an account of the founding of the *Political Quarterly*, see Leonard Woolf, *Down Hill all the Way*, (London, 1967), p. 206 ff.
61. The *Labour Magazine* was called *Labour* after 1933.
62. The exceptions were the contributions by Norman Leys in the 1920s.
63. For Dutt's estimate of this journal's role see R. P. Dutt, 'Our First Quarter of a Century', *Labour Monthly*, 28 (1946), pp. 193–4.
64. Its circulation rose rapidly in the 1930s. See H. Pelling, *The British Communist Party: A Historical Profile*, (London, 1958), p. 84.
65. See two articles by H. Rathbone 'The Problem of African Independence', *Labour Monthly*, 18 (1936), pp. 161–172 and pp. 237–249.
66. The Fabian Colonial Bureau was founded in 1940 with Arthur Creech Jones as Chairman and Rita Hinden as Secretary.
67. See Margaret Cole, 'The Fabian Society', *Political Quarterly*, XV (1944), pp. 245–56.
68. Founded by G. D. H. Cole, Clement Attlee and Stafford Cripps, it concentrated on research rather than propaganda.
69. This was 'Protection of Colonial Peoples: A Study in British Colonial Policy', *New Fabian Research Bureau Series*, No. 10 (1933).
70. The Aborigines' Protection Society was founded in 1837 and the British and Foreign Anti-Slavery Society in 1839. These two organizations were amalgamated in 1909.
71. See Ch. 6 for details about this survey.
72. W. R. Crocker refers to the 1931–2 reduction in administrative officers as 'beyond the minimum requirements of the Service.' See *Nigeria. A Critique of British Colonial Administration* (London, 1936), p. 195.
73. See J. M. Lee, *Colonial Development and Good Government*, (1967).

PART II

CHAPTER 3

THE MEANING OF COLONIAL TRUSTEESHIP

For two centuries the twin themes of self-interest, and the obligations of civilized states for less fortunate peoples had appeared as part of the raison d'etre for the possession of colonial territories. Mercantilist policies reflected the first of these themes, as did the doctrine of social imperialism which flourished in England towards the end of the nineteenth century. This doctrine reflected the widespread belief at that time in a close relationship between the maintenance of colonial possessions abroad and social security and reform at home.[1] In its extreme form, this theory emphasized national self-interest at the expense of other European nation states, and, if necessary, of the native inhabitants of colonial possessions. It was clearly related to doctrines of Social-Darwinism current in the late nineteenth and early twentieth centuries.[2] On the other hand the work of the humanitarians and evangelists in the late eighteenth and nineteenth centuries attests to the existence of beliefs profoundly opposed to those which emphasized self-interest.[3] However, whatever the contrast between these two viewpoints,[4] both justified British colonial expansion in the late nineteenth century and were often used together in argument as though in no real conflict.

The history of the formation of the League of Nations, and the establishment of the mandates system, makes clear that in the twentieth century a new consideration was influencing attitudes to questions of colonial possessions.[5] This new impetus was towards internationalism and came from people who believed that industrialized nations would continue to struggle for access to the resources and markets of the colonial world and that, as this had already been a fertile source of war, there should be some system for regulating international relations on these (and other) issues. Rather belatedly those supporting international arbitration turned their attention also to the question of some system of trusteeship for the protection of the native inhabitants of these colonies.[6] In the event the doctrine of trusteeship was written into the League Covenant and the Permanent Mandates Commission was set up to see that mandated territories were governed according to trusteeship principles.[7] At the same time the Open Door principle, made obligatory in the Mandated territories, was supposed to provide equal access to colonial areas.[8]

Although the idea of trusteeship suggested eventual independence for colonial areas, it was sufficiently vague to allow a variety of interpretations and could therefore be espoused by people with widely differing views. However it did seem to rule out the argument that African territories were the estates of Britain, to be used for British advantage, an idea now seldom expressed to justify the possession of colonies. Although this ideology undoubtedly survived among some people,[9] the events of the immediate post-war period made it difficult to use the argument baldly and not appear to be denying the theme of trusteeship. It was replaced in this period by the theory of the 'dual mandate', which was first developed at the end of the nineteenth century[10] and now provided a new conservative ethos.

There were three main explanations of past imperial experience and future imperial obligations held by those who wrote about British-African politics in the period between the wars. The largest group were the supporters of the dual mandate, a theory which rationalized British activities in Africa from the 1880s onwards but which also partook of the 'aura' of trusteeship. The second group which believed in State action for protection or development consisted of many people of liberal or socialist persuasion, some obviously influenced by J. A. Hobson, and many of them reformers. Whether they had spent most of their lives in Africa or Britain, all these people had a record of protest against the cruder forms of exploitation in Africa,[11] and many of them, particularly in the 1930s, were highly critical of Britain's failures in the fields of education, public health and developmental projects generally. The Marxist-Leninists were the smallest group with what was undoubtedly the most closely-knit ideology. They were important because they apparently provided the basic texts for African nationalist propaganda after 1940.[12]

The supporters of British conservative policy in Africa saw both the economic and political motives, which they believed inspired British individuals and statesmen to support interventionist policies in Africa in the late nineteenth century, as perfectly understandable and perfectly reputable. According to the conservative argument, the advanced society of Britain, anxious to preserve her position in the world of nations, and to maintain and improve her internal economy, looked outward to Africa, recently discovered and explored by individuals of outstanding personal qualities.[13] These individuals were exemplified as products of British society, but frequently appeared in heroic proportions. It was they who opened the door to these riches, so desired by industrial Europe, but the door could only be kept open by assuming political control. In fact some writers were critical of the British Government of the time for allowing companies to do for so long what the Government itself should have undertaken.[14] Not only did the Europeans have the brains, the capital and the enterprise to make productive those lands which the Africans had allowed to go 'wasted and ungarnered', but according to many writers, British intervention in Africa could have been justifiably carried out by force with the desirable result of putting an end to African barbarism. In Lugard's view, for example,

> it was the task of civilization to put an end to slavery, to establish Courts of Law, to inculcate in the natives a sense of individual responsibility, of liberty, and of justice, and to teach their rulers how to apply these principles; above all, to see to it that the system of education should be such as to produce happiness and progress.[15]

These were the two aspects of the dual mandate, the economic advantages for the civilized world and the moral advantages for barbarian Africa. The outstanding statement of this ideology in this period was that of Sir Frederick Lugard,[16] a strong supporter of trusteeship principles, and Britain's permanent representative on the Mandates Commission from its inception until 1936. Lugard's arguments were partly a reaffirmation of the nineteenth century belief that British presence must inevitably have a civilizing effect on African people, whether it came in the guise of explorer, missionary, trader, or administrator.[17] They also contained overtones of social imperialist thought, as the following passage suggests.

> Let it be admitted at the outset that European brains, capital and energy have not been and never will be, expended in developing the resources of Africa from motives of pure philanthropy; that Europe is in Africa for the mutual benefit of her own industrial classes, and of the native races in their progress to a higher plane; that the benefit can be made reciprocal and that it is the aim and desire of civilized administration to fulfil the dual mandate.[18]

He considered it 'a cheap form of rhetoric which stigmatises as "common greed" the honourable work by which men and nations earn their bread and improve their standard of life'. This passage suggests that Lugard was familiar with the charges of exploitation made by Hobson and Lenin, and their supporters, but he saw no need to apologize for the economic motives which led to European expansion and which still kept Britain in Africa. The dual mandate implied that British and African interests were reciprocal. While the British brought the many advantages of civilization to Africa, they also helped to provide civilization with those

> raw materials and foodstuffs which cannot be grown in the temperate zones, and are so vital to the needs of civilized man that they have in very truth become essential to civilization.[19]

But not all writers dwelt on the economic aspects of British expansion with the same candour that characterized Lugard's writing. Conservative ideology tended to play down economic motives and emphasized instead Britain's protecting and civilizing mission and the inevitability of her political involvement in Africa, once these territories were opened up to Europeans. Some writers interpreted Britain's role in Africa as a kind of historic necessity from which she could not draw back;[20] some saw her involvement as the only possible action for a self-respecting and powerful nation.

> We just had to do what we did, or else confess ourselves as decadent people in whose veins a tepid skimmed milk fluid ran instead of the warm red blood of a purposeful and puissant race.[21]

Margery Perham, however, represented Africa as a kind of quicksand into which Britain was drawn in an attempt to put down disorder and provide good administration.[22] Once Britain was committed her responsibilities gradually increased, both for protecting Africans from unscrupulous individuals,[23] and it was sometimes suggested, unscrupulous nations, but also for providing administrative stability in societies which were being destroyed by European impact.[24] This view was shared by Philip Kerr[25] who also advanced the argument, common to many writers in conservative journals, that Britain was forced into imperial adventures by the threat of intervention by other states. Not only was this necessary to secure the requirements of industry, without which British civilization would have suffered, but she was forced into it in the interests of the natives 'who would have fared worse in other hands'.[26] This note of apology, so often accompanied by emphasis on the British civilizing mission as the basis of nineteenth century imperialism, often conveyed the impression that the writer was answering a criticism of imperialism from 'enemies within our gates disguised as friends'[27] as one writer called the critics.

The emphasis on Britain's civilizing mission was given a particular slant by L. S. Amery, who contrasted the British love of order and hatred of anarchy with the barbaric or broken down civilizations they found in Asia and Africa.

> Again and again in our Imperial history the desire on the part of the Englishman on the spot to put things straight, to get rid of corruption and oppression, to bring law and order, personal freedom and opportunity to the common man, have counted for at least as much as any conscious desire for power or thought of gain.[28]

The habit of myth-making around the lives and experiences of late nineteenth century explorers, missionaries and administrators in Africa needs little documentation. Sir Charles Lucas summed up what a great many articles and books were meant to convey in this, and in earlier periods, by people writing about David Livingstone, Cecil Rhodes, Sir George Taubman Goldie, Sir Frederick Lugard and others. He believed that the empire was the result of deeds not words, and that Britain's success depended on the work of a few outstanding individuals who were representative of all that was best in the British race.[29] According to one writer the 1890 pioneer column which first entered Rhodesia were people of this kind.

> . . . they were the spearhead which began to break down the wall of isolation and savagery . . . [and] ought to have a niche to themselves in that Imperial Valhalla where 'Deeds that won the Empire' are commemorated.[30]

But by 1920 the great adventures were over and the myth needed recreating. Now the emphasis was on British genius for government both in the creation of superior institutions at home, and also in the administration of colonial peoples abroad. This was a favourite theme in the columns of conservative journals such as the *United Empire,* the *National Review* and, indeed, the *Journal of the African Society,* and it was in these journals that the idea found its most uninhibited expression. Sir Frederick Lugard believed that

> To our race it has been given to build up an Empire on the basis of Freedom, and to lead the way in representative and democratic institutions.[31]

Sir Charles Lucas declared himself an old fashioned man, believing

> that an all ruling providence has given to every people its talent, its specific work to be done, that to our people has been given the work of carrying justice and freedom through the world . . . a better world for the fact that the British have peopled some lands with their own race and taken the rule of others into their own hands.[32]

On another occasion Sir Charles Lucas talked of the British Empire as though it was some sort of mystical entity, the creation of which had been due to something he called 'the quality of the race' which produced it. Its special genius for governing others was reflected in the British sense of justice, love of fair play, in British constancy and tenacity.[33] These qualities were not always appreciated by the public in Britain who knew too little of the work of administrative officers in colonial territories. Sir Hugh Clifford tried to redress the balance in an article in the *Journal of the African Society* in which he described how

> that little bit of coloured bunting has been carried of recent years into so many obscure and distant places; and even in my own time I have seen it cast a shade beneath which not thousands but millions of our fellow creatures have sought and found rest, peace and security from the thunder-storms of injustice, oppression and misrule, amidst which for untold generations, until that Flag was raised to protect them, they have lived in perpetual misery.[34]

This passage, and many others, implied not only that Africans had been badly governed in the past, but that the British possessed some innate capacity for good government, not possessed by Africans. The *National Review* and the *Round Table* publicized this view throughout the inter-war period, using arguments with strong racist overtones to suggest British superiority in the field of government.[35]

The irrational nature of some of these views, and the rather extreme language in which they were often expressed, invites amused comment. Yet the conservative viewpoint should not be dismissed lightly. There were many people who were convinced of Britain's civilizing mission but who emphasized the aspect of sharing the riches of Western civilization with Africa, and who made no judgments of a racist kind about African backwardness. The two governors, Sir Donald Cameron and Sir Gordon Guggisberg, for example, both expressed the comparatively liberal view that their main concern was with the intellectual, moral and material development of the African people.[36] Sir Donald Cameron, writing in 1939, said that

> during the last twelve years we have breathed into the minds of these people a very clear conception of the free institutions that have characterized British rule; we have taught them consistently in the spirit of the Mandate and our own colonial policy that we are but trustees until they can 'stand by themselves'. We have set them on that road by teaching them the art and practice of local government within the tribal areas with a degree of success that has surprised me as the author of that policy in East Africa.[37]

Other administrative officers were equally deeply committed to what seemed genuine civilizing work and believed that this was the ultimate purpose for which the British were in Africa. C. K. Meek, for example, believed that the British Government had 'endeavoured to fulfil the highest ideals of trusteeship'[38] while another anthropologist, R. S. Rattray explained his role as a kind of liaison officer between the British Government and the African people.

> I have tried to make the people understand that we are here among them to help them by grafting on to their institutions such of our own as will enable them to take their place in the commonwealth of civilized nations.[39]

The conservative writers of the period, many of whom had lived through, or taken part in the 'scramble' for Africa in the late nineteenth century, believed this had occurred as a kind of natural result of Britain's economic growth and her political prestige, and that any advantages accruing to Britain were more than balanced by the valuable contributions which Britain had made and was continuing to make in Africa. However the liberal-humanitarian philosophy of the nineteenth century survived among a number of people, who, while they believed that Britain had a mission to civilize (and Christianize) Africa, were at the same time critical of the exploitive nature of much that had been done in the past.[40] J. H. Harris, for example, regular writer for the *Contemporary Review,* and author of several books attacking the ruthlessness of much British pioneering,[41] wanted to see a genuine trusteeship policy. Harris wanted the British Government to offer protection from all kinds of exploitation in Africa, and to undertake the tasks of education and development.

> The whole idea of trusteeship and tutelage implies that a day is coming, remote as it may be, when the 'ward' or the 'pupil' will arrive at a stage of manhood, in which he will be capable of managing his own estate, and in every other respect taking good care of himself and his interests.[42]

This liberal paternalist doctrine involved a comfortable faith in the good intentions of many administrators and missionaries and in the good results of their work. These writers, many of them Christian missionaries, tended to lay stress on the importance of preserving what they thought was 'desirable' in African societies for they envisaged an ultimate synthesis of African and European culture. A trusteeship policy implied eventual independence but this belonged to the distant future. Ultimately, then, they were conservative and preservationist in their thinking.

But a number of prolific writers adopted a much more radical position about the future of the African colonies. These writers, many of them clearly influenced by the work of J. A. Hobson,[43] can be distinguished by their emphasis on the necessity for development rather than preservation. Their debt to Hobson's ideas is clear, both in their analysis of the origins of imperialism and in their emphasis on the part played by the doctrines of Social-Darwinism. In their view British imperial expansion was due, in the main, to economic motives. The emphasis on overseas trade, investment of capital or the search for cheap labour varied from one writer to another but most of them would have agreed with the statement by Leonard Barnes that

> with a few relatively insignificant exceptions, every part of this enormous area and these enormous populations had been brought under British control for the sake of increasing Britain's material strength in general and her overseas trade in particular . . . trade and investment provided the main motive force.[44]

Leonard Woolf emphasized the importance of more markets and wrote of the story of African imperialism as one of 'atrocities, exploitation and hypocrisy'.[45] E. D. Morel's account referred to 'broad and bloody avenues from one end of Africa to the other' in the interests of economic gain and political prestige.[46]

A second facet of this argument about the origins of imperialism was that political direction was often, but not necessarily, subordinated to the interests of private capital.

> But where, as in some parts of Africa and Malaya, political control and economic direction are intimately coordinated, and where the docility of the conquered had made it easy to the conquerors to achieve their ideals, we see established in a single generation what capitalist Europe conceives to be the perfect type of society. In these rich but unhappy countries the natives have no political rights. In some of them they have no rights whatever in land. They are forced, none the less effectively because the means of compulsion are indirect, to work for European owners of land and capital for rates of pay which governments make common cause with capitalists to keep at subsistence level.[47]

Here we have the implication of the corruption of the state by the capitalist class, interested in the profits of the colonies.

One of the most important threads in the arguments of these critics was their attack on Social-Darwinism which had contributed to the conservative ethos about imperialism and was still present in the Lugardian arguments about the superiority of British civilization and the British race. Norman Leys believed that the populations of Europe in the nineteenth century were prone to see the control of alien people as a symbol of strength and glory. He and Leonard Barnes, in particular, felt a deep revulsion for what they saw as the destructive and arrogant beliefs of nineteenth century Britain.[48] They deplored the strange faith of that period, that civilized nations should maintain their standards at the expense of other people.[49] According to the crudest of Social-Darwinian doctrines the superiority of their own culture conferred upon them the right to destroy the cultures of others and to make use of whatever wealth they controlled. Leys believed that

> the root ideas of the new [imperial] policy were that the peoples of the tropics were, essentially and permanently, inferior to Europeans, in every human sense, and in particular both that they were incapable of free institutions, and that they conducted their own institutions so badly as to justify alien government irrespective of their wishes, so that, in Burke's phrase, they were 'doomed to live upon trust'. It followed that the wealth of these countries inhabited by these 'lesser breeds without the law'—and it was soon found to be enormous— should not be left for hands so incompetent to neglect and abuse.[50]

This is a reference to the ideas of the period of the 'new imperialism' of the late nineteenth century but it also applies with some force to the arguments of the dual mandate. Barnes, too, in his comments on the work of the heroic individuals of the Empire provided a remarkable contrast to the picture presented by Lugard and other conservatives, of the civilized European bringing peace and order to Africa.

> To rob and exploit the 'lesser breeds' too weak for self defence against machine guns and high explosives, to disintegrate their distinctive cultures, to pull down their traditional livelihoods, to conscript them as protesting and bewildered auxiliaries of industrialism—all this came to be seen not as a chaotic fury of looting, but as a beneficent process of tidying up a disorderly world, of spreading the salt of civilization more evenly over the earth and of sweeping the scum of barbarism away into inconspicuous corners.[51]

These arguments followed those of J. A. Hobson quite closely and were essentially an attack on the ideas of the age of the "new imperialism". The fact that they also represented a direct attack on the theory of the dual mandate, indicates to what extent that conservative doctrine was a restatement of earlier themes. Lugard argued that

> Europe benefited by the wonderful increase in the amenities of life for the mass of her people which followed the opening up of Africa . . . Africa benefited by the influx of manufactured goods, and the substitution of law and order for the methods of barbarism.[52]

These critics saw no such necessary reciprocity. In their view, increase in European amenities had been bought at the cost of great suffering in Africa and the growth of unhealthy doctrines of Social-Darwinism in Britain.

The individuals who wrote in this vein were critics of their own society. They remained unimpressed with the products of the English public schools, and with the supposed special virtues of the Anglo-Saxon race. They were highly critical of these assumptions which were supposed to confer rights over less fortunate people. They were critical also of the economic system of capitalism, which seemed to them to have emphasized material wealth and technological prowess at the expense of the individual's sense of belonging.[53]

There was a dilemma for these critics, however, for they did in fact value the individual freedoms of Western society and they did see Africans as backward, and needing assistance.[54] Hence, they too were compelled to occupy a paternalist position vis-a-vis African colonies. Yet they differed fundamentally from the supporters of the dual mandate, for whom Britain had an indefinite and prosperous future in Africa. They argued flatly that there was no dual mandate. Britain's rule had begun in exploitation and continued in exploitation. The question was whether the 'single' mandate, as Barnes called it, was to be carried out and African colonies prepared for independence.

There were overtones of Marxist thought apparent in the arguments used by these critics of British colonial policies. But their position was fundamentally different from that of the Marxist-Leninist contribution to the debate which appeared in the *Labour Monthly* from 1921 onwards. The writers in this journal[55] saw the period of imperial expansion as arising inevitably out of the economic dynamic of capitalist society. They condemned the myth-making around the lives of the great Empire builders; and they dismissed the theories of Britain's civilizing mission as sheer hypocrisy. Apart from the determinism of the ideology expressed in this journal, it is important in connection with their views on African affairs that they were advocates of revolution in their own society.[56] Their interpretation of imperialism as the highest stage of capitalism, involving the exploitation of the resources and cheap labour of the colonies, left no room for reformist politics, for the State apparatus would, according to the Marxist belief, support imperialist interests. Attacks on Labour Party policies were therefore as frequent in this journal as attacks on imperialism.[57]

The work of Lenin on imperialism[58] relied to a considerable extent on the work of J. A. Hobson whose criticism of imperialism was published in 1902.[59] Both writers argued that the need to export capital was the basis of imperialist adventures in the late nineteenth century. But Hobson's theory of 'underconsumption'[60] at home was a criticism of the way capitalism worked. He believed that the export of British capital led to the exploitation of indigenous people of Africa and Asia, through various malpractices including the appropriation of land and the use of cheap labour. However he believed that these areas should be developed under some sort of international control, while the British capitalist could solve his immediate problem by raising the wage levels, increasing consumption and raising living standards at home. In other words there was an alternative to the export of capital, and one which would reduce, rather than inflame, existing tendencies to aggressive nationalism and militarism.

Lenin, on the other hand, saw imperialism as a stage in the development of capitalism which was inevitable and which would have inevitable consequences in the areas colonized.[61] There was no alternative course which could be pursued under the capitalist system. Because Lenin viewed the State as the instrument of finance capital, his theory did not, as did Hobson's, involve any additional argument about the corruption of the State or of public opinion by imperial interests.

The Leninist interpretations of imperialism were used or assumed throughout the whole of the period by the contributors to the *Labour Monthly*. Britain was the first state to reach the stage of industrial capitalism which provided the strength for her to carry out a policy of dominating territories all over the world for 'trade, tribute and monopolies'. The British Empire 'is conquered territory added to the estates of the British bourgeoisie for the purpose of large scale exploitation.'[62] In this article, Dutt attacked several of the old shibboleths about the Empire. It was not acquired in a fit of absence of mind. There were no links of a racial, religious, geographical or sentimental kind but only the link of exploitation. The myth about the great settlers, pioneers and explorers concealed the truth of free-booting, piracy, slave-trading, plunder, penal settlements and the extermination of natives.

These writers attacked all theories of Britain's civilizing mission. They argued that backwardness was not cured by colonial rule, which, in fact, meant continued exploitation, becoming always more subtle.

Colonization, notwithstanding all that its defenders may say, is a socially backward system, retarding the economic development of Africa, and the cultural progress of the Africans. The colonies will always be backward, so long as they are looked upon as estates of the Crown to be exploited for the benefit of Europeans.[63]

Administration and developmental works, according to this

theory, provided the framework for more successful exploitation by Europeans. The removal of this parasitic growth was essential before real development could occur.[64] The British Government, therefore, had no role to play in Africa except perhaps that of the outside enemy. For in answer to the charge that independence would result in chaos, one writer declared that

> it is the process of the developing struggle against imperialism which enlightens the masses as to the aims of imperialism, and at the same time trains a corps of the population who become the leaders of the mass of the people in building for the nucleus of the State which comes into being when freedom from imperialism has been secured.[65]

The imminence of war towards the end of the 1930s, involving considerable debate about the possibility of appeasing Hitler in some way in connection with his demand for colonies, provoked several angry articles insisting that the colonies be given independence and not treated as pawns in the big power game.[66] In 1939 a statement 'Colonies and War', which was the text of a statement adopted by the Central Committee of the C.P. of Great Britain, was published in the *Labour Monthly*. It was a call to the working classes of Britain to reject the appeal to fight as a nation against fascism and a demand that they show their solidarity with the exploited peoples of India and Africa.

> ... the people of Britain must be quite clear that they have nothing in common with the imperialists and their aims for the re-division of the world. They must give their fullest and their most practical support to the people of India and the Colonies in their struggle against imperialism . . . Between the British people and the people of the colonies there is a complete unity of interest for the overthrow of the imperialist ruling class.[67]

The British working class did not respond to the challenge but the propaganda of the Marxist-Leninist arguments found fertile soil in protest movements within Africa.[68]

The propaganda of nationalist movements in Africa after the Second World War used the arguments of Hobson and Lenin on the exploitation of African resources and of African labour. Nationalist leaders were undoubtedly influenced by Lenin's argument that independence would only be achieved as a result of a revolutionary situation developing in the colonies.[69] The appeal of Leninist dogma was largely due to the fact that it was the only coherent explanation of the origins of imperialism, and of its operations and future intentions, which left room for African nationalist leaders to play a role in determining their own political future. All other accounts of imperialism involved the continued operation of some kind of paternalist policies. Even Hobson had advocated the development of Africa under international control.[70] The critics of British imperial policy, who attacked the theory of the dual mandate as cant and argued that Britain had only one mandate—to prepare Africa for independence as soon as possible—even they drew back from the proposition that Britain could leave Africa in the near future. It was almost unknown for British writers discussing African problems in this period to project themselves forward to a time when Africans would be governing themselves in independent states. In a sense the Marxists avoided this issue and resolved the dilemma by arguing that imperialist powers would never grant independence until forced to do so, and that, in the meantime, the inevitable revolutionary struggle for independence would unite the Africans in each colony and provide the national solidarity required to operate as political units.

The idea that African colonies should be granted independence in the not too distant future found wide acceptance in the decade after the Second World War. This represented a remarkable change from attitudes current in the inter-war period, and may be explained by a number of factors, the relative importance of which it is difficult to determine. Among them were the profound influences of the war on British society, including a loss of prestige in the face of the greatly enhanced importance of Russia and the U.S.A., both ideologically committed to ending colonial rule; the influence of events in India; and the increase of political agitation in the colonies, compelling counter measures. It was clear that the colonies now had to be prepared for independence and the more conservative arguments of the inter-war period had to be rejected. The need for development of all kinds was recognized belatedly, when Britain could no longer contemplate undertaking major projects.

NOTES

1. For an analysis of these ideas see B. Semmel, *Imperialism and Social Reform*, A. M. McBriar, *Fabian Socialism and English Politics*, and I. Henderson, 'The Attitude and Policy of the Main Sections of the British Labour Movement to Imperial Issues, 1899-1924', B. Litt. thesis, University of Oxford, 1964.
2. See B. Semmel, *Imperialism*, p. 29 for a distinction between 'internal' and 'external' Social-Darwinism.
3. See H. D. Hall, *Mandates, Dependencies and Trusteeships*, (London, 1948), p. 99, for reference to early theories about trusteeship obligations.
4. Often summarized as the 'Rhodes' tradition and the 'Livingstone' tradition.
5. See H. R. Winkler, *The League of Nations Movement in Great Britain, 1914–1919*, (New Jersey, 1952), particularly Ch. VIII, 'The Idea of Colonial Trusteeship'.

6. *Ibid.,* Ch. VIII, for an account of the debate of the period before 1919 on these issues.

7. For the most cynical view of the intentions behind this scheme see George Padmore, *Africa and World Peace,* (London, 1937), p. 177. According to his view, these arrangements allowed the war victors to acquire territory on the pretext of holding it in trust for the indigenous inhabitants.

8. The mandates system is also analysed in W. K. Hancock, *Survey of British Commonwealth Affairs,* (London, 1940), Vol. 2, Part 1, Ch. 2, p. 111 ff. Unlike Padmore, Hancock concludes that the system represented 'an important advance upon former attempts to secure by international convention a just colonial order'.

9. This was the ideology of The Empire Resources Development Committee, a propaganda body set up in 1917 which advocated the control of the economic resources of the colonies in the interests of Britain. See W. K. Hancock, *Survey,* Vol. II, Part 1, p. 106 ff.

10. See Bernard Porter, *Critics of Empire,* (London, 1968), p. 48 ff. Benjamin Kidd was one of the first to develop the idea that Britain should develop tropical products 'as a trust for civilization' in *Control of the Tropics,* (London, 1898). Porter finds widespread support for this aspect of the dual mandate in the early part of the twentieth century.

11. For example, over the alienation of tribal land, forced labour, and inequitable taxation.

12. In *How Britain Rules Africa,* (London, 1937), p. 333, George Padmore discussed the question of apparent conflict between Marxist attacks on European nationalism and support for nationalism in Africa. According to Padmore the objectives of a nationalist movement determined whether it was progressive or reactionary.

13. See F. D. Lugard, "The White Man's Task in Tropical Africa", *Foreign Affairs,* 5 (1926), pp. 57–68 for an account of how the discovery of steam gave access to new places, led to the growth of industry, demands for raw materials and the growth of population.

14. See, for example, F. D. Lugard, *The Dual Mandate,* p. 14, Margery Perham, *Native Administration in Nigeria,* (London, 1937), p. 27, and Edwin W. Smith "Northern Nigeria", *Empire Review,* XXXIX (1924), p. 436.

15. F. D. Lugard, *The Dual Mandate,* p. 5.

16. *Ibid.*

17. For a discussion of this view see A. P. Thornton, *Doctrines of Imperialism,* Ch. IV.

18. F. D. Lugard, *The Dual Mandate,* p. 617.

19. *Ibid.,* p. 43.

20. See, for example, R. C. F. Maugham, *Africa as I have known it.* (London, 1921), p. 23. 'It fell upon Britain to shed upon this long neglected portion of Darkest Africa the light of civilization for which she had long been athirst'.

21. J. Stanley Little, 'Empire Old and New', *United Empire,* New Series, XVI (1925), p. 97.

22. M. Perham, *Native Administration in Nigeria,* see pp. 9–15.

23. See, also, L. Haden Guest, *The New British Empire,* (London, 1929), p. 290 and Major A. G. Church, *East Africa: A New Dominion.* (London, 1927), p. 242.

24. There will be further discussion of this question in Chapter IV.

25. See Philip Kerr, 'From Empire to Commonwealth'. *Foreign Affairs.* 1, 2 (1922–23), pp. 83–98.

26. This was the expression of Sir Charles Lucas in *The Partition and Colonization of Africa,* (London, 1922), p. 98. Similar views may be found in the articles of Sir Hugh Clifford and Sir Humphrey Leggett.

27. Major G. Bell, 'Then and Now', *United Empire,* New Series, XVI (1925), p. 210.

28. The Rt. Hon. L. S. Amery, 'Ideals of the British Commonwealth', *United Empire,* New Series, XXVI (1935) pp. 506–9. This article was republished in *The Forward View* (London, 1935). Donald Fraser in *The New Africa,* (London 1927), thought it doubtful that Africa could have advanced out of barbarism without the help of European administration.

29. Sir Charles Lucas, 'The Meaning of the Empire to the Labour Democracy', *United Empire,* New Series, XI (1920), pp. 110–121.

30. See Mrs. Tawse Jollie, *The Real Rhodesia,* (London, 1924), p. 18.

31. Sir Frederick Lugard, 'Growth of Empire', *United Empire,* New Series, XIII (1922), p. 746.

32. Sir Charles Lucas, 'The Meaning of the Empire to the Labour Democracy', *United Empire,* New Series, XI (1920), p. 119.

33. Sir Charles Lucas, 'Balance of Power within the Empire', *United Empire,* New Series, XIII (1922), pp. 17–26. See also J. S. Little, 'False Analogies', *United Empire,* New Series, XIII (1922), pp. 71–73.

34. Sir Hugh Clifford, 'United Nigeria', *J.A.S.,* 21 (1921–22), p. 4.

35. See, for example, A. C. G. Hastings, 'The Real Nigeria', *National Review,* 88 (1926–27), p. 764 and Captain C. E. Cookson, 'Experimenting with Africa', *National Review,* 106 (1936), p. 51.

36. See, for example, F. G. Guggisberg and A. G. Fraser, *The Future of the Negro,* (London, 1924), p. 65.

37. Sir Donald Cameron, *My Tanganyika Service and Some Nigeria,* p. 286.

38. C. K. Meek, *Europe and West Africa,* p. 20.

39. R. S. Rattray, Preface to *Ashanti,* (Oxford, 1923), p. 12.

40. For an account of the various strands of liberal thought on the possession of colonies in the period before World War I, see Bernard Porter, *Critics of Empire.*

41. e.g. *The Chartered Millions,* (London, 1920), and *A Century of Emancipation,* (London, 1933).

42. J. H. Harris, *Slavery or 'Sacred Trust'?* (London, 1926), p. 109.

43. J. A. Hobson, *Imperialism: A Study.* But another book by J. A. Hobson, *Problems of a New World,* was published in London in 1921. He spoke of the victors fighting over 'desirable lots' in Africa, and of the growing British parasitism on the colonies.

44. Leonard Barnes, *Skeleton of Empire,* (A Fact Pamphlet, 1931), p. 10.

45. Leonard Woolf, *Imperialism and Civilization,* (London, 1928), p. 79.

46. E. D. Morel, *The Black Man's Burden,* (London, 1920), p. 7.

47. Norman Leys, 'The Tropics and the League of Nations', *Socialist Review,* XVIII, 96 (1921), p. 72.

48. Both J. H. Oldham and Leonard Barnes analysed the views of several writers of the 19th and early 20th centuries who advocated the right of the strong quite baldly. See *Christianity and the Race Problem,* (London, 1924), p. 115 f. and *The Duty of Empire,* (London, 1935), p. 88 f.

49. *Ibid.,* p. 84 'To the fin de siècle imperialists expansion had become an economic and social necessity of the first importance, the modern form of the struggle of nations for existence.'

50. Norman Leys, *Kenya,* (London, 1924), p. 86.

51. Leonard Barnes, *The Duty of Empire,* p. 87.

52. F. D. Lugard, *The Dual Mandate*, p. 615.

53. They were writing before it became apparent that modern industrialized society appeared to produce this result, whether it was organized along capitalist lines or not.

54. Only Leonard Barnes developed the idea that Britain had actually destroyed viable social systems in Africa.

55. These writers were usually members of the British Communist Party which 'consisted to a remarkable degree of persons of non-English origin'. See Henry Pelling, *The British Communist Party*, p. 15.

56. For example see George Padmore, *Africa and World Peace*, p. 237. 'Our contention is that there can be no peaceful solution to the Colonial question within the existing social order'.

57. See, for example, M. Spector, 'The Empire Labour Conference', *Labour Monthly*, 7 (1925), pp. 548–52.

58. Vladimir Ilich Lenin, *Selected Works* (London 1936–39), Vol. 5, 'Imperialism and Imperialist War, 1914–17'. This was written in Russia in 1915 and translated into English in 1920. See T. Kemp, *Theories of Imperialism*, (London, 1967), p. 30, for a comment on Lenin's views of Hobson's work.

59. J. A. Hobson, *Imperialism: A Study*. Hobson had been profoundly disturbed by the events in South Africa before and during the Boer War. The publications of these two men are generally regarded as the classic statements of the economic theories of imperialism. It has been argued that their use of the word 'imperialism' to denote a stage in the development of capitalism, and implying the exploitation of less developed areas, gave the word a new and specific meaning which it has since retained. See R. Koebner and H. D. Schmidt, *Imperialism: The Story and Significance of a Political Word, 1840–1960*, (Cambridge, 1964).

60. Based on earlier classical economic theory. See D. K. Fieldhouse (Comp.), *The Theory of Capitalist Imperialism*, (London, 1967).

61. For an analysis of Lenin's arguments see W. H. B. Court, 'The Communist Doctrines of Empire', an appendix to W. K. Hancock, *Survey*, Vol. II, Part I.

62. R. Palme Dutt, 'The British Empire', *Labour Monthly*, 5 (1923), p. 208.

63. George Padmore, *How Britain Rules Africa*, p. 387.

64. Padmore argued, for example, that Britain had no intention of allowing industrial growth in Africa.

65. H. Rathbone, 'The Problem of African Independence', *Labour Monthly*, 18 (1936), pp. 161–172 and 237–249.

66. G. Graham, 'The Demand for Colonies', *Labour Monthly*, 18 (1936), pp. 364–73, R. Bridgeman, 'Colonies and War: Today's Big Issue', *Labour Monthly*, 20 (1938), pp. 45–53, and R. F. Andrews, 'Hitler and Colonies', *Labour Monthly*, 21 (1939), pp. 145–51.

67. See 'The Colonies and War', *Labour Monthly*, 21 (1939), pp. 751–758.

68. George Padmore, who later worked with Nkrumah in Ghana, may have been one of the most influential writers as far as West Africans were concerned. His book, *The Life and Struggles of Negro Toilers* (London, 1933), concluded with a chapter called 'Revolutionary Perspectives'.

69. The earliest work of K. Nkrumah, *Towards Colonial Freedom*, (London, 1947), follows this argument closely.

70. J. A. Hobson, *Towards International Government*, (London, 1915), and 'The Open Door' in C. R. Buxton (Ed.), *Towards a Lasting Settlement*, (London, 1915).

CHAPTER 4

THE PROBLEMS OF SOCIAL CHANGE

One of the major issues which concerned these writers in the inter-war years involved the problems of social change in societies apparently disrupted by contact with the West. The analysis of the nature of this disruption varied a great deal. But almost all British writers were convinced that control of the colonies must be continued until Africans were better equipped to come to terms with Western economic and social influences of all kinds. It was generally assumed that British activity in Africa had seriously disrupted existing social systems, and that individual Africans were finding it difficult to absorb unfamiliar ideas. As a result a variety of paternalist policies were advocated, some of them involving the notion of Africans participating in political life, but none of them predicting the rapid end of colonial rule and the complete transfer of political power to the Africans. Only the Marxist writers advocated the ending of colonial rule, although they did not believe that independence would be granted until a revolutionary situation had developed.

By 1920 the theory of trusteeship had been embodied in the Covenant of the League of Nations, but in such general terms that it could be interpreted to suit any view of colonial rule, except that of the extreme right or left. The Communist left continued to regard expressions of trusteeship as cynical cover for policies of exploitation. The Social-Darwinism of the extreme right was transformed and muted in the theory of the dual mandate although the more conservative spokesmen continued to refer in the most general terms to the advantages for the Africans of the British civilizing mission. But there was, in this period, a growing body of opinion which specifically advocated the end of laisser-faire policies in Africa. These reformers made the assumption that the spread of administration had been carried out so far in the interests of the metropolitan power, and not with the intention of pursuing any specific policy which might affect the nature or direction of change in Africa. They now advocated direct intervention by the

British Government, using the colonial administration, and other more specialized agencies, to carry out a positive programme of change.

Part of the explanation for growing support for interventionist policies may be discovered by examining British beliefs about the nature of African society, and about what effects British contacts had had on Africa so far. Conclusions on these two questions convinced all but a small minority that British presence and British paternalism would be essential for a considerable time to come.

What then was African society thought to have been like before Europe intruded, or at least before an alien administration affected it significantly? The answers to this question revealed an almost universal attachment to the dichotomy between 'primitive' Africa and 'civilized' Europe, implying that African societies were all alike. In particular the word 'primitive' was used in the most cavalier fashion. It was used in this period to refer to societies which were believed to have simple and undifferentiated social structures; to refer to religious beliefs, and ethical and moral standards, believed to be inferior to those of the West; and to describe societies which had a low level of technology. It was used to refer to societies which were thought to be despotic and cruel on the one hand, or societies pure and uncorrupted on the other.[1] In fact it seems clear that the use of the word to refer to African societies which all had a comparatively undeveloped technology was due to an attachment to social evolutionary theory. The idea of a clear dichotomy between 'primitive' and 'civilized' was explained according to the theory that African societies were at a different and earlier stage in the developmental process, an idea fundamental to the theory of social evolution.

The second half of the nineteenth century saw the development of social evolutionary theories, which grew up independently of biological theories, and embodying the two Enlightenment beliefs that there is inevitable progress in history and that societies are natural systems for the operation of which laws can be discovered.[2] These early social anthropologists[3] wanted to discover the plan underlying the history of mankind, but they were not interested in what they regarded as the minutiae of history. Most of their work was hypothetical and involved attempts to reconstruct the distant past by conjecture, using the existing body of ethnological literature for comparative purposes. In this way they established a hierarchy of institutions and beliefs, arranged in ascending order. It was argued that some existing societies were living exponents of the culture stages through which advanced societies had already passed.[4] The explanation for the apparently slow progress of some societies and the rapid advance of others was thought to be the task of the historian. This left the social evolutionists free to choose their examples of 'savagery' or 'civilization' at random, disregarding the question of historical time. The implication of social evolutionary theory was that all societies could be classified according to the stage of development they had reached, thus providing a hierarchy of societies with Western European states heading the list.[5]

While social evolutionary theory accorded well with Western confidence in the possession of a superior technology, and fostered the prevalent belief in the possession of superior social institutions, it gradually lost ground in the discipline of social anthropology in the twentieth century. Although the nineteenth century anthropologists introduced the comparative method, now an essential part of the social sciences, the data on which they worked was often inadequate and arbitrarily chosen. In the hands of the social evolutionists, who were armchair theorists, the comparative method became a vehicle for extravagant and unscientific conjectures about the laws of social progress, with cavalier use of apparent evidence, which suited *a priori* arguments. They have been criticized for their neglect of the time factor in history which led them to disregard evidence of cultures which had apparently declined. Moreover a closer examination of 'savage' societies in the twentieth century has suggested far greater complexity than the evolutionists believed. Such examination has cast doubt on the notion that there has always been clear progress from simple and undifferentiated social structures to more complex ones.

During the first three decades of the twentieth century there were many criticisms within the discipline of social anthropology of the grand designs of the evolutionists and many attempts to put the work of the social anthropologists on a more scientific basis. One of the main results of this concern with methodology was the insistence on the necessity for careful, patient field work to take the place of conjecture.[6] The main attack on both evolutionists and diffusionists came in the 1920s and 1930s from the functionalist school,[7] and concerned the whole nature of the discipline of social anthropology. Essentially their criticisms were directed towards the historical bias of both evolutionists and diffusionists,[8] by which they meant their search for origins. They argued that if social anthropology was to discover the universal characteristics of all societies, the historical element should be regarded as irrelevant.[9] Thus the idea that societies are natural systems was retained, but the emphasis was no longer on explanations of developmental stages,.nor on questions of the relationships between different societies, but rather on the way in which all facets of a given society were related.

An examination of the views of laymen interested in British-African problems of all kinds, but probably unfamiliar with the current rather esoteric debates about the theory and methodology of social anthropology, reveals an attachment to the general theory of social evolution, in some cases made quite explicit. Although, as indicated, the theory had by this time come under strong attack within the discipline of social anthropology, its major tenets continued to exercise great influence.[10]

Several of the individuals, who wrote widely about Africa between the wars, made their acceptance of social evolutionary views quite explicit, and put their theoretical position quite clearly. Norman Leys, for example, one of the chief critics of British policies in Africa, stated

> History displays a process of social development that is common to all mankind. It proceeds through the same stages, though not without retrogressions, so that in every continent men once lived in tribes, trembled under priests, made to themselves kings and oligarchies to obey ... at the same stage of social development, men evolve the same institutions, acquire the same ideas and beliefs, and follow the same practices, in every age and in every continent.[11]

Lord Lugard, the most respected figure in the British world of 'experts' on Africa, revealed a similar commitment to social evolutionary theory in his discussion of social attitudes to land. Lugard quite clearly believed that private ownership of land represented the pinnacle of a long process of development.

> Conceptions as to the tenure of land are subject to steady evolution, side by side with the evolution of social progress from the most primitive stages to the organization of the modern state. In the earliest stage, the land and its produce is shared by the community as a whole; later the produce is the property of the family or individuals by whose toil it is won, and the control of the land becomes vested in the head of the family. When the tribal stage is reached, the control passes to the chief, who allots unoccupied lands at will, but is not justified in dispossessing any family or person who is using the land. Later still ... the conception of proprietory rights in it emerges, and sale, mortgage, and lease of the land, apart from its user, is recognised ... These processes of natural evolution, leading up to individual ownership may, I believe, be traced in every civilization known to history.[12]

A further example, less committed to the exact stages of the evolutionary processes may be found in J. H. Oldham's writings.

> The centuries of slow growth and progress which separate the more advanced from the more backward peoples of the world cannot be left

out of account . . . There is nothing derogatory to the dignity and self-respect of any people in recognizing and accepting facts, or in beginning the upward climb from whence they are.[13]

It is clear that Margery Perham was also familiar with social evolutionary theory. But if she believed it offered insights, she also believed that modern political developments had made rapid change possible so that the rigid concept of developmental stages had to be qualified.

> I do not think that we need form the fatalistic conclusion that the African must tread every step of the long road we have trodden away from tribal society, and sojourn as we have done in the wilderness of feudalism, despotism and individualism. Are we not today trying to create by political art some of the advantages we have lost by nature? Should this not qualify us to help the African to carry over into the twentieth century whatever was socially valuable in the first?[14]

Examples of social evolutionary beliefs occurred regularly in the journal articles and published literature of the period. But before examining, in any greater detail, the nature of British beliefs about African society, it is necessary to look at the implications of this attachment to social evolutionary theory.[15] Concerning the accuracy of the statements quoted above, it is perhaps necessary to go back to the general criticism of the theory offered earlier. It is certainly true that societies known to historians have exhibited great diversity in institutions, in ideology and in economic and technological development. However the theory of inevitable stages of growth implies a teleological view of history, and the certainty of overall progress, which many historians would now find untenable. On the other hand the extreme functionalist view—that all societies are the result of a unique adaptation to environment and therefore not able to be compared—has also come under attack in recent years.[16] Whatever the outcome of this debate within the discipline of Social Anthropology, it is clear that the view of social evolutionary theory, held by laymen between the wars, is no longer tenable.

The social evolutionary framework, into which African social systems were believed to fit, affected the attitudes of British observers to the question of the nature, possibility and speed of social change. It therefore influenced, fundamentally, their attitudes to British policy. As far as Britain's position in Africa was concerned the implications were clear. Under 'natural' circumstances it would take many centuries for Africa to 'catch up' with Europe, even supposing that progress in Europe was minimal. For although there was no conception of a fixed rate of progress in social evolutionary theory, some developmental stages were believed to be far behind others. The intervention of a paternalist order was seen as essential if this 'catching up' process was to be foreshortened.

Three examples of the extreme form of the social evolutionary argument made the point that African societies could not be suddenly abandoned to make their own efforts to come to terms with the problems of rapid social change.

> In Africa, the European finds himself face to face with a nation, or nations, who are, culturally, in the early morning of their history. For the greater part without learning, as we understand that word, these people inherit traditions that go far back in man's history, and it is by slow and gradual evolution, rather than by any violent substitution of alien methods of thought for his own traditional ideals that the African may be expected to advance most safely.[17]

The same idea was expressed by Robert Stokes.

> How can the African, having no experience of modern civilization, be expected to evolve for himself within a reasonable time the apparatus of civilization which it has taken the whole of the rest of the world some millenia to evolve?[18]

The final example of this pessimistic view about the rate of progress included also the implication that there were stages which could not be leaped over.

> On the veldt you have great masses of humanity, emerging from the lowest depths of barbarism, abysmally ignorant, and lacking every code of honour, morality and religion . . . It is suggested you should raise them as a body to the same psychological level as white men. It has taken centuries for the white man to arrive to the level on which he stands today, and to expect the native races of Africa to rise by a single bound is to demand an acrobatic feat in evolution of which humanity is quite incapable.[19]

Social evolutionary theory presupposes the unity of mankind and therefore has no necessary racist implication. This does not mean that laymen may not have held some version of social evolutionary theory and also provided the explanation for the level of progress of different societies in racist terms. Certainly racist views of all kinds were common in this period. However, many writers, who sought an explanation for these apparently different levels of progress, provided explanations in terms of physical environment, the depredations of the slave trade, the ravages of disease and the general inaccessibility of particular areas.[20] But whatever the explanation for backwardness, a wide gulf was believed to exist between African and European society, and the effects of Europe on Africa were therefore bound to be rather drastic. The existence of social evolutionary beliefs did not necessarily mean a conviction that there was a fixed time for passing through each stage or even that each stage had to be encompassed. But the belief in a vast gulf between the two kinds of society suggested that abnormal change would have to occur and that somehow the shock would have to be cushioned. Africans had to be taught how to operate in their new milieu and they had to be protected from the ravages of more sophisticated societies.

It might be expected that a commitment to social evolutionary theory, along with the constant dichotomy between 'primitive' and 'civilized', would mean that observers of African society would be in broad agreement about what they had found in Africa.[21] But, at this non-expert level, all comments on African societies must be seen also as a reflection, in some sense, of people's views about their own society. In observing African societies, Westerners saw the values or shortcomings of their own in new perspective. For this reason, while African political structures and social customs were often dismissed as comparatively so barbaric, they were also sometimes idealized because something of value, apparently missing in Western society, seemed to have been preserved in Africa. In some cases writers expressed ambivalent attitudes about what they had observed in Africa.

The most uncritical appraisals came from those conservative writers who made much of Britain's civilizing mission and who had little first hand experience of Africa. Sir Reginald Coupland, the historian of the slave trade, wrote of Africa as 'the homeland, first and last of that swarming fecund negro race, the most backward among the races of mankind'.[22] Ifor Evans referred to 'the all too prevalent abuses in religion and morals' to be found in Africa.[23] These observations suggested unquestioning acceptance of the superior virtue of British society and customs.

It is ironic that the supporters of Lenin, who were most scathing in their attacks on Britain's claim to be a civilizing force in Africa, were also prone to thinking in stereotypes about Africa. The European writers in the *Labour Monthly,* for example, made no attempt to analyse African societies in detail. They were simply barbaric survivals which were doomed to extinction in the final stage of capitalist development.

But many writers attempted an analysis of the structures and beliefs of African societies, some of them emphasizing that, contrary to general opinion, Africans were deeply religious people.[24] They referred, too, to the security of African tribal life and the apparent harmony which was being disrupted by Western impact. Others made a contrast between Western industrial society, which was thought to be characterized by a harsh materialism and individual insecurity, with African organic society which provided material security for all, and elevated the spirit of brotherhood. Not surprisingly the most obvious expression of this sort of view came from the left wing critics of Western society, one of whom wrote that Africa's lesson

> is the intimate sense of brotherhood and common humanity, of Ubuntu, the capacity of social self-sacrifice on behalf of others, the solidarity of a cooperative communism swallowing up all egoistic competition.[25]

However a number of writers who stressed the security of tribal life as opposed to the supposed insecurity of the individual in Western society, also emphasized the shortcomings of tribal society. These included an absence of individual independence, and material conditions which may have been equally shared but were none the less deplorable for that. Norman Leys, for example, said that

> In tribal society there are no paupers, no unemployed, no idle rich, no prostitutes, no prisons, no man goes hungry as long as his fellow clansman has enough. But there is another side to the picture. When all are mutually dependent, none has independent mind or character. And we in our own society would not barter our personal liberty for anything . . .[26]

Others referred to the insanitary conditions, the poor food and malnutrition, and the unpleasant customs (such as the circumcision of girls) which were typical of African tribal life.[27] Even some of the more prized communal aspects of African society were open to criticism, because they inhibited change. These included communal land ownership and communal grazing and watering of stock; the customs of lobola, according to which all cattle were of equal value; witchcraft which threatened the more obviously successful members of society; and numerous customs connected with community crop planting which inhibited innovation.[28] But probably the most important observation concerned the vulnerability of these societies to calamities of all kinds. Many of those who believed in the importance of human welfare in terms of adequate food, good health and the application of rational solutions to human problems were appalled at what they saw in Africa. One writer believed that what seemed most valuable in African society, 'its integrated solidarity and mutual dependence', was in fact its greatest weakness.

> The fear of calamity was eclipsed by group dependence. The incentive to thrift was reduced to a minimum. Foresight, the most dynamic force in advanced society, was smothered in group respon-

sibility for individual need. Thus the native was an easy prey to famine, pestilence, tyranny and exploitation, which with the background of meagre military equipment and training, rendered him powerless when opposed by the older individualistic civilizations.[29]

Many writers, then, were ambivalent about African societies which seemed to offer security, but also to restrict the individual freedoms so valued in the West. But, in any case, the finely drawn pictures of communal societies were supposed to be those of a people so far untouched by Western influences.[39] And no one supposed that any of these societies could survive unchanged. The current views about the way in which change was occurring as a result of Western impact provided a further impetus for support for paternalist policies.

An analysis of attitudes to the question of European impact suggests overwhelming support for the idea that the main agents of change had been economic influences of various kinds and that, so far, the result of that impact had been to disintegrate African society. In other words the influences had been essentially destructive. Although there was general agreement on this issue, the language used to describe the changes which had occurred varied according to the political views of the writer, as did the conclusions reached as to what solutions should be attempted. Many writers spoke of the destruction and disintegration of tribal society, referring often to the institutions of that society which had been seriously undermined by rapid economic change.[31] They referred also to the apparent moral deterioration of African people faced with situations which were new and unfamiliar.[32] Both of these arguments were present in the following passage:

> Fifty years ago Africans lived wholly within a communal way of life that gave guidance for every act and at every stage of growth. A man's whole being was steeped in his tribal life as the hand of a dyer is subdued to the colour in which he works. That way of life, though limited, was complete. It was intelligible. It formed what we called a cosmos. Today that little cosmos is breaking down into chaos. Forces play on the African that he cannot resist and, at the outset, fails to understand. The elders of the tribe lament the depravity of the young. A feeling that the house of life is crumbling at the foundations and collapsing in the roof produces profound unrest. The African way of life is suffering that most desperate of maladies: it is losing faith in itself.[33]

There were several implications in this sort of writing which were common to a great many contributors to the literature. The first was the tendency to generalize about African societies as though there were no significant differences between people as unlike as the Masai, the Baganda, the Ibo or the Fulani. The second implication was that these societies had been untouched and unchanging for a very long time before European impact, a suggestion which ignored the centuries of Arab and European slave trading, Moslem invasion and proselytizing, and often savage internal conflict.[34] It was generally believed by these writers that none of these societies could absorb change readily and that they found all aspects of European culture profoundly disturbing, unsettling and even incomprehensible. As a result the picture drawn was always one of destruction rather than growth, with the accompanying fear of chaos of some kind.

The emphasis on the African cut adrift from his own society but not yet assimilated into the security of a new system, presumably a synthesis of African and European institutions and values, was given picturesque form by Hugh Wyndham. He wrote of the African's loss of contact with his own society, as he went out to work to satisfy new material wants. In the process he learned to despise his own tribal background.

> He may end as a highly trained mechanic, dancing in evening clothes, and in the intervals whispering pan-African politics of which the first plank is to turn all Europeans out of Africa neck and crop. But his mental and spiritual being is all the time in its primitive state. He becomes an individual drifting about without any real anchorage in the society he sees so rapidly developing around him, and therefore, at the same time, a menace to the maintenance of the standard of the imported civilization which has cut him adrift from his natural environment.[35]

This passage presented overtly many of the anxieties felt by other writers, concerned with European impact. First there was the argument that the change was only superficial. The evening clothes covered what was, perhaps, formerly a naked tribesman. This reflected the general doubt about how successfully the enormous gulf between 'primitive' and 'civilized' could be bridged. The second anxiety was reflected in Wyndham's reference to pan-African politics. The British clearly had a task in Africa whether it was seen in terms of a civilizing mission at the level of ideas (releasing the African from irrational beliefs) or in developmental terms. Yet the Africans seemed to have a tendency to reject British administrative presence and to become subversive. To what extent would this reaction impede or even prevent the advance of civilization? The third point, closely related to the first, was that reflected in Wyndham's reference to 'natural environment'. This implied that it was somehow right and normal for the African to live in a tribal society—more natural, in fact, than his living in a 'civilized' society. If we assume that Wyndham was not suggesting some essential biological difference between the African and the white man, he presumably referred to the fact that the African had been socialized into the tribal system and could not therefore be easily re-directed to feel at home in a European system. Again the emphasis was on the absence of any elements of continuity from one to the other.

It followed, then, that there was a need for a long and slow process of penetration from outside tribal society, if it was to be transformed successfully so that the 'standards of the imported civilization' (to use Wyndham's phrase) were maintained. Most writers clearly did not think that this gradual change was occurring, for their emphasis was on the destruction and disintegration of tribal society. It was fundamental to most of these arguments that the African, in close contact with European society, threw overboard the security of his tribe. He was a man of two worlds, at home in neither.[36] The answer lay in some sort of regulation of the rate of change, in paternalist policies which would cushion the shock.[37] Sometimes the emphasis was on the administrative policy of indirect rule, which was supposed to prevent too rapid change; sometimes it was on the necessity for a restraint on commercial and industrial activity so that teachers and missionaries could undertake the transformation of African society before the individual lost contact with the economic and social security of tribal life.

The particular emphasis on education and Christian missionary activity was largely the work of writers who had worked as missionaries in Africa and who shared with the radicals a particular language in describing the European impact on Africa. Whereas the conservative view tended to be that European impact had had many undesirable results, in spite of the best efforts of the Europeans involved, the liberal and radical critics of colonial rule were out-spoken in their criticism of the ruthless and exploitive nature of most European enterprise in Africa. Sometimes these critics made the distinction between what had occurred in West and East Africa, in so far as land rights were concerned.[38] However, like the more conservative writers, they tended to generalize about Africa as a whole, when they wrote of the growth of a new industrial proletariat, of the creation of an undesirable class society and the introduction of all the evils of the nineteenth century industrial revolution in Britain.[39] Two particularly prolific writers, J. H. Harris and J. H. Oldham, were directly critical of particular examples of European exploitation in East Africa. J. H. Oldham was fearful that the Christian message would be rejected by people who were trying to defend themselves against the inroads of political domination and economic exploitation. He wanted to see missionaries make a more positive effort to understand African traditions and social customs, which they had so far failed to do, in order to graft Christianity on to them before African society was destroyed.

But the most radical arguments came from those who, while they regretted the disintegration of tribal life, also regretted the spread of all the evils of capitalist society into Africa. These writers were aware that tribal society could not survive the impact of Europe and were even encouraged at the signs of the African's liberation from old fears and irrational beliefs. But, to use the words of Leonard Barnes,

> European economic penetration of Africa has set up conditions to which the clan-bond, the tribal structure, the old unity of African life, is no longer relevant. We are destroying the solidarity of blood related societies in which all members were productively active and of whose cooperative character and significance all members were fully and directly aware. We have split the whole basis of social relationship, and are putting in its place a society which is no society, a society divided against itself and riven by the conflict of opposed group interest. We are, in a word, introducing into African life our own type of class society with all our own unhealed social wounds.[40]

The ambivalence of the views of some of these radical writers left them with something of a dilemma. The conservative writers, confronted with the problem of disruptive social change, found a political solution in indirect rule[41] which they believed would help maintain social stability. They were also prepared to support the idea of limited state intervention in the areas of education, public health and improved agriculture. But they maintained their faith in the dual mandate, according to which there was no necessary conflict between British and African interests in Africa. Others who were critical of much colonial and imperial practice, and who had inherited the humanitarian traditions of the nineteenth century, saw Africa as 'just one more battlefield between Christian understanding of man and the values of modern secular civilization.'[42] They wanted indirect rule policies so that the Christian message could be grafted on to traditional beliefs; and they hoped for a genuine application of trusteeship principles in Africa, using the British administrative service as a kind of buffer to prevent exploitation, until the work of education and Christianization had transformed African society. While many of these liberal Christians were critical of the secular values of their own society they saw themselves as the agents of all that was best in British society

The dilemma for those with radical views about their own society lay in the fact that they did not want to see it reproduced in Africa. Yet they were critical of the conservative reaction in support of indirect rule policies because they believed that tribal institutions were clearly unsuitable to the new milieu in which the African now found himself. More than this, in spite of their emphasis on the spirit of cooperation in the tribe, they believed that tribal institutions inhibited change and elevated the irrational in human relations. Nor did they put much faith in the colonists or missionaries, both groups seen as agents of the civilizing process by conservative and liberal writers.[43] Barnes' doubts, for example, were such that he sometimes approached the problem from a Marxist viewpoint and expressed the determinist idea that African societies were going through a necessary period of destruction before a revolutionary situation developed.[44] These were his views in the late 1930s. Leonard Woolf, writing in 1920, predicted that the European state could not become 'an instrument for good rather than evil in Africa' unless the economic beliefs and desires of Europe were transformed.[45] In effect both of them were hopeful of a transformation of a major kind in their own society as a precursor to changed policies in Africa.

Yet none of these writers were convinced Marxists, hoping for and expecting a revolution to occur. They suspected the interests of private capital but they did not regard the State as the necessary instrument of these interests. They therefore committed themselves to support for a new kind of radical paternalism. They supported the idea of State intervention to carry out planned change over a wide area of activities; they supported the idea of increased African participation in political life outside the tribe; and they supported the idea that an economic and social revolution must be begun in Africa in the interests of the African people.

NOTES

1. In recent writing it has been usual to avoid the word 'primitive' to refer to whole societies. It may be used to refer to the ancestral stages of an organism, or to describe the earliest known beginnings of a particular phenomenon, e.g. tools, implying simplicity of form, even inferiority.
2. See E. E. Evans-Pritchard, 'Social Anthropology, Past and Present', *Man,* 50 (1950), pp. 118–124.
3. Sir Edward Burnett Tylor (1832–1917) was probably the most influential figure among these nineteenth century anthropologists. For an account of his achievement see John Bowle, *Politics and Opinion in the Nineteenth Century,* (London, 1954), pp. 264–273.
4. Known as the Theory of Survivals.

5. See C. Levi-Strauss 'Race and History' in U.N.E.S.C.O., *The Race Question in Modern Science,* (Paris, 1956), for a criticism of the view that Western culture is superior to all others.

6. See T. K. Penniman, *A Hundred Years of Anthropology,* (London, 1935).

7. Two of the earliest functionalists were B. Malinowski and A. R. Radcliffe-Brown.

8. See Daryll Forde, 'Anthropology and the Development of African Studies', *Africa,* 37 (1967), pp. 389–404.

9. It is necessary here to distinguish between this use of the term 'historical', meaning a search for origins and an inevitable order in social development, and the more general use of the term.

10. Most writers on Africa between the wars were not explicit about the source of their social evolutionary beliefs although Norman Leys mentioned Tylor and Frazer as giving a true picture of primitive life.

11. Norman Leys, *The Colour Bar in East Africa,* (London, 1941), p. 56.

12. F. D. Lugard, *The Dual Mandate,* p. 280.

13. J. H. Oldham, *Christianity and the Race Problem,* p. 214.

14. M. Perham, 'The System of Native Administration in Tanganyika', *Africa,* 4 (1931), p. 312.

15. Some writers made specific time comparisons with life in Britain. Leys, for example, compared Africans of thirty years before with people of Britain 2,000 years ago. Perham believed that Bantu life resembled our own as pictured by Tacitus in *Germania,* Cullen-Young spoke of modern Africans as the cultural contemporaries of our ancestors.

16. See M. G. Smith, 'History and Social Anthropology', *J.R.A.I.,* 92, Part 1 (1962), pp. 73–85, E. E. Evans-Pritchard, 'Social Anthropology, Past and Present', *Man,* 50 (1950), pp. 118–124, and Daryll Forde, 'Anthropology and the Development of African Studies', *Africa,* 37 (1967), pp. 389–404. The functionalists have been attacked for their synchronic studies, which were carried out on the methodological assumption that societies were unchanging; for their neglect of history; for their denial of the value of the comparative method.

17. L. J. Cadbury, 'Cocoa Colony', *Geographical Magazine,* 5, 3 (1937), p. 168.

18. Robert Stokes, *New Imperial Ideals,* (London, 1930), p. 161.

19. The Hon. Sir Arthur Lawley in the chair at a talk given by Robert Williams 'More Milestones in African Civilization and some Problems', *United Empire,* New Series, XV (1924), pp. 82–95. The Chairman's opening remarks were recorded.

20. The historians Sir Reginald Coupland, Sir Charles Lucas and Margery Perham all contributed explanations of this kind, which have since been repeated many times in historical texts about Africa.

21. In this analysis, the more specialist work of the anthropologists is being ignored.

22. Sir Reginald Coupland, *The Empire in These Days,* (London, 1929), p. 7.

23. Ifor Evans, *The British in Tropical Africa,* (London, 1929), p. 7.

24. See, for example, W. C. Willoughby, *The Soul of the Bantu,* (London, 1928), Diedrich Westermann, *The African Today and Tomorrow,* (New York, 1934), Margaret Wrong, *The Land and Life of Africa,* (London, 1935), Richard C. Thurnwald, *Black and White in East Africa,* (London, 1935).

25. Leonard Barnes, *The Duty of Empire,* (London, 1935), p. 97. For another example of the same idea see J. H. Oldham and B. D. Gibson, *The Remaking of Man in Africa,* (London, 1931), p. 53.

26. Norman Leys, *A Last Chance in Kenya,* (London, 1931), p. 110.

27. Many writers, using fairly crude stereotypes, developed arguments about the barbaric practices of African people.

28. See Sir Alan Pim, 'British Protectorates and Territories', *United Empire, New Series*, XXV (1934), pp. 266–79.

29. See Charles W. Coulter, 'Environment and Social Conditioning of the Rhodesian Native', in J. Merle Davis (Editor), *Modern Industry and the African*, (New York, 1933), p. 46.

30. Emphasis on the virtues of communal societies may have owed something to the writings of Freud, who stressed the high price paid for civilization in terms of human happiness. It was also in the tradition of Rousseau.

31. See, for example, Wilfred Robertson, 'European Civilization and African Reactions', *National Review*, 101 (1933), p. 358; Donald Fraser, *The New Africa*, (London, 1927), p. 157; C. W. Hobley, *Kenya, From Chartered Company to Crown Colony*, (London, 1929), p. 183.

32. See, for example, Captain L. M. Dundas, 'The African Native', *Empire Review*, 51 (1930), p. 450 and W. R. Crocker, *Nigeria—A Critique*, p. 207.

33. Basil Mathews, *Consider Africa*, (New York, 1936), p. 15.

34. See G. St. J. Orde-Browne, *The African Labourer*, (London, 1933), p. 7, for the rare view that the African had had forced upon him the characteristic of adaptability.

35. Hugh Wyndham, 'The Colour Problem in Africa', *International Affairs*, IV, 4 (1925), p. 176.

36. For picturesque expression of this commonly held view see Basil Mathews, *Consider Africa*, (London, 1935), p. 13, who speaks of the tribal African as 'flotsam and jetsam on the sullen tide of commercialism.'

37. See, for example, J. H. Driberg, *The East African Problem*, p. 57, 'The fusion of cultures, the assimilation of one culture to another, is a process requiring infinite patience, measurable in centuries rather than in decades.'

38. For example Leonard Woolf, *Imperialism and Civilization*, p. 83 f; Leonard Barnes, *Skeleton of Empire*, p. 52 and Norman Leys, 'Kenya and the Gold Coast—a Contrast', *N.S. and N.*, 15 April, 1933.

39. For examples of these criticisms see E. D. Morel, *The Black Man's Burden*, p. 7 f; Leonard Woolf, *Empire and Commerce in Africa*, (London, 1920), p. 353 f; John H. Harris, *Slavery or 'Sacred Trust'?*, p. 160 f; Leonard Barnes, *Empire or Democracy?*, (London, 1939), p. 160 f; and Norman Leys, *Kenya*, p. 306 f.

40. Leonard Barnes, *Empire or Democracy?*, p. 160. See also here Barnes' references to the African's likely escape into 'a millenial world'.

41. This accounts to some extent for the widespread support for indirect rule policies in this period, but not necessarily for the origins of the policy.

42. See J. H. Oldham and B. D. Gibson, *The Remaking of Man in Africa*, (London, 1931), p. 18. 'Is love or force the ultimate power in the Universe?'

43. See for example Leonard Barnes, *The Duty of Empire*, p. 168. Barnes argued that they destroyed the foundation upon which an enlightened society might be built.

44. See for example, *Empire or Democracy?*, p. 160 f.

45. See Leonard Woolf, *Empire and Commerce in Africa*, p. 361.

CHAPTER 5

THEORIES ABOUT RACE

The theme of trusteeship, popular in the 1920s and 1930s seemed to imply an ultimate end to colonial rule in Africa, once her people had made sufficient progress towards certain rather ill-defined goals. The certainty that Africans were as capable of progress as were Europeans would have made the paternalist role easier to define.[1] As it was, a great many writers of varying political opinions, referred to the current state of uncertainty about race questions[2] and commented on the importance of this question in considering any issue involving imperial policies in the African colonies. Some of the current uncertainty was expressed by writers who posed questions for which they believed there were no reliable answers. J. H. Oldham, for example, argued that it was possible that Africans would be unable to maintain, unaided, the complex organization of a modern state, although he hoped that this was a mistaken view. Lord Hailey, pondering a similar question, felt 'some hesitation and uneasiness' when he contemplated the politics of Liberia and Haiti. While some writers deplored the popularity of scientific racism, which provided all kinds of supposed evidence to support existing prejudices, they also pointed to the prevailing ignorance about race questions, due to the absence of reliable information.

We know practically nothing on these subjects, and the reason is that nearly everything written on them is pseudo-science, the product of racial and political bias. We do not know, for instance, what the real causes are which have produced the dying out of the natives of the Pacific Islands, which has followed the appearance of the white men and the introduction of Western civilization. We do not know whether there is any truth in the oft-repeated dogma that two types of civilization cannot exist in close contact, where there is political equality, without the lower type dragging the higher type down to its own level. We have no real knowledge, I think, of the results of inter-marriage between widely different races. Yet such knowledge is indispensable to a rational solution . . . of most of the problems which I have been discussing.[3]

It is clear, then, that in this period, although there was plenty of dubious 'evidence' about race differences and race capacities, many people were wary of such evidence and were uncertain, uneasy and prepared to suspend judgement on questions of race.

Some of those concerned over race questions, and the importance of such questions for making rational political decisions, were predisposed to disbelieve evidence which appeared to support the theory of innate differences between races. Two such people were Sir Gordon Guggisberg, Governor of the Gold Coast in the 1920s and A. G. Fraser, first Principal of Achimota. They stated in the preface of their book that 'divergent views are held about the intellectual capacity and future development of the native of Africa'.[4] They recognized that some saw Africans as occupying inferior positions permanently but they believed

in the absence of theoretical proof to the contrary, biological or otherwise, that the African races are capable of eventually attaining the mental development of the Europeans.[5]

These two writers, then, were 'pro-African' on this issue in spite of the absence of convincing evidence one way or the other. On the other hand many people were predisposed to accept racist interpretation of culture differences and of historical events. One such writer was F. S. Joelson, editor of the paper *East Africa* and author of several books and articles.[6] He believed that

though a few missionaries go to the extreme of saying that white and black are in all things equal, the reasonable man recognises the falsity of such an unnatural idea: nor will he preach it. For all that, many coloured converts have undoubtedly an absurd idea of their own importance, and maintain their equality with the white man . . . [the missionaries] . . . are weakening the white man's prestige by unconsciously, but nevertheless certainly, encouraging the doctrine of the equality of the races.[7]

Joelson went on to speak of miscegenation as 'unnatural' union and to comment on the characteristics of the negro which made it clear that he could not achieve results 'comparable with those of Europe'.

There was at this time, then, considerable doubt and confusion about so-called racial differences, and an examination of the literature dealing with Africa suggests that many people held a quite irrational commitment to a particular point of view. It is clear that the individual with first-hand experience of African people was not, ipso facto, best qualified to make rational judgements about race issues involving Africans. The interested observer in Britain was often more familiar with current literature about questions concerning racial differences and, therefore, sometimes capable of more dispassionate judgement. But attitudes to other questions clouded the issue. Those who were reluctant to see the end of colonial rule sought rationalizations for their position. And one of these was that the African people would never be able to govern themselves. On the other hand many of the reformers, those who wanted to see Africa transformed, were bound to believe that African people had the same potential as Europeans.

Attempts at race classification, first begun on the basis of skin colour in the eighteenth century, assumed, in their theoretical framework, the existence of racial stereotypes or 'ideals' and encouraged a belief in 'pure' races.[8] By the second half of the century race classifications became more complex as scholars, who were engaged in the discipline of physical anthropology, became increasingly involved in measuring the human body, and particularly the cranium, in order to classify race groups more accurately.[9] These early attempts all dwelt on the recording of group differences, implying that some fairly rigid classifications were possible. The conclusions to be reached from their findings were frequently extended to include theories about the relationship between cranial capacity and intelligence, and about the supposed correlation between physical characteristics and class or national superiority.[10]

The discoveries of Mendel[11] which were to lay the foundation of genetics, made possible the clarification of a number of important points in connection with the classification of races. It became apparent that races could not be defined rigidly, either spatially or in terms of time.[12] The idea that race groupings were 'evolutionary units in space and time' had to be discarded,[13] as did earlier theories about the blending of inherited characteristics.

However the theory of genetics had made little impact on scholars by 1920 so that reliance on anthropological evidence continued. It was still commonly held that different races could be clearly identified, while the idea of an existing relationship between physical racial characteristics and particular cultural traits was still frequent. The racist theories developed in Europe in the nineteenth century[14] still found their firm supporters, and even those who were disposed to question such beliefs remained confused and uncertain. This uncertainty among many laymen was a reflection of the absence of reliable scientific information. In 1931 E. A. Hooten wrote

Anthropologists have not yet reached the point of agreement upon criteria of race which will enable psychologists to isolate with any degree of facility the racial types which are to be studied. Psychologists have not yet been able to develop mental tests which anthropologists are willing to trust as fair gauges of mental capacity. Neither group has yet perfected its technique of measurement. Until we know exactly how to distinguish a race and exactly what intelligence tests test, we shall have to hold in suspension the problem of racial mental differences.[15]

However, in 1935 the two scholars Julian Huxley and A. C. Haddon attempted to provide the public with 'a popular presentation of the facts with some interpretation of them in terms of scientifically acceptable genetic doctrine'.[16] The authors deplored the vast body of pseudo-science which existed on the subject of race,[17] and pointed out that even in the field of anthropological writings, genetic discoveries had not been adequately incorporated.[18]

The level of ignorance is perhaps reflected in the fact that the works of Sir Arthur Keith,[19] one time President of the Royal Anthropological Society,[20] continued to promote confusions between race and culture. Sir Arthur Keith deplored the trend away from the recognized relationship between race and nation. He postulated what he called the group theory of evolution that

> during the whole period of human evolution mankind had been divided into a vast number of isolated local communities, each inhabiting a delineated area of territory.

These groups maintained themselves because of an innate spirit of antagonism towards one another.[21] Thus Keith believed in pure races inherently antagonistic while at the same time he identified race and nation. He saw the existence of race prejudice as part of 'the evolutionary machinery which safeguards the purity of the race.'[22] He spoke of the mixing of the races, in the geographical area between India and Britain, as having 'queered Nature's plan of evolution', but argued that Nature immediately set out to repair the damage by creating new races out of the fusion of old elements.[23] Both the confusion about what he believed constituted a pure race, and the anthropomorphism were reminiscent of the nineteenth century.

Nor had the earlier confusion between race and linguistics been cleared up.[24] C. G. Seligman,[25] author of *The Races of Africa* first published in 1930, declared that he recognized

> that questions of race should first and last be determined by the study of physical characters, yet in no part of Africa is there in existence anything approaching an anthropological survey.[26]

In the absence of this supposedly decisive anthropological survey,

Seligman combined limited anthropological data with linguistic evidence to provide an account of race differences in Africa. He claimed that 'linguistic criteria are constantly applied to large groups of mankind and, indeed, if intelligently used, often fit quite well.'[27] He failed to see that although the study of linguistics does provide valuable information about human relations in terms of their culture and history, there is no necessary genetic similarity between speakers of related languages.

The existence of centuries of linguistic confusion between the concepts of race and culture is clear from an examination of the entries under 'race' in the Oxford Dictionary. Such confusions continue in terms such as 'the British Race' and 'primitive races'. These confusions do not necessarily imply a belief in the existence of a relationship between the culture of a particular group and its biological peculiarities; nor does the term 'primitive race' necessarily imply a biological explanation for a culture evaluated as inferior to one's own. Yet modern justifications for segregationist policies are frequently couched in terms which suggest a close causal relationship between race and culture, race and intelligence and race and morality.[28]

In the inter-war period there was great confusion over the use of the term.[29] The word 'race' was used, without qualification, to refer to groups of people who occupied defined geographical areas, groups with apparently similar physical characteristics, groups with a distinctive culture or speaking the same language, and finally, to refer to all Africans as opposed to all Europeans. These two categories of black and white were the ones used most frequently in comments of a racist kind, so that a stereotype of 'the African' was created and used as a comparison with 'the European'. This simple identification of many diverse cultural groups according to skin colour not only perpetuated the myth about the necessary connection between physical appearance and cultural achievement. It also made meaningful discussion almost impossible, because it ignored cultural diversity in both Africa and Europe, and implied that there were two sorts of culture which were closed systems.

Among those writing about African affairs in the inter-war period, there were comparatively few who became involved in discussion about actual physical differences between race groups.[30] There were, however, occasional echoes of some of the scientific debates of the time in mention of brain size[31] and comparative intelligence testing of various groups, isolated according to the criteria of skin colour and hair form. In particular R. A. C. Oliver, who had written a manual entitled *General Intelligence Tests for*

Africans, published several articles on this question in the journals *Oversea Education* and *Africa*.[32] A few writers advocated the extension of existing work on the mental capacity of Africans because the results might have a direct bearing on colonial education policy.[33] Others were prepared to believe that fairly conclusive results had already been obtained. In 1937 the *Empire Review* printed an article which quoted the conclusions of an expert in mental disease in Nairobi

> that there is accumulating evidence that the native brain differs materially from the European brain, and that there is a definite racial inferiority in quantity as well as quality in the actual brain tissue.[34]

Undoubtedly the most popular issue referred to by laymen in this period was that of miscegenation, and discussions of this issue frequently revealed a belief in the existence of groups which were racially pure. A great many people expressed doubt about the outcome of miscegenation, many of them counselling caution. Many believed the result to be disastrous for the white man in terms of prestige and the 'debasement of racial standards'.[35] On the other hand some writers argued that the 'mixing of blood' improved the negro strain.[36] Lugard, for example, thought the Sudanese and negroid people, who were not pure negro, made better soldiers. He argued that the

> alien immigrants in the northern tropical belt (of Africa) afforded better material for social organization, both racially and through the influence of their creed, than the advanced communities of negro stock.[37]

He advanced the theory that these differences in intelligence, which he had observed, were due to the fact that the 'pure negro stock' was lower on the scale of evolution and had a less highly developed brain and nervous system than other groups, apparently able to be distinguished partly by lighter skins.[38] The arguments against miscegenation included theories about race mixture resulting in a general lowering of the intellectual level achieved by the white race. J. H. Oldham, for example, committed himself to a belief in the possibility of biological determinism in history.[39]

> In view of what the white man has actually accomplished in history it is evident that certain qualities that make for human progress are present in that race. The lack of historical achievement up to the present among the black peoples suggests that while they may possess other desirable qualities, those which have made white civilization possible may not be distributed among them to the same degree. We cannot be certain that this is so, but it is possible, or, as many would say, probable.[40]

A similar argument was developed by Major Archibald Church, who concluded like Oldham, that 'racial purity' was therefore desirable.[41] Much of the opposition to miscegenation was much less reasoned than this and found expression in reference to the tragic consequences of intermarriage[42] and to the creation of racial mongrels.[43] Perhaps the most picturesque expression of opposition to miscegenation came from a writer who referred to both the half-caste and the Europeanized African as 'neither flesh, nor fowl, nor good red herring'.[44]

It is clear that this sort of opposition to miscegenation implied a belief in racial purity and the necessity to maintain that purity. An article by Sir Frederick Lugard, from which the following passage was taken, also indicated a confusion between race and nation.

> By promoting the migration of British men and women the Mother Country can assist in keeping the strain predominantly British in these great and growing communities. The vital importance of this purity of blood has been brought home to us very vividly by the school of American writers, more especially Mr. Stoddard's recent books, *The Rising Tide of Colour* and *Revolt against Civilization*. The facts cited and the logical conclusions drawn are so arresting that I wish every Englishman could read them.[45]

These books referred to by Lugard committed their American author to a racist philosophy of history. According to Stoddard civilization sprang from 'the creative urge of superior germ plasm. Civilization is thus fundamentally conditioned by race'.[46] He wrote of some peoples being 'congenital barbarians incapable of progress' and warned against the dire consequences of allowing these inferior races into civilized communities. He also believed that part of the explanation for the decline of all known civilizations lay in the fact that civilized life impeded the processes of natural selection. This was a restatement of an argument common to the Social-Darwinians in the nineteenth century.

This belief in a hierarchy of races, of which the Negro was on the lowest rung, was on a par with other beliefs still current between the wars about the sexual over-indulgence of the African,[47] and his lack of sensibility and character.[48] Some of these ideas flowed strongly from the beliefs of an earlier period.[49] But there were two aspects of the question of race differences which seemed to have received particular attention in the inter-war period. One was the question of a difference between European and African 'mentality', a word in constant use between the wars. The other was the question of whether or not Africans would ever be able to master the art of good government. The interest in these two issues at this time presumably reflected the fact that the doctrine of trusteeship implied the need for education and for progress towards self-government.

However, the discussion about African 'mentality' had also been raised in learned circles by Lucien Lévy-Bruhl, a professor at the Sorbonne who, in 1910, wrote a book which was translated as *How Natives Think*.[50] This was followed in 1923 by another book called *Primitive Mentality*.[51] Bruhl stated that primitive mentality was due 'neither to incapacity nor inaptitude'[52] and seemed to be attempting an analysis of the profoundly different 'world view' of African societies when compared with those of Europe. He believed that according to the African cosmos all objects and entities were 'involved in a system of mystic participation and exclusion: it is these which constitute its cohesion and its order';[53] whereas the European saw the world as reflecting the operation of immutable natural laws.[54] Bruhl aimed at scientific objectivity, but it is clear that many people have since regarded his work as reflecting racist value judgements. In particular he was attacked for his use of the word 'pre-logical' to describe African thought processes. The writer and anthropologist, J. H. Driberg, explicitly denied the argument (which he said was Bruhl's) that the African was incapable of thinking logically.[55] He did not deny that Africans held beliefs which would have been regarded as irrational in Western society, but he argued that they were rational for the African in his circumstances. He attempted to demonstrate the ability of the African to draw accurate inferences from his observations.[56]

In the same year the Reverend J. W. C. Dougall, educationalist and missionary,[57] joined in the debate in a memorandum published by the International Institute of African Languages and Cultures.[58] He put the issues clearly in his introduction by asking

> Is there a fundamental disparity between Africans and ourselves in modes of thought? Can they assimilate Western civilization, not merely accepting its scientific discoveries and inventions, but making its intellectual assumptions and methods really their own?

He pointed to the existence of a conflict between the belief in the unity of the human race and the actual observations of missionaries and others, which he believed had now developed into a general theory arguing a 'fundamental disparity in the psychology' of European and African. Dougall produced a closely reasoned argument to show that no such disparity existed.[59] But he also concluded that there was some ambiguity in the position of Lévy-Bruhl who, although he argued that 'pre-logical and mystical are co-existent with the logical', also seemed to want to say that there was some fundamental difference between the two cultures.

The confusion between concepts of race and culture apparent at this level of the debate found much cruder expression in those debating more general political issues. Those who were convinced of the African's inferior mentality argued that there was a definite limit to his educability, that he was more susceptible to propaganda (usually thought to be of a sinister kind) than the European, and that it would be unjust to the African to burden him with political power and responsibility.[60] The difficulties faced in educating Africans arose, according to these arguments, from his inability to grasp the 'real points at issue',[61] the impossibility of his requiring lasting knowledge[62] and from the fact that he lacked initiative, balance and perseverance.[63] These were judgements about the African as a member of the African 'race' and not comments on the great gulf which existed between European and African cultural values. The conclusion drawn was that the process of educating the African might make him more easily indoctrinated with Pan-Islamic or Pan-Negro doctrines[64] or 'false ideas of rights and grievances'.[65] According to these views, such an outcome would indicate not success but failure in the educative process.

Doubt about the ability of the African to master the arts of good government were common throughout the inter-war period, and some journals promoted the idea that good government was preferable to self-government.[68] It is not always possible to attribute this scepticism about the political capacity of the African to beliefs of a racist kind. It was sometimes a comment on the wide gulf between British and African political practice which could be interpreted in social evolutionary terms.[67] However some of these arguments clearly implied some innate incapacity for good government, and many reputable scholars made statements which had strong racist implications. Sir Charles Lucas, for example, was convinced of the need for paternalist government in Africa for

> if we consider the African races, or at any rate the Negro and Bantu races . . . their outstanding features are, on the one hand their strength and vitality, and on the other their inability to do without European guidance.[68]

If it is assumed that even the most unsophisticated debater would have admitted that Africans once governed themselves, there must have been some particular implications behind these arguments that British presence was required in Africa to provide good government. It seems clear that most of those who supported colonial policies on the grounds of the inability of Africans to govern themselves were convinced that, in the nineteenth century, Britain took over control of societies which were unprogressive, corrupt and despotic. Their arguments implied that the African systems in existence before the intervention of Europe were so undesirable as to indicate some racial limitations in political capacity.[69]

Many writers knew that confusion was rife in these arguments about African mentality and political capacity, and attempted some kind of objectivity. The three colonial governors Sir Gordon Guggisberg, Sir William Gowers, and Sir Donald Cameron were among this group. All attributed 'backwardness' to environmental factors, and recorded their belief that the African was not inferior in intelligence to the European.[70] Sir William Gowers stated that after thirty years in Africa he could see no evidence that would lead him to believe

> that the native of Africa is on the whole naturally or fundamentally inferior to the so called white races in reasoning power or capacity for development.[71]

Some writers denied the proposition that it was not possible to understand the African mind. One writer argued that

> the complexities and illogicalities have no other origin than in the natural difference between two human minds whose starting points of experience are not the same.[72]

For others the accidents of environment and opportunity had limited the outlook of the African, but he was capable of living on equal terms with the European.[73] Some writers explained apparent differences in evolutionary terms. The uniqueness of the African would disappear if he were compared with medieval Europeans,[74] while others compared African societies with those of Europe a thousand years earlier than this.

Several writers combined an attack on racist dogma with theorizing about its origins in economic conflict and national arrogance.

> Race prejudice in a dominant race is self-justificatory arrogance. Men hate whom they have injured, despise him for his subjection, and blacken his character in order to justify his oppression. Having enslaved they complain of servile qualities . . . and say these [men] are unfit to govern themselves.[75]

Racist beliefs were thus under attack from some whose observations convinced them that Africans were intelligent people; from others whose view of history convinced them that Westerners were parochial and arrogant on the issue;[76] and from several writers who were convinced that there were no genuine scientific grounds for supporting theories of African inferiority. This last named group included Norman Leys, Leonard Barnes[77] and W. M. Macmillan.[78] In the view of Norman Leys

> There is no scrap of evidence to suggest that mental capacity and ability in any group have improved in the course of the evolution of its ideas. The opinion of scientists, anthropologists and philosophers alike is that the minds of our ancestors 5,000 years ago were not inferior to our own. Our sole gain lies in a laboriously acquired and precariously as well as laboriously transmitted mass of knowledge and ideas and habits, no part of which is ever the sole achievement of any single man or any isolated community.[79]

Norman Leys was the propagandist most anxious to break down the racial stereotype and allow Europeans to see Africans as 'just people', who had the same aims as men on other continents.[80] For Leys, and other writers who were sympathetic to his viewpoint, colonial rule was not justified by race differences. They shared a faith in reformist politics and developmental programmes which would transform African societies, and prepare them for independence.

NOTES

1. See, for example, Sir Godfrey Lagden, *The Native Races of the Empire*, (London, 1924), p. 74, 'It is no easy matter to make a forecast of the future because it is beyond our powers to realize the intellectual height which the natives as a whole can reach. The mere fact that a few here and there have shown outstanding ability gives us no clue.'
2. See, for example, J. H. Oldham, 'Report of the Commission on closer union of the Eastern and Central African Dependencies', *International Affairs*, VIII (1929), p. 229; M. Perham, 'Future Relations of Black and White in Africa', *Listener*, 28 March, 1934; Basil Mathews, *The Clash of Colour*. (London, 1924), p. 117 of the 1928 edition; Major A. G. Church, *East Africa: A New Dominion*, p. 57 f.
3. Leonard Woolf, *Imperialism and Civilization*, pp. 104–5.
4. F. G. Guggisberg and A. G. Fraser, *The Future of the Negro*.
5. This quotation is from the introduction to the book mentioned above, which was signed by Guggisberg.
6. See bibliography.
7. See F. S. Joelson, *The Tanganyika Territory*, (London, 1920), p. 96.
8. For comment on this, see W. MacGaffey, 'Concepts of Race in the Historiography of North East Africa', *Journal of African History*, 7, 1 (1966), pp. 1–17.
9. Craniometry was begun in 1842 by a Swedish scholar, Retzius, who devised methods for measuring the skull. He introduced the divisions of mankind into Brachycephalic and Dolichocephalic. For the application of these ideas to Africa see Christine Bolt, *Victorian Attitudes to Race* (London, 1971), p. 15.
10. For discussions of these theories, see F. H. Hankins, *The Racial Basis of Civilization*, and J. Barzun, *Race*, (London, 1938).

11. First published in 1866, but not further developed until 1900. See C. L. Brace and M. F. Ashley Montagu, *Man's Evolution* (New York, 1965), pp. 25–32.

12. See 'Genetics: race and genetics', an entry in the *International Encyclopaedia of the Social Sciences*, (1968).

13. See the essays of R. W. Holm and N. A. Barnicot in A. Montagu (ed.), *The Concept of Race*, (New York, 1964), for a discussion of this idea, and the fact that it was encouraged by early race classifications.

14. For detailed analysis of the racist theories developed in Europe in the first half of the nineteenth century, see P. D. Curtin, *The Image of Africa,* and E. W. Count, 'The Evolution of the Race Idea in Modern Western Culture during the period of the pre-Darwinian 19th Century'. *Transactions of the New York Academy of Sciences,* Second Series, 8 (1946), pp. 139–165. For the later period see A. C. Haddon, *History of Anthropology,* and T. K. Penniman, *A Hundred Years of Anthropology.*

15. E. A. Hooten, *Up from the Ape,* (New York, 1931), p. 596.

16. See Julian Huxley and A. C. Haddon, *We Europeans,* (London, 1935), p. 7.

17. They referred in particular to a continuing belief in a 'blood-tie', in a literal sense, in the racial origin of group sentiment, and in 'pure' races.

18. See *We Europeans,* p. 63.

19. See bibliography.

20. From 1912 to 1914.

21. Sir Arthur Keith, *A New Theory of Human Evolution,* (London, 1948).

22. Sir Arthur Keith, 'The Evolution of the Human Races', *J.R.A.I.,* 58 (1928), p. 316.

23. *Ibid.,* p. 318.

24. See Christine Bolt, *Victorian Attitudes to Race,* pp. 12–13.

25. C. G. Seligman, some time Professor of Ethnology, University of London. President of the Royal Anthropological Institute, 1923–35.

26. *The Races of Africa,* (London, 1930), p. 9.

27. *Ibid.,* p. 10.

28. See 'Race', in the *International Encyclopaedia of the Social Sciences* (1968) . . . it is beyond dispute that the overwhelming bulk of the response repertory of any human breeding population can be learned by any other human breeding population'.

29. Norman Leys attempted to check some of this confusion. See *Kenya,* p. 84. He pointed out that most of the names given to East African people were based on language distinctions. Also Major A. Church, *East Africa: A New Dominion,* p. 53, 'Common origin for speech is not synonymous with common racial origin'.

30. The first classifications to be made on the basis of blood groups were carried out in the 1920s and early 1930s, using only O, A and B blood groups, O being universally present. See W. C. Boyd, *Genetics and the Races of Man* (Oxford, 1950), p. 221.

31. Margery Perham thought there was no firm evidence of a relationship between brain size and intelligence. See M. Perham, 'Future Relations of Black and White in Africa', *Listener,* 28 March, 1934. The archaeologist L. S. B. Leakey pointed to the existence of a school of thought in Kenya which believed the European and African to be fundamentally different. He thought there was no scientific evidence for a relationship between brain size and intelligence. See *Kenya: Contrasts and Problems,* (London, 1936), p. 164.

32. See R. A. C. Oliver, 'The Adaptation of Intelligence Tests to Tropical Africa', *Oversea Education,* IV, 4 (1933) pp. 186–191 and V, 1 (1933),

pp. 8–12, 'Comparison of Cultural Achievement', *Oversea Education*, V, 3 (1934), pp. 107–111 and 'Mental Tests in the Study of the African', *Africa*, VII (1934), p. 4.

33. See, for example, C. W. Hobley, *Bantu Beliefs and Magic*, (London, 1922). See the revised edition 1928, p. 333.

34. Sir Ernest Graham Little, M.D., M.P., 'The British Empire and Backward Races', *Empire Review*, 66 (1937), p. 270.

35. The expression of C. W. Hobley, *Kenya: From Chartered Company to Crown Colony*, p. 223.

36. This view was widespread in the 19th century. See Christine Bolt, *Victorian Attitudes to Race*, p. 23.

37. See F. D. Lugard, *The Dual Mandate*, p. 204. See also p. 68 f and p. 574.

38. Sir Reginald Coupland also believed there were advantages for the negro in miscegenation. See *The Empire in These Days*, p. 201.

39. J. H. Oldham was confused on this issue. For on p. 62 of *Christianity and the Race Problem* he says "Theories which attempt to isolate a racial factor and find in it the explanation of civilization are highly speculative and have little of the cautious attitude which belongs to true science."

40. See J. H. Oldham, *Ibid.*, p. 180.

41. See Major A. G. Church, *East Africa: A New Dominion*, p. 207 f.

42. See Sir John Chancellor, 'Southern Rhodesia and its Problems', *J.A.S.*, 26 (1926–27), p. 2.

43. See Robert Stokes, *New Imperial Ideals*, p. 200.

44. Wilfred Robertson, 'European Civilization and African Reactions', *National Review*, 101 (1933), p. 362.

45. See Sir F. Lugard, 'Growth of Empire', *United Empire*, New Series, XIII (1922), p. 738.

46. See Lothrop Stoddard, *The Revolt against Civilization*, (London, 1922), p. 2.

47. See, for example, C. W. Hobley, 'Some Native Problems in Eastern Africa', *J.A.S.*, 22 (1922–23), p. 191, and 'Achimota', *Round Table*, XVI (1925–26), p. 90.

48. For an example of this kind of argument see W. R. Crocker, *Nigeria. A Critique*, p. 202 f.

49. See Christine Bolt, *Victorian Attitudes to Race*, p. 136.

50. In French, *Les Fonctions Mentales dans les Sociétés Inférieures*.

51. Bruhl's work on the subject included other books published in the 1930s.

52. See *Primitive Mentality*, p. 29.

53. *Ibid.*, p. 35.

54. For an account of Lévy-Bruhl's theories, see *The Encyclopaedia of the Social Sciences*, (1969).

55. See J. H. Driberg, *The Savage as he Really is*, and *At Home with the Savage*, (London, 1932).

56. See, also, Edwin W. Smith, *The Golden Stool*, (London, 1927), p. 84, for a discussion of Bruhl's arguments.

57. The Reverend J. W. C. Dougall was first Principal of the Jeanes School at Kabete, Kenya, and subsequently educational adviser to the Protestant Missions in Kenya and Uganda.

58. J. W. C. Dougall, 'Characteristics of African Thought', (*I.I.A.L.C.* Memorandum X, 1932), pp. 1–30.

59. J. H. Driberg had stressed the element of rationality in African modes of thought. Dougall, on the other hand, emphasized the survival of irrationality in Western culture and concluded that the African's 'social tradition has

encouraged the persistence in the individual of the pre-logical modes of thought characteristic of the unconscious.'

60. See, for example, W. R. Crocker, *Nigeria. A Critique*, p. 206.

61. See, for example, William Jesse, 'Natives in East Africa', *National Review*, 103 (1934), p. 734.

62. See, for example, Captain L. M. Dundas, 'The African Native', *Empire Review*, LI (1930), p. 450.

63. The view of C. W. Hobley, 'Some Native Problems in Eastern Africa', *Journal of the African Society*, XXII (1922–23), p. 191.

64. 'The Indian Problem in East Africa', *Round Table*, XII (1921–1922), p. 359.

65. The words of G. K. Peto, 'Kenya and Madagascar: A Comparison and a Moral', *Empire Review*, LII (1930), p. 33.

66. e.g. *The Round Table.*

67. The view expressed by Sir F. Lugard in his article 'Growth of Empire'.

68. See Sir Charles Lucas, *The Partition and Colonization of Africa*, (London, 1922), p. 204 f.

69. For many people, the instability in new African States can be explained in this way.

70. See Sir Donald Cameron, *My Tanganyika Service and Some Nigeria*, (London, 1939), p. 244, and Sir Gordon Guggisberg, *The Future of the Negro*, p. 48.

71. See Sir William Gowers, 'Uganda and Indirect Rule', *United Empire*, New Series, XXIV (1933), p. 102.

72. See Thomas Cullen Young, *Contemporary Ancestors*, (London, n.d.), p. 57.

73. See, for example, Sir Daniel Hall, *The Improvement of Native Agriculture in Relation to Population and Public Health*, (Oxford, 1936), p. 87 and L. S. B. Leakey, *White African*, (London, 1937), p. 39.

74. See, for example, A. Victor Murray, *A School in the Bush*, (London, 1929), p. 96 and p. 315.

75. Sir Sydney Olivier, 'Colour Prejudice', *Contemporary Review*, 125 (1923), p. 456.

76. See, for examples, of this group:—C. R. Buxton, *The Race Problem in Africa*, (London, 1931), p. 50, Basil Mathews, *The Clash of Colour*, p. 133, and Donald Fraser, *The New Africa*, p. 186.

77. See Leonard Barnes, *The Duty of Empire*, p. 67.

78. W. M. Macmillan, *Africa Emergent*, p. 31.

79. N. Leys, *Kenya*, p. 70.

80. See, in particular, *A Last Chance in Kenya*, p. 116.

CHAPTER 6

DEVELOPMENT AND RESEARCH

An important element in the paternalist faith of the inter-war period was the new emphasis on Britain's role as that of a kind of development agency, responsible from now on for applying Western knowledge and skills to the special problems of Africa. The comparatively advanced technology of Britain had already made possible major changes in Africa, especially in the provision of the sort of infra-structure which could assist in the growth of trade.[1] Some of these changes had been promoted by the Colonial Office,[2] but there had never been any systematic development programme for African colonies. Nor was widespread support for development policies typical of any period before World War I.[3] However in the period between the wars the advocacy of interventionist policies for the purpose of development in Africa was undertaken by people of almost all political persuasions.[4]

The word 'development' was used constantly and ambiguously in this period. In the discussion of politics and social change it often referred to the process whereby African societies appeared to be more nearly approximating to Western norms, often involving the idea of some fixed social evolutionary processes. In the field of economics it was often used as a label for those operations of private capitalists, including investments in mining, in plantations, and in industrial concerns, which were thought likely to increase general productivity. But increasingly the word was used to describe the nature of projects which should be carried out by the British or Colonial governments and which were either planned to benefit the African people or, it was argued, likely incidentally to do so. By the end of the 1930s the word 'development' was most frequently used to describe a process of social, political and economic change, which had been, and should be, directed by Britain so that African colonial territories could be transformed into viable states. It was conceded that private capital had a part to play but it was no longer believed that development and welfare inevitably followed capital investment.[5]

It was part of the nineteenth century laisser-faire doctrine that the investment of capital in profitable enterprises would result in economic development and improved human welfare. Africa may even have seemed to offer particularly good 'developmental' opportunities because of the existence of largely untouched natural resources, a large body of unskilled workers, and a market so far barely opened up.[6] The rejection of this doctrine and the growing attachment to the idea of planned development, implying interventionist policies, may be seen as partly the outcome of earlier British experiences in Africa in the economic sphere; partly the result of the growth of new economic orthodoxies in Britain from 1900 onwards; and partly due to changing interpretations of Britain's role in Africa.

The slave trade had provided the first major commercial impact on Africa and the transformation of this trade into 'legitimate' commerce had been accompanied by a gradual increase in political control. The spread of administrative services, backed up by small armed forces, brought comparative peace to vast areas which could be opened up for trade. This resulted in a gradual increase in knowledge about African geography and resources, further extended by European wartime activities in Africa. The demand for tropical goods was considerable from 1900 and increased during the first World War, yet the problems associated with satisfying these demands were becoming increasingly apparent.[7] The economic and political experiences connected with past exploitation of African resources suggested that there was no longer any long term profit in 'despoliation'.[8] Nor were the Chartered companies any longer able to operate successfully, as the freedom which they had enjoyed because of their administrative undertakings was curtailed. Nor were conditions in Africa always conducive to the success of private business ventures. The communications problem was probably the vital one,[9] but the labour force was both unskilled and often unwilling to seek European employment,[10] while the subsistence economy was only very slowly being transformed into a market economy.

While the difficulties faced by private enterprise, operating in a laisser-faire situation, were being identified, support in Britain for Free Trade policies had begun to decline and tariffs were increasingly being applied for political ends. The idea of developing the resources of the Empire as a whole, according to what one advocate called a policy of 'constructive imperialism',[11] began to take shape in the late 1890s and at first most clearly concerned the Dominions. It was greatly strengthened by the siege mentality which developed during the first World War and resulted in increasing support for notions of imperial self-sufficiency. This ideal lay behind the establishment of the Tariff Commission in Britain in 1903,[12] and the promotion of a Dominions Royal Commission set up in 1912 to study Imperial policy.[13] The growth of protectionist attitudes towards the colonies was particularly reflected in the formation of a committee in 1917 in Britain which undertook to analyse a variety of problems connected with British economic interests, including the safeguarding of Empire supplies from foreign control and the development of Empire resources.[14] The same spirit was reflected in attempts during and immediately after the war to gain monopoly control over the supplies of various goods produced in the colonies, including palm kernels, jute, tin and copra.[15]

In the post World War I period the idea of exercising fairly stringent controls over colonial products by the exercise of tariff policies was thought by some writers to be contrary to the spirit of trusteeship. Yet the accompanying idea that the colonies should be developed was not also rejected. It was supported as an essential ingredient of the theory of trusteeship. Much of the sense of mission which was apparent in the debates of the time about the obligations of Trusteeship was based on a belief in the possession of, or access to, superior knowledge and skills which could be made the basis for promoting change in Africa.

Western faith in scientific progress, in technological innovation and in the discovery of rational solutions to human problems was highlighted by contrasting European society with examples of what was thought to be fairly typical of African society.[16] Economic activities were seen to be largely centred on subsistence agriculture which could provide no resources for development. Social systems were underpinned by ritual and the survival of many irrational beliefs.[17] Political life was such as to deny individual freedom and initiative and produce stagnation rather than progress.[18] Although many of the critics of British industrial society found much that was praiseworthy in the communal societies of Africa, most of them stressed the existence of many undesirable features as well, and asked themselves how these societies could best be transformed in order to retain what was valuable.

An analysis of the literature advocating developmental projects reveals that there were a variety of interpretations of Britain's obligations in this field, and of the purposes for which the British and Colonial governments should undertake such projects. But all arguments implied support for paternalist policies of a positive kind. All of them, if carried out, would have required considerable capital, a large body of skilled administrators, and the involvement of many people with specialized knowledge and skills. There is evidence of some support for development theory in Colonial Office policy in the period under discussion,[19] but it was not made the basis of a real programme until the period after 1940.[20] The Colonial Development and Welfare Act of that year represented a new approach to development policy.[21] This change may be attributed in part to the propaganda for development policies from a wide cross section of the British intelligentsia interested in Africa, in the preceding two decades.[22]

In the context of general debate about the African colonies, there were at least four main arguments which provided the basis for development propaganda, and which were used to explain why British intervention was thought to be necessary. Those writers who wanted to emphasize the need for the British Government to assist in creating those conditions which would ensure the success of private ventures, expressed themselves as supporters of the dual mandate, arguing that the interests of Europe and Africa were inextricably linked. Those who preferred to emphasize Britain's obligations in Africa believed that developmental programmes were an essential part of trusteeship. A third group went further than this and claimed that Britain must now intervene for planned development, in order to make up for past neglect and to correct the unfortunate results of the earlier introduction of British capital. Finally many writers believed that material progress was necessary if there was to be progress in other areas, and that the colonies could not provide the necessary resources to undertake development schemes.

The supporters of the dual mandate tended to emphasize British interests in Africa, and to speak of the potential wealth of the colonial areas, in both material and human resources, if only developmental projects could be carried out. The Liberal Member of Parliament, F. C. Linfield, for example, who was one of the members of the East African Commission of 1925,[23] advocated development planning through a National or Imperial Development Board.[24] According to his argument African wealth would help solve Britain's problems in providing employment, creating wide demands for British goods and increasing the supply of raw materials for British industry.[25]

> We have within the Empire millions of acres of fertile land and enormous mineral resources only awaiting development by the provision of roads, bridges, and railways.[26]

It was typical of writers who stressed British interests in Africa that they emphasized the importance of transport and communication. Exploitation of resources by private capital, one form of development, waited on the provision of certain services which should be provided by the State. The emphasis was on the fact that Britain controlled vast untapped resources which should be used in the interests of providing wealth for Britain. In 1925, for example, the Right Hon. L. S. Amery exhorted Britain to think imperially, in order to rival the prosperity of the United States.

> We have the territory, we have the resources, we have the men, we have the capacity to achieve an even greater prosperity than theirs.[27]

In the 1920s African interests were given little consideration by these advocates of development. It was generally assumed that the operations by private capital would ultimately benefit Africans in much the same way as they benefited the working classes of Britain in providing employment and, therefore, higher standards of living. In fact an occasional writer in the 1920s used the argument that economic development in Africa was a vehicle for the moral regeneration of the African people who would be encouraged to adopt habits of work and thrift.[28]

None the less some of the dual mandate supporters dwelt on the advantages, both for Britain and Africa, of the extension of health and education services. In the early 1920s, for example, one writer urged large scale education by the State in order to prevent the growth of pan-African politics. He argued that training in trades

> renders the native a useful and cooperative member of a productive community, and will increase his stability in enabling him to assist in the development of his own continent, which is the most certainly valuable investment that Europe can make today.[29]

The views of those who supported trusteeship policies were oriented differently from those who thought primarily of British interests in Africa. These were the people who stressed the second half of the mandate and, in some cases, were actually dubious about the advantages, for Africans, of economic development. Some feared the disruptive nature of much British enterprise and advocated British Government control over private enterprise.[30] This group of paternalists stressed the obligation of Britain for African welfare and either ignored, or played down the question of British interests.

> European governments . . . have taken responsibility for guiding the development of African peoples. The security of law of which they are the guardians, the resources of science which they can command and organize, the comprehensive measures for the improvement of health, agriculture and education which they alone can devise and carry out

are indispensable for the material, moral and social advancement of the peoples of Africa.[31]

They talked of measures which directly concerned human welfare, rather than of economic development. This aspect of their writing reflected not only their primary interest in moral and social questions but also the fact that they believed that British interests had exploited Africa in the past. This view was apparent in an article by Sir Bernard Bourdillon, in which he contrasted the theory of exploitation, according to which Africa was a mine of material and human resources to be exhausted as soon as possible, with the development theory which gave first place to the welfare of the Africans.[32] A similar point of view was expressed by Julian Huxley in articles which examined a number of aspects of government policy in East Africa.[33]

Some of the writers, who stressed the obligations of the British to carry out her trusteeship undertakings, saw no conflict between economic development and more general welfare programmes. Rather they took the view that whereas economic development had already occurred in Africa, Britain had consistently failed to carry out her promises in the welfare field. These had been made first at the Berlin Conference in 1885 when the European powers had agreed to regulate

> the conditions most favourable to trade and development and the means of furthering the moral and material well-being of the native populations in certain regions of Africa.[34]

According to Major Church, and to Donald Fraser[35] who also referred to the Berlin and Brussels meetings, Britain had previously failed to accept her responsibilities. Her right to be in Africa and to control African resources depended upon whether or not she was prepared to promote economic development but also the 'moral and educational advance' of the people. These views were expressed early in the inter-war period, in an appeal to the Under Secretary of State from the Anti-Slavery and Aborigines Protection Society for a conference along the lines of previous ones held at Vienna, Brussels and Berlin.[36] This was to be an attempt to establish principles which would have application to all the colonial areas, and provide a basis for government action.

> We have asked that any such conference should define anew the exist-ing international obligations for the suppression of slave-owning and slave-trading, secure an international agreement to abolish forced labour for private profit, lay down the broad lines of protective measures for migration and for labour contracts, obtain effective inter-national action for controlling the traffic in spiritous liquors, establish

an international bureau for the study and prevention of tropical diseases, making provision for giving security and adequacy of land tenure for indigenous populations.[37]

This programme dealt with the main concerns of most post-war liberal writers. The choice of items which should command the special attention of the members of any such conference indicated their belief that Europeans had regularly exploited Africans in the past, and that Colonial Office policy had failed to provide adequate safeguards. They wanted to suggest irresponsibility on the part of the British Government rather than any fundamental objection to capitalist enterprise by Europeans in Africa. They remained convinced of Britain's mission to transform Africa, but now stressed the importance of a positive policy, which would promote African welfare and prevent European exploitation.[38] The reformist and humanitarian aspects of the liberal tradition had survived from the nineteenth century, but with a growing mistrust of laisser-faire colonial policies.

There was however a group of more radical reformers, who often used the language of Hobson and Lenin in describing British imperial adventures in the past, but who did not advocate revolutionary solutions to African problems. They differed from the liberal writers in believing that the European impact on African society had had disastrous results in the past, and that there was very real conflict between European and African economic interests. Whereas the liberal argument seemed to involve no more than measures to ameliorate the worst examples of exploitation or neglect, these socialist critics wanted to see a change in the basic relationship between Europeans and Africans.[39] A denial of the dual mandate theory was characteristic of this group of writers. Norman Leys, for example, was convinced that the presence of Europeans in Africa had almost invariably led to the dispossession of African lands, the exploitation of African labour and the neglect of the African people. Leonard Barnes believed that the industrial revolution, which he saw occurring in Africa, was being promoted in the interests of European society. Although he admitted that in some areas Africans had been enriched by economic development, he argued that 'extensive African impoverishment can also accompany what from the European standpoint appears as the winning of fabulous wealth'.[40]

There was a doctrinaire quality about the writings of this group of critics, particularly on the question of past (and present) exploitation of African resources in the British interest. But their solutions were never as fully elaborated as their criticisms. The

anger and pessimism in much of their writing implied a
revolutionary ardour, but, unlike the Marxists, they did not
advocate a colonial revolution. The writing of some of these
radicals, including E. D. Morel, Leonard Woolf and Norman Leys,
whose contributions were largely made in the 1920s (or earlier),
reflected the faith in the reform of imperial policy which was
characteristic of the first two decades of the twentieth century.

Norman Leys, who wrote specifically about Kenya, advocated
determined British government intervention to prevent the
exploitation of Africans by Europeans. He wanted the British
government to undertake piecemeal reforms on questions of land
ownership, labour contracts, and small scale production to increase
the freedom of the African to work out his own future.[41] The key
to development of all kinds lay in education and he argued that it
was urgently necessary 'that a scheme should be drafted which will
provide schools for most of the children in the country in twenty
years.'[42]

In his 1928 publication, *Imperialism and Civilization,* Leonard
Woolf attached similar importance to these questions of land,
labour and education. However, whereas Leys' approach was that
of a pragmatist anxious to solve the most urgent problems of one
colony, Woolf was an idealist, using Africa as just one of his
examples in the development of his ideas about internationalism.
Woolf believed that the development of the mandated areas in
Africa should be controlled by a much strengthened Mandates
Commission which should put into effect a code of native rights.[43]
Success in the mandated areas would lead to the extension of the
same principles to other colonial possessions.

However both Leonard Woolf and E. D. Morel wanted to limit
the operations of private capital, an idea also developed by
Leonard Barnes who was much more clearly influenced by
communist doctrine about the Empire. E. D. Morel believed that
tropical Africa needed the assistance of Europe to provide means
of communication, technical instruction, internal security and
medical and health services.[44] But his knowledge of the Congo and
West Africa convinced him that development by the company
promoter and planter should give way to development by African
peasant proprietors, stimulated by Western advice and Western
trade.[45] Leonard Woolf elaborated a programme of development
which also emphasized the use of the land, rather than any kind of
industrial development, and which envisaged first of all the
discouragement of private capital enterprise and finally the
gradual expropriation of all foreign capital.[46]

This identification of private capital as inimical to African interests was followed up by Leonard Barnes, and others, writing at a later period but now demonstrating a more realistic approach to the problem. Barnes, for example, specifically attacked the operations of private capital in Africa, but recognized the necessity for vast capital resources for developmental projects. This capital should come from Europe, but controlled by a body responsible to the British Government, while capitalist enterprises already established in Africa should be transferred to public ownership.

> Colonial development would probably be financed first by a national investment board in Britain on the basis of plans prepared by the Colonial Office in consultation with Colonial governments, and later perhaps by some international board of colonial development. In any case, all new development would be socialized in the sense of being ab initio publicly owned enterprise conducted in the general interest of the inhabitants of the Colony, and not in the special interests of creditors, whether residents or absentees.[47]

In a later book, Leonard Barnes set out a development programme involving two ten-year periods during which African colonies would gradually be prepared economically and politically for independence.[48] This programme made clear the part Britain still had to play before African territories could become viable states.

> The development of Africa can only take place by means of a merger of land and labour on the one hand with capital and technology on the other. The land and the labour will be provided by Africans and the capital and technology by Europeans. In the view of democrats, the object of this merger is to give Africa mastery of the technology and capital, and not to give European capitalists mastery of African labour and African land . . .[49]

There was a utopian quality about the solutions offered by these critics of colonial policy. But there were two important writers in the period who made the most explicit statements in support of planned development, and who faced up most clearly to the problems associated with such a policy. They were Lord Hailey and Professor W. M. Macmillan. Both made clear that development programmes had to be seen as a government responsibility requiring planning and expenditure.[50] Both emphasized the importance of thinking of the colonies as eventually becoming self-governing territories, and both questioned the value of the administrative policy of 'indirect rule', in preparing for this day.[51]

In his book *Africa Emergent,* published in 1938, Professor Macmillan provided a detailed analysis of the nature and cause of African 'backwardness' and of the particular problems which confronted African people in contact with European civilization. He argued that whatever the truth about the origins of imperialism it was clear that the weakness of Africa had 'exposed Africans to oppression if not by European capitalists then by slave dealers and warlike chiefs among their own people'.[52] He condemned the 'supine governments' of earlier periods for their failure to carry out any work of reconstruction[53] and argued that the economic development of the colonies was 'a necessary part of the process of securing their independent status in the world'.[54] Macmillan was not ideologically opposed to the operations of Western capital in Africa,[55] but believed that it was the duty of the State to enforce the conditions under which European enterprises might operate in African colonies. Private enterprise could contribute to economic development in the interests of Africans if their operations were controlled, but it was still the duty of the British government to provide the capital for other development of all kinds, including transport and communications and most particularly in providing health services and educational facilities.

Although Professor Macmillan castigated the British government in a manner which would perhaps have been unbecoming in a colonial civil servant, his conclusions were not so very different from those of Lord Hailey. *The African Survey,* carried out under the direction of Lord Hailey, was published in 1938 and in the months after its publication, a variety of articles by Lord Hailey, and others, debated the conclusions of the survey and a variety of general questions raised by its publication.[56] In an address to the African Society in 1939 Lord Hailey analysed changing attitudes in Britain to the possession of colonies. He identified what he called three earlier stages in Britain's attitudes to her colonial possessions,[57] none of which any longer applied.

I think we no longer look on overseas possessions in the light of their material advantages to us. We are fully prepared to accept all the humanitarian principles that are embodied in the mandatory system ...

Hailey believed that there were two major factors influencing Britain's policies. One was the international interest aroused everywhere in Europe over the question of colonies, the other the growth of collectivism.

Everywhere in Europe the State is now accepted as an all-pervading influence which, if it does not initiate, is at all events responsible for all the agencies which make for the social development of the people, and the world is asking—What are these States who hold these territories doing in Africa? ... so that we are, in effect, getting a new interpretation of our colonial obligations; not a negative one intended merely to prevent exploitation but a positive one.[58]

In this speech Hailey thus rejected the idea of the dual mandate and emphasized Britain's responsibilities towards the African people. In other articles and talks he urged development of all kinds, paid for where necessary by grants or loans from the British treasury and involving planning and research into particular African problems.

Lord Hailey's *Survey* was the most important of several publications in the late 1930s which dealt with the problem of development in the African colonies. The work of S. H. Frankel,[59] which was part of the Survey project, not only provided a vast quantity of statistical information but also attempted an analysis of past and future impediments to African development. He stressed African dependence on British capital[60] but also the importance of 'non-material capital accumulation, which consists in the spread of knowledge, education and scientific enquiry, and new adaptations to ecological conditions.'[61]

Several other publications indicated the growing interest in 'development' in the late 1930s. One was a collection of papers[62] read at a Conference called by the Royal Empire Society to discuss Empire development. British interests were paramount in these discussions. On the other hand, some of the. publications of the Royal Institute of International Affairs in this period provided valuable discussion and information about colonial problems.[63] In particular a considerable proportion of *The Colonial Problem* was concerned with general problems of development, with an attempt to provide some sort of guide to solutions. The authors of this report emphasized that the interests of the native population were primary, and dealt with such problems as the building up of internal capital, the prevention of undue drainage of wealth from the colonies, and problems connected with a proper balance between agricultural production for home consumption and for export. Like *The African Survey,* this volume attests to the existence of a new 'development' orthodoxy which might well have provided the basis for considerable changes in imperial policy.

It is possible to regard all 'development' in Africa as involving the application of Western science and technology to the particular problems of the Continent. Even the investment of private capital was made in the belief that African resources could be made productive by the application of Western technology. Yet the information available to either private investors or to governments was decidedly scanty in this period.[64] Nor was there available the sort of information which might have been made the basis for large scale welfare projects, such as an attack on the tsetse fly or on the disease of malaria. Many writers stressed that development projects could only be successful if based on adequate research into problems peculiar to Africa.

Public interest in and advocacy of research projects in the colonies received considerable impetus from the remarks made in the Report of the East African Commission of 1925.[65] This all-party commission[66] recommended a loan of £10 million to East Africa, half of which they believed would be spent in Great Britain, thus incidentally providing work in industries affected by the depression.[67] On the provision of scientific and research services in the colonies, the report was an indictment of the Imperial Government.[68] It referred to the Amani Institute of Tanganyika, originally set up by the German Government, for scientific purposes.

> It was lying derelict, its laboratories unoccupied, its costly apparatus dismantled, the living quarters deteriorating, the magnificent and priceless collection of books and scientific records and specimens unused.

The Commissioners made several references to the government's failure to act on questions of research and suggested that some of the £10 million loan be used for research purposes.

Major A. G. Church, one of the Commissioners, made the advocacy of research one of his major interests. In the book which he wrote on his return from East Africa,[69] he referred to the absence of reliable information of all kinds on East Africa, the importance of which he felt should be brought home to the Colonial Office and the various Colonial governors.[70] He referred to the neglect of the Amani Institute and the Imperial Institute, which he believed was starved for funds.

> Our greatness as an Imperial power will ultimately be based upon our achievements in this field. Our claim to guide the destinies of so large a proportion of the world's people will rest upon the application of the work of our research workers to develop the vast potential resources . . . for the material advantage of every people.[71]

Most of the early advocates of research projects spoke of the resulting economic advantage for Europe as well as for the Africans, demonstrating their belief in the dual mandate. The 1920s was a period of expanding commercial and industrial activity in Africa,[72] and to some writers the absence of reliable information was a factor seriously inhibiting development. It is apparent that the British government was influenced by the propaganda for research in the late 1920s[73] but the onset of the depression had the effect of curtailing British government expenditure in Africa. But while financial support from the British government dwindled in the early 1930s, striking evidence of interest in research in Africa was provided by the inauguration of the five year Plan of Research by the International Institute of African Languages and Cultures; by the setting up of a department of Social and Industrial Research and Counsel by the International Missionary Council; and by the promotion of the African Survey. The five year Plan of Research was to be an investigation into the results of contact between Europeans and Africans in order to provide important information for missionaries, traders and settlers as well as for educationalists and administrators.[74] Missionary activity in the research field resulted in a study of the effects of modern industry upon African tribal life in Central Africa.[75]

The idea for what was ultimately to be called the African Survey originated with General Smuts in 1929, when he delivered the Rhodes lecture at Oxford. He said that it was time to consider how far the resources of modern knowledge were being applied to Africa, as well as the possibilities of coordinating the experiences of territories under the charge of different governments.[76] A committee under the chairmanship of Lord Lothian, and including Lord Lugard, Dr. J. H. Oldham and Professor Julian Huxley among its members, was set up to plan such a survey.[77] The finance was provided by the Carnegie Corporation, and Chatham House (home of the R.I.I.A.) undertook to provide a centre for the project and to administer the funds. Sir Malcolm (later Lord) Hailey was chosen to direct the enquiry but was unable to begin work until 1935. He was assisted by other scholars who began work in 1933, and by Professor S. H. Frankel and E. B. Worthington who were commissioned to write special memoranda.[78] The Survey far exceeded its original intentions in scope and was widely regarded as an outstanding success.[79]

In Chapter XXIV of the Survey, the one section of this imposing document which was endorsed by the Committee responsible for the Survey,[80] Lord Hailey gave a resumé of the work of a variety of research institutions working partly or solely in Africa,[81] and recorded attempts to coordinate this research.[82] He concluded that this research, currently of vital importance to the future of Africa, was suffering from inadequate funds and lack of responsible central coordination. He advocated 'liberal assistance' from the British Treasury, preferably in the form of grants-in-aid, so that the colonies could carry out adequate research.[83] This, he believed, should be coordinated by a committee either of the Privy Council or of the Cabinet which should operate through existing institutions.[84] He noted the valuable work of many organizations disseminating information about Africa but considered that there should be a central African bureau which would become an information bureau and a central point of contact for all those individuals and organizations interested in Africa.[85] Hailey regarded these matters as urgent.

> History will doubtless look back on this period as being the most critical stage of African development; errors that are made now for lack of the knowledge which a well-considered scheme of special study might supply may well create situations which the future can rectify only at the cost of great effort and much human distress.[86]

Logically the application of scientific knowledge to African problems meant intervention on a grand scale. This would have meant the British Government abandoning old laisser-faire policies and undertaking an active interest in African affairs, in order to plan development, provide the finance to carry it out, and undertake research into major problems. The slow response of the British government to this challenge may have been partly due to the highly fragmented nature of the administrative services in Africa which operated with a minimum of control from the Colonial Office.[87] It may also be partly accounted for by the nature of pre-Keynesian orthodoxy concerning the legitimate purposes of government spending, particularly as the economy was mainly recessive in this period. Another explanation may be found in the conservatism of the administrative service which came largely from the class in English society which deplored any rapid change in the colonial situation.[88] This conservatism may have been decisive, in view of the very limited amount of time spent in debating colonial issues in the Houses of Parliament, and in the absence of electoral interest in African affairs. However in the late 1930s a new interest in colonial affairs was provoked by Germany's demand for the return of her African colonies.

The debate which raged over the issue of German colonial claims[89] compelled attention to the question of British obligations in Africa. While Germany appealed for the return of her colonies on the grounds of self-interest, British propagandists made much of British responsibilities for the development of backward peoples, as the raison d'être for her control over these areas. The political climate at home and abroad was now such as to place increasing importance on evidence that trusteeship policies were in fact being carried out. The publication of *The African Survey* was made at this time and provided one of the major texts for the new 'development' orthodoxy.

In the 1920s those dual mandate supporters, who were interested in African development, stressed Britain's neglect of valuable resources. At the same time more liberal thinkers attempted to persuade the British Government to intervene more positively in Africa to prevent exploitation and to implement social reforms of various kinds. By the late 1930s the emphasis had shifted to the extent that the dual mandate argument had lost respectability. There was now a more positive liberal paternalist view, which represented a reaffirmation of Britain's civilizing mission, purged of its evangelical overtones. This view stressed the responsibility of the trustee power in all colonies for a general development programme which would prepare Africans for eventual independence.

The liberal position of the late 1930s had taken on a radical tinge which satisfied many people with a mildly reformist conscience who believed that Britain had a long period ahead of her in Africa. However, some writers, like W. M. Macmillan and Leonard Barnes, who made major contributions to the debate in the 1930s, kept alive the sense of urgency and the attack on complacency. Leonard Barnes approached the Marxist position in his opposition to the operations of private capital in Africa and his pessimism about Britain ever really undertaking development programmes. Professor W. M. Macmillan, on the other hand, could see private capital playing some useful part in African development and was hopeful that the British government would see the necessity for more positive policies.[90]

The passage through the British Parliament in 1940 of the Colonial Development and Welfare Act represented a victory for the developers. Under the Act it was proposed to provide assistance to Colonial Governments of up to £5 million a year for ten years,

> not only for schemes involving capital expenditure necessary for Colonial development in the widest sense, but also for helping to meet recurrent expenditure in the Colonies on certain services such as agriculture, education, health and housing.[91]

At the same time separate provisions were made to assist in colonial research, as suggested by Lord Hailey.[92]

Whatever the success or adequacy of the programme,[93] it represented a major change of policy. In the 1920s the colonies were still largely thought of as an extension of Great Britain and collectivist demands were made on behalf of British interests. By the late 1930s the eventual separation of the African colonies from Great Britain could be envisaged, and there was fairly general acceptance of a new kind of collectivism, which involved British Government intervention in the interests of Africa.

NOTES

1. For a contemporary account of these changes, see Allan McPhee, *The Economic Revolution in British West Africa*, (London, 1926).
2. See, for example, I. F. Nicolson, *The Administration of Nigeria, 1900–1960,* for an account of 'planned development' in Southern Nigeria from 1905 to 1912.
3. See J. D. Fage, 'British and German Rule. A Synthesis and Summary', in P. Gifford and W. K. Louis (Eds.), *Britain and Germany in Africa*, p. 696.
4. The Marxists were an exception.
5. See, for example, L. P. Mair, *Native Policies in Africa,* (London, 1936), p. 2. '. . . public opinion has passed beyond the stage which accepts as automatic and inevitable the connection between intensive economic exploitation of tropical territories and the advancement of their inhabitants.'
6. See S. H. Frankel, *Capital Investment in Africa,* (London, 1958), p. 24. He refers to the 19th Century belief that concentrated financial activity in Africa was bound 'to be rapidly creative'.
7. See, for example, Charles Wilson, *The History of Unilever,* Part 1, (London, 1954), for a record of attempts by this company to control palm oil supplies in the period after 1910.
8. The term used by Frankel to describe the activities of slave traders and those in the French and Belgian Congo who traded in indigenous products. See *Capital Investment in Africa,* p. 37.
9. See S. H. Frankel, *Capital Investment,* p. 32. Professor Frankel analysed the impediments to African development and concluded that railways were crucial. Once railway construction was undertaken 'the transformation of the African Continent had commenced'. In the same section the author argued that human porterage was one of the main factors which ravaged the economic powers of the indigenous populations of Africa.
10. See G. St. J. Orde-Browne, *The African Labourer,* for a contemporary analysis of labour problems.
11. See W. A. J. Hewins, *The Apologia of an Imperialist,* Vol. 1 (London, 1929), p. 60 for an account of what was essential to this doctrine. The activities of the Round Table group, which aimed at imperial federation, are described in Walter Nimocks, *Milner's Young Men.*
12. See W. A. J. Hewins, *The Apologia,* Ch. III, for an account of the foundation of the Tariff Commission.
13. See W. K. Hancock, *Survey,* Vol. 2, Part I, p. 98 f, for details concerning this Commission. Although the scheme finally proved abortive, this Commission attempted to establish an Imperial Development Board, the British members of which were to represent the Crown Colonies and Protectorates as well as Britain.
14. *Ibid.,* p. 97.
15. *Ibid.,* p. 113 f.
16. The author and archaeologist, L. S. B. Leakey, who was brought up among the Kikuyu,.made a plea, very rare for this period, for Europeans to examine African agricultural methods and cures for disease which he said were 'a curious mixture of ignorance and knowledge.' See *Kenya Contrasts and Problems,* (London, 1935), p. 122 f.
17. For a harsh judgement of African life generally, see W. J. W. Roome, *Can Africa be Won?,* (London, 1927), p. 18 f. His views were shared by many of the most convinced supporters of Britain's civilizing mission.

18. W. M. Macmillan warned against the tendency to idealize African society. See *Africa Emergent*, (London, 1938), p. 16, 'The newest anthropological studies give more evidence than one had feared of native African ignorance and incapacity, of the cruelty and sometimes the essential injustice of tribal institutions, of a hard and on the whole unsuccessful struggle with nature'.

19. For example, the Colonial Development Fund of 1929 was partly a reflection of belief in the necessity for government action in the colonial field, as well as in the area of domestic politics. See E. A. Brett, 'Development Policy in East Africa', p. 89 for this view.

20. See W. K. Hancock, *Survey*, Vol. 2, Part 2, p. 236–298 for an analysis of West African problems in this period. See, also, S. H. Frankel, *Capital Investment in Africa*, p. 170–172, for an analysis of the amount of public capital invested in Africa between 1870–1936.

21. See J. M. Lee, *Colonial Development and Good Government*, p. 5.

22. *Ibid.*, for an examination of the ideas which lay behind official policy in the post 1940 period.

23. Cmd 2387, (1925). This Commission was sent to East Africa to report on the possibilities of speeding up the economic development of the area.

24. In fact a Joint East Africa Board was set up in 1926. It was an unofficial body, representing people with business interests in East Africa and M.P's. It aimed 'to unite all interest in East Africa in support of a common policy of development.' See K. M. Stahl, *The Metropolitan Organization of British Colonial Trade: Four Regional Studies*, (London, 1951), p. 189 f. The government set up the East Africa Dependencies Trade and Information Office in 1925. For details, *Ibid.*, p. 183.

25. See E. A. Brett, 'Development Policy in East Africa', for an analysis of the basis of support for development in East Africa.

26. F. C. Linfield, 'Empire Development', *Contemporary Review*, 128 (1926), p. 324.

27. Rt. Hon. L. S. Amery, 'Economic Development of the Empire', *United Empire*, New Series, XVI (1925), p. 146.

28. See, for example, A. Wigglesworth, 'Regeneration of Africa', *United Empire*, New Series, XIV (1923), p. 535–8. (Alfred Wigglesworth was the founder of a company involved in the production of sisal in East Africa.)

29. Captain J. E. T. Philipps, 'The Tide of Colour. I. Pan Africa and Anti-White?', *J.A.S.*, 21 (1921–22), p. 311.

30. See, for examples, J. H. Oldham, *White and Black in Africa*, (London, 1930), p. 42, and J. H. Harris, *Slavery or 'Sacred Trust'?*, p. 101.

31. J. H. Oldham and B. D. Gibson, *The Remaking of Man in Africa*, p. 12.

32. Sir Bernard Bourdillon, 'Native Production in the African Colonies and protectorates', *United Empire*, New Series, XXVIII (1937), p. 145–9.

33. Julian Huxley, 'East Africa: Politics and Native Questions', *Contemporary Review*, 132 (1930), pp. 459–469, and 'The Future of Colonies', *Fortnightly Review*, 154 (1940), pp. 120–30.

34. See Major A. G. Church, *East Africa. A New Dominion*, p. 73. Major Church used this argument and quoted from the Berlin agreement.

35. Donald Fraser, *The New Africa*, p. 60.

36. For details of this appeal, see the *Anti-Slavery Reporter and Aborigines Friend*, April, 1919, p. 2.

37. *Ibid.*, p. 2.

38. See Bernard Porter, *Critics of Empire*, p. 53, for the view that 19th Century humanitarians believed that 'the imperialists' motives had only to be purified for their activities to benefit the African'.

39. For an account of much that is relevant to an understanding of this group of radicals, see I. Henderson, 'The Attitude and Policy of the main sections of the British Labour Movement to Imperial Issues, 1899–1924'.

40. Leonard Barnes, *Empire or Democracy?*, p. 152 f.

41. See Norman Leys, *Kenya*, Ch. XVI.

42. *Ibid.*, p. 405.

43. See Leonard Woolf, *Imperialism and Civilization*, p. 129 f.

44. See E. D. Morel, *The Black Man's Burden*, p. 189.

45. Morel's position is analysed by Bernard Porter, *Critics of Empire*, p. 254 f.

46. Leonard Woolf, *Empire and Commerce in Africa*, p. 362.

47. Leonard Barnes, *The Duty of Empire*, p. 29.

48. Leonard Barnes, *Empire or Democracy?*, p. 283.

49. *Ibid.*, p. 260.

50. They both pointed to the inadequacy of the 1929 Colonial Development Fund as it was operating in the 1930s. See W. M. Macmillan, *Warning from the West Indies*, (London, 1936), pp. 197–198, and Lord Hailey, 'Present Trends in Colonial Policy', *Listener*, 10 August, 1939.

51. See W. M. Macmillan, *Europe and West Africa*, p. 62 and Lord Hailey, 'Some problems dealt with in the African Survey', *International Affairs*, XVIII (1939), pp. 194–210.

52. W. M. Macmillan, *Africa Emergent*, p. 23.

53. He believed the missionaries had done some such work.

54. *Ibid.*, p. 23.

55. See W. M. Macmillan, *Europe and West Africa*, p. 66 f.

56. For articles about the Survey see the Supplement of the *Journal of the Royal African Society*, Volume 38, 1939. In this supplement a number of experts and interested observers commented on the survey and provided support for development policies of all kinds.

57. The first stage:—the view that colonies provided closed markets for exports and a source of raw material and cheap labour.
    The second stage:—the application of Open Door principles and the denigration of the value of colonies.
    The third stage:—the scramble because of the increasing competition from other European nations.

58. This speech by Lord Hailey was recorded in the *J.R.A.S.*, XXXVIII (1939), p. 381.

59. *Capital Investment in Africa.*

60. *Ibid.*, p. 424.

61. *Ibid.*, p. 429.

62. The Royal Empire Society, *The Crucial Problem of Imperial Development*, (London, 1938).

63. See R.I.I.A., *The Colonial Problem*, (London, 1937) and *The British Empire*, (London, 1937).

64. But some information *was* provided by the Imperial Institute, established in 1892 for the promotion of the development and the industrial use of the raw materials of the Empire. It was said to perform the three functions of 'intelligence, investigation and education'. See Lt. Gen. Sir William Furse, 'Aiding Primary Production' in F. S. Joelson (Ed.), *Eastern Africa Today and Tomorrow*, (London, 1929), pp. 144–148. Sir William Furse was the Director of the Institute.

65. Cmd 2387.

66. The members of this Commission were all Members of Parliament. They

were, W. G. A. Ormsby-Gore (Conservative), Major A. G. Church (Labour), and F. C. Linfield (Liberal).

67. In this the commissioners anticipated the arguments to be used in justifying the Colonial Development Fund in 1928.

68. For an account of the Government's expenditure on the Colonies in the inter-war period, and a description of the institutions related to the Colonial Office, see Kenneth Robinson, *The Dilemmas of Trusteeship*, (London, 1965), p. 29 f.

69. Major A. G. Church, *East Africa. A New Dominion*.

70. *Ibid.*, p. 59.

71. *Ibid.*, p. 109.

72. For an account of development in East Africa in this period, and for details of the relationship between the Imperial Government, the Colonial Governments and private interests, see E. A. Brett, 'Development Policy in East Africa'.

73. See Kenneth Robinson, *The Dilemmas of Trusteeship*, p. 34. The author gives an account of the appointment of specialist committees and advisors.

74. For details of this plan see 'A Five Year Plan of Research', *Africa*, 5 (1932), pp. 1–13.

75. This was the book *Modern Industry and the African,* edited by J. Merle Davis, the preparation of which was financed by the Carnegie Corporation and the Phelps-Stokes Fund. See the introduction to the 1967 Cass edition by Robert Rotberg.

76. See Jan Christian Smuts, *Africa and Some World Problems*, (Oxford, 1930), including the Rhodes Memorial Lectures delivered at Oxford in 1929.

77. For a history of the planning of the Survey, see Stephen King Hall, *Chatham House,* (London, 1937) and Lucy Mair, 'The Social Sciences in Africa', *Human Organization*, XIX, 3 (1960), pp. 98–106. See also the foreword of *The African Survey*, written by Lord Lothian.

78. Professor S. H. Frankel, *Capital Investment in Africa,* and E. B. Worthington, *Science in Africa,* (London, 1938).

79. For articles about the value of the Survey see the Supplement of the *Journal of the Royal African Society,* Volume XXXVIII, 1939, and other articles, recorded in the bibliography by R. Coupland, Sir John Harris and George Catlin.

80. In the foreword Lord Lothian indicated that Lord Hailey was responsible for any expressions of opinion in the Survey, except for Ch. XXIV which had been discussed by the whole Committee and endorsed.

81. See p. 1620 f.

82. See p. 1625 f.

83. See p. 1629.

84. See p. 1631.

85. See p. 1634.

86. See p. 1629.

87. For a discussion of the absence of 'a central direction of major lines of policy', see Lord Hailey, *An African Survey*, Introduction, p. XXV.

88. See J. D. Fage, 'British and German Colonial Rule', in P. Gifford and W. R. Louis (Eds.), *British and Germany in Africa*, p. 699.

89. For details of the main lines of this debate see W. M. Schmokel, 'The hard death of Imperialism: British and German Colonial Attitudes, 1919–1939', in P. Gifford and W. K. Louis, *Britain and Germany in Africa*, pp. 301–335.

90. W. K. Hancock referred to W. M. Macmillan's programme as that of the missionaries brought up to date and 'restated in terms of twentieth century

experience in science, economics and administration'. See a review of *Africa Emergent, Spectator,* 17 June, 1938.

91. *Statement of Policy on Colonial Development and Welfare,* Cmd 6175, (1940).

92. *Ibid.,* para. 8. A Colonial Research Advisory Committee was to be set up and £500,000 a year allocated for research expenditure.

93. See J. M. Lee, *Colonial Development and Good Government,* esp. p. 111 f.

CHAPTER 7

EDUCATION

The doctrine of trusteeship implied the eventual independence of African colonies although there was wide difference of opinion about when this might occur. It also implied some degree of responsibility on the part of trustee powers for promoting the sort of development policies which would make independence possible.[1] During this period there was growing conviction that education was the key to development of all kinds. It became part of the paternalist faith of the time that a broad programme of education, which could not be generated from inside Africa, must be provided by Britain in order to transform African society.

In British society considerable conflict in the field of educational policy had followed changes towards more democratic political practices, the growth of industrial mass society and collectivist political theory.[2] The nineteenth century idea that the mass of working class children needed no more than primary education died hard. Although the first demands for secondary education for all were made by the Trade Union movement in the last decade of the nineteenth century, this principle was not embodied in official statute until 1944.[3] A second area of conflict, also dating back to the last decades of the nineteenth century, when some schools first began specializing in science and technical education, concerned the rival claims of a liberal and vocational education. The Butler Act of 1944, based on the findings of earlier expert committee reports,[4] attempted to provide for a system of secondary schools in England which had different curricula, but equal status.

The gradual extension of secondary education to all and the widening of the scope of educational curricula implied increasing mobility within English society. These developments brought home to observers the fact that, although education could be viewed as part of the process of socialization into existing society as well as a means of providing access to accumulated knowledge, it could also be a potent means for promoting social change.[5] In Britain the rate of social change was not such as to cause alarm.

But similar observations were now being made about the effects of education in African societies, and here the impact seemed much more revolutionary.

It is apparent that by the 1920s the experiences of British educators in both Britain and Africa had led to a recognition of the importance of educational practices in shaping society. As far as Africa was concerned crucial questions were now being asked about how far the culture of one society could be 'transferred' to another society; and how far it was necessary, for both political stability and educational success, to attempt a synthesis of the two cultures. This new view suggested a growing tolerance of other cultures, a new liberalism in the approach to education. But this was only one side of the picture. This new approach was also a result of the apparent failures of the missionary absolutism of the earlier period which seemed to have contributed to political instability. In the past missionaries had counted themselves successful if their work in the field of education had produced black Englishmen, Africans who seemed to have assimilated Western culture. But these mission educated Africans were anathema to many administrators and others. They were 'cheeky' and demanded social equality and political rights. Many of the radicals of the inter-war period believed that the new tolerance for things 'African', this advocacy of partial Africanization of the education system was, in reality, a conservative reaction on the part of those who were determined not to think in terms of social equality or even in terms of African participation in political life. In other words it indicated a desire to slow down the rate of change.

Until the end of World War I most education services in Africa had been provided by missionary bodies as part of their programme of evangelization, although the beginnings of secular education were evident in some colonies.[6] The early missionary endeavour in the field of education had involved the more or less authoritarian indoctrination of the Christian beliefs of the society from which the teachers came. These early missionaries undoubtedly failed to consider the outcome of imposing their own beliefs and presumptions on societies with a different scale of values. Although they may have been regarded as conservatives in their own society, they were responsible for introducing radical concepts into African society. By their emphasis on the individual rather than the communal group, by their challenge to the values of the older generation of Africans, the missionary teachers began a revolution in African society.

The literature of the 1920s and 1930s about missionary goals and methods dwelt frequently on this aspect of past missionary work. The most obvious attack came from those who were supporters of gradual change in Africa and advocated the retention of African institutions through the administrative device of indirect rule.[7] They saw missionaries as responsible for the disintegration of African society by their attempt at a wholesale introduction of Western ideas and customs.[8] Missions had seen little or nothing 'to respect or preserve' in Africa, and were guilty of confusing Christianity with Western civilization and even with English social habits.[9] These writers, for whom political stability was more important than the spread of Christian beliefs, saw some sort of conflict between missionary and secular goals in Africa. They did not believe that Africans could be effectively socialized into a Western system in less than several generations. They therefore argued that the Christian desire for converts had the effect of introducing changes too suddenly and too superficially.[10]

Other writers, particularly missionaries themselves, saw missions as one of the several disruptive forces which had entered African society in the nineteenth century, but believed in the possibility of their now providing a new kind of social cohesion, necessary in a society already disrupted by other forces anyway.[11] In any case, a re-examination of missionary aims, and the way in which missions worked, would be necessary in the light of the growing acceptance of education as a State responsibility. Although mission schools still provided much of the education available,[12] missionary resources were no longer adequate to meet the demands for education in Africa, and many of their schools were already subsidised by the colonial governments. The Church, which had earlier had a favoured position as a pressure group,[13] because it provided what were often the only social services available, now gradually lost its special place as the State undertook more responsibility.

This then was a period of readjustment for missionaries who now had to operate within the secular framework as far as teaching was concerned.[14] Their writing in this post-war period indicated an awareness of criticism of past educational practices, and suggested a growing commitment to the idea of a synthesis of European and African culture, the need for a clear distinction between Christianity and English social habits, and the need for a more equal partnership between Europeans and Africans.

These conclusions were partly a response to problems encountered in Africa by missionary organizations.[15] But much of the general enquiry arose out of the fact that the Phelps-Stokes

Commissions on education in Africa,[16] originally planned by missionary interests,[17] were in fact highly critical of much past effort in the education field.[18] Apart from their influence on missionary thinking, these Phelps-Stokes Commissions into African education were to have considerable influence on the general debate about education in the African colonies, because they publicized the educational ideas developed at the negro schools of Tuskegee and Hampton in the United States.[19] The Reports referred to the work at these schools and emphasized the importance of education as a community project.[20] Although the reports made reference to the necessity for the development of technical and professional education in the future, they concentrated on the necessity for providing the three 'R's' which were essential to promote the development of character through religion, to teach the rules of health and hygiene, to inculcate agricultural and industrial skills and to improve family life.

> Some would follow blindly the Europeans and adopt the European customs by processes of imitation. They would cast aside their own native customs as undesirable evidences of savagery and barbarism. Unfortunately the conceit of Western civilization has too often encouraged this superficial imitation of European customs and the disregard of everything native. It is to be hoped that this will be discouraged.[21]

Much of the argument about what direction African education should take consisted in a disagreement about emphasis rather than a complete rejection of other points of view. However it does seem clear that the early Phelps-Stokes Commission insistence on the need for education to promote the regeneration of African societies was in some conflict with the view that Africa should be offered the best and broadest education that Britain could provide.[22]

A further important influence on thinking about education in Africa were the criticisms, now being widely made, about the education system in India.[23] Probably the most influential book on this question was *Indian Unrest* by Sir Valentine Chirol,[24] first published in 1910. In this book, Chirol made a number of criticisms of education in India which seem to have provided an authoritative text for writers dealing with education in Africa. A number of such writers referred explicitly to Sir Valentine Chirol's works on India,[25] and many of them developed ideas which suggested his influence.[26] He criticised the elitist nature of the system in India, the use of the English language, the exclusive training of the intellect to the neglect of religious and moral teachings, and the fact that Indian education seemed largely unrelated to the environment. Many writers, dealing with the methods and goals of education in Africa, emphasized the need for mass education at a village level, the necessity for using the vernacular at all but higher levels, the need for religious and moral teaching, and the importance of relating all education to the African environment. This re-examination of the educational methods used in India came at a time when many Englishmen felt new humility about their own society, with its apparent potential for self-destruction and its inability to organize economic life effectively.

There was also, at this time, a rapidly growing body of literature about people of alien societies.[27] Many of these books were written by missionaries and administrators who had lived in Africa or the Pacific, and who provided ethnographic accounts of societies with which they were familiar. By the 1930s this body of literature was being augmented by the work of anthropologists, trained in the new functional theories and imbued with the idea that field studies were essential to an understanding of other cultures.[28] One educationalist in the late 1930s referred to a number of books of this nature and commented

> Malinowski and other functional anthropologists have introduced a new conception into the discussion that has proved very fruitful. They insist that every custom, idea or belief, of a social group fulfils some vital function, has some task to accomplish and represents an indispensable part in an organic whole. This living unity shows pattern in its parts and the parts build themselves up into a patterned whole.[29]

It is difficult to estimate the extent of the influence of the new functional theories,[30] but it is clear that they bolstered the conservative reaction against the promotion of rapid change.[31] This new anthropological knowledge also undoubtedly provided educationalists with new material about African educational systems,[32] and perhaps helped to qualify educational theory generally by requiring that it take cognisance of educational practice in widely differing societies. Of particular importance in determining how Britain could provide education for Africans was the view that all educational practice in an integrated society normally involved the transmission of that society's cultural heritage from one generation to the next. How then were outsiders to replace the continuous course of instruction to tribal members, which was the basis of indigenous African education?

There were, then, a number of influences which affected attitudes to education in Africa and qualified any preconceived ideas based on knowledge or experience of the English educational system. These influences included the contemporary re-appraisal of past missionary work; the spread of particular theories about negro education which had earlier developed in the United States; the existence of serious criticisms of the kind of Western education provided in India; and, finally, the growth of a large body of serious literature about African societies which were now recognised to have their own systems of education.

Some of these influences clearly made for a more cautious and conservative approach to education problems. But while it was now increasingly recognized that Western education in the colonial situation did have revolutionary implications this was not seen as a reason for drawing back, but rather for trying to determine ultimate goals and satisfactory methods. Even those who pointed to past British arrogance about possessing a monopoly of the essential features of 'civilization', even they were convinced that Britain had something to contribute to education in Africa. It was not usual for either conservatives or radicals to counsel inaction.[33] From the point of view of the convinced paternalist this was, in fact, one area which could no longer be neglected, because education could provide the key to stability and progress in the colonies. The charge of past arrogance was rejected by some but met in a variety of ways by others. Arthur Mayhew, for example, managed to demonstrate his conviction of the superiority of European culture, while he denied any suggestion of racism and revealed an educated sensibility about other cultures.

> Assuming, then, not only a universal capacity for cultural develop-
> ment, but also its universal necessity, and refusing to mistake dif-
> ference in stages of development for difference in racial ability, we
> are bound as educationalists to have in view an ultimate good, a
> common civilization for the whole world, a framework, as it were,
> of universally accepted values, and within this framework a rich variety
> of local cultures, not mutually repellant or suspicious, but each ready
> and able to borrow and absorb what it is able to absorb without loss
> of identity.[34]

According to this writer the aim of education was the harmonious development of aspects of both European and African cultures. Another writer used the word 'renaissance' to describe what this process would mean in Africa.[35]

While the idea of a synthesis is undoubtedly an accurate way of describing the likely outcome of close contact between people of widely different cultures, it often had particular connotations in this context. It was now believed that there had to be a careful selection of what was to be passed on,[36] even of what was to be allowed to survive in the existing culture, in spite of the obvious difficulty in directing either process. This new orthodoxy can be discovered in the writings of missionary educationalists, in the public statements issued by the Colonial Office Advisory Committee on Education; in the conclusions reached at conferences attended by missionaries, administrators and educationalists; and in the writing of many of those who saw the close connection between educational policy and political development in Africa.

According to Professor Murray, a new interest in education among missionaries was first made apparent at the Edinburgh Missionary Conference of 1910,[37] and was reflected in support for several later conferences which discussed education problems. This did not mean a diminution in the central importance of religious teaching but, rather, that unquestioning evangelical zeal was giving way to a new appraisal of the problems confronting European missions in Africa.[38] The books and articles of many people with interest and involvement in missionary activity in the inter-war period reflected a determination to avoid the kind of total condemnation of African life and customs which had been characteristic of an earlier period. Now the emphasis was on teaching the African to value his own heritage as well as to learn from the West. While some missionary educationalists emphasized the importance of leaving open 'the road to Western knowledge'[39] it was argued that few would be capable of travelling that road for a long time to come. They therefore stressed the importance of education at the village level,[40] a careful consideration of environment in education policies,[41] and the use of the vernacular at all but highest levels. The same emphasis may be found in the two memoranda[42] issued by the Colonial Office Advisory Committee on Education in Tropical Africa[43] in 1925 and 1935. In fact education was to be the means of a kind of moral regeneration of African society.

> Its aim should be to render the individual more efficient in his or her condition of life, whatever it may be, and to promote the advancement of the community as a whole through the improvement of health, the training of the people in management of their own affairs, and the inculcation of true ideals of citizenship and service.

The committee also placed great importance on religious teaching and moral instruction which should find expression

> in habits of self discipline and loyalty to the community. With such safeguards, contact with civilization need not be injurious, or the introduction of new religious ideas have a disruptive influence antagonistic to constituted secular authority.[44]

These views seemed much more tolerant of the survival of African culture than had those of the early missionaries and undoubtedly reflected a new relativism about other societies, as well as an attempt to meet practical difficulties. But they also reflected the fear that a broad Western education would promote subversive ideas. Education was not to be the means of introducing Africans to world civilization but the means of achieving stable, even compliant, populations in colonial Africa. These conclusions emerged from the Missionary Conference at High Leigh in 1923,[45] and from the later one at Le Zoute in Belgium in 1926.[46] In an address to the Le Zoute Conference Sir Frederick Lugard claimed that it was now recognized that it was more important to educate the mass of the people

> in a manner which shall improve the standard of life and conduct of the community, than to endeavour to make imitation Europeans of a small section by a literary education crowned by a University degree.[47]

In summing up the work of the Conference on the question of education Edwin Smith stated that it adopted a programme with more emphasis on religion and less on book-learning. The aim of education

> is not the mastering of books and the passing of examinations, but the elevation of the tone and character of the community in which the school is placed.[48]

He recorded the importance of the ideas of Hampton and Tuskegee in the United States and the influence of Dr. Jesse Jones.[49]

Some of the same emphasis on the 'development of native society as a whole'[50] was expressed in articles in the journal *Oversea Education,* first published in 1929.[51] But this journal contained sophisticated arguments about all aspects of African education. Regular articles appeared concerning the problems of teaching particular subjects in Africa, and the extent to which methods suitable to the English milieu would have to be modified. Problems connected with language difficulties and the use of the vernacular were debated frequently. But most important were the articles which questioned how far the school in Africa would have to bear burdens which it did not have in England;[52] whether it was necessary to separate out the issues of mass and elite education.[53] Many of the writers in this journal had had wide educational experience in Africa,[54] and while they shared some of the prejudices held by other groups in the community, they were obviously deeply involved in issues of immediate importance.[55]

There were, however, many other writers who expressed firm

beliefs about what should be the nature and direction of educational policy at this time who had no such expertise. They contributed to the discussion because they recognized that the issue raised important political considerations. And although the ideas of the so-called experts filtered through to some extent, most of the views expressed by administrators, politicians and others were closely related to political convictions generally.

One prevalent view was that the provision of Western education spread disaffection and subversive ideas and that it would lead in the future to the training of a body of agitators. According to this view education had often produced individuals divorced from their social milieu, no longer prepared to engage in traditional agricultural occupations and even holding a contempt for manual labour.[56] These products of the education system were neither European nor African, according to some writers. They had lost any moral basis for action and no longer accepted the responsibilities imposed by their clan and family. They were 'loose-charactered, deraciné, non-producing, inefficient and often unemployable' according to G. Howard Jones who spoke of these products of the education system in West Africa being turned loose into 'a narrow and flooded market'.[57] Another writer was alarmed at what had occurred in India due to the policy of Westernization and was fearful that Achimota might produce

a class of useless, discontented, disaffected miserable men, and of such are the firebrands of agitation . . . once versed in uncritical summaries of John Stuart Mill and Mrs. Besant . . . such leaders might become in time a very dangerous political force.[58]

These views on blunders in matters of Indian education were shared by the Earl of Selborne[59] who emphasized the need for character training and a bias towards practical education. Many writers, sharing these fears about the outcome of introducing Western ideas, talked of the importance of moulding a people suited to their agricultural environment. Coupland thought it desirable to keep the African 'rooted in Africa and to help him to become the best possible kind of African, not something half and half or hybrid, still less a synthetic European'.[60] This view seemed to imply some kind of racial barrier to complete Europeanization as well as the existence of fixed European and African stereotypes.

These conservative arguments stressed the futility of training people for jobs which were not available and of divorcing Africans from their traditional social milieu. They stressed, too, the political dangers inherent in educating people to aspire to equality with

Europeans. These views reflected their interest in maintaining the political status quo and their desire to preserve existing inequalities. More positively these writers stressed the inculcation of the kind of political virtues which a subject people should have. The emphasis was on what was called political 'responsibility', obedience, a sense of duty, courage and self-sacrifice. These virtues should be inculcated to take the place of old clan loyalties and responsibilities which had been destroyed.[61] The observation that the impact of Western civilization had done much to destroy the traditional order in Africa inspired this conservative emphasis on discipline and obedience.[62] But, in particular many observers found fault with the 'literary' or intellectual education which had been provided in the past.[63] Referring to Indian unrest, Lugard believed

> the fundamental fault lay in the failure to recognise that the time must come when this purely intellectual type of education and emancipation of thought would produce its inevitable results, under-mining respect for authority, whether of the State or of the parents.[64]

Apart from the greater emphasis on 'moral' training, the solution lay in education which was more clearly tied to the needs of the community. Hence the demand that education should provide training in agricultural and industrial skills and in general questions of hygiene. This bias was sometimes expressed in doubts about the value of the three R's;[65] sometimes in articles deploring the fact that Africans were educated out of employment opportunities which would satisfy them;[66] and occasionally on the grounds that Africans should be educated to contribute to their own advance. Hence Lugard's statement that

> the object which education in Africa must have in view must be to fit the ordinary individual to fill a useful part in his own environ-ment, with happiness to himself, and to ensure that the exceptional individual shall use his abilities for the advancement of the community and not to its deterioration, or to the subversion of constituted authority.[67]

Much opinion reflected this suspicion, expressed by Lugard, that Western educated intellectuals were likely to engage in subversion against the colonial administration. The conservative reaction was not the advocacy of some liberalization of colonial administration in order to involve the educated African in the processes of government, but rather a retreat to less education or a different kind of education. They saw, correctly, that an educated elite was dangerous to the maintenance of political stability. They therefore advocated more widespread education of an industrial and agricultural nature, designed to improve productivity and the general standards of the people, but designed also to prevent social unrest and the growth of revolutionary cadres within African society.

The conservative reaction away from Western education in the 1920s and 1930s was also sometimes due, as has been noted in the case of many missionaries, to a general loss of confidence. Professor W. M. Macmillan made this observation as early as the mid-1930s. He believed that this loss of European self-confidence had produced

> a reaction in educational programmes from the old disposition to sweep away African institutions wholesale to the opposite extreme of attributing to them a more definite sense of community value than they really contained . . . There was danger . . . of forgetting that the African was a human being whose ideas were not to be ordered for him from the outside; and further that there was absolute need for educated Africans.[68]

Professor A. Victor Murray expressed concern at the failure of Europeans to treat Africans as equal human beings when he wrote

> There is a certain meanness about a good deal of African education. The Native is looked upon as a tool to be fashioned rather than as a new partner in the age long process of bringing the world out of darkness into light. And so everything is so utilitarian, so very much ad-hoc, so patronizing.[69]

Both Macmillan and Murray spent considerable time in British colonial territories in Africa in the 1920s or 1930s as observers of British administrative and educational practice and of race relations generally. Their observations achieved an objectivity and perspective which were usually lacking in the arguments of those who had been deeply involved in British-African administration or politics or who were committed to particular views about imperialism generally. Both writers rejected the conservative position already described and expressed many of the current dissatisfactions felt by Africans and by many Europeans about the progress being made in education in Africa.

The most frequent criticisms of existing practices in African education, and of this new orthodoxy about Africans needing a particular kind of education, took three forms. These were criticisms of the general provisions being made and the absence of facilities of all kinds; criticisms of current theories about the preservation of aspects of African culture, which, said the critics, implied some limitation on what sort of Western education should be provided; and finally criticism of arguments about the primary importance of character training.

The most extreme critics of British educational policy stated baldly that Britain had failed in her responsibilities. Leonard Woolf, for example, argued that the need to educate the African had been agreed on at the Berlin Conference in 1885 but

> no European government in Africa has made a serious attempt to begin the education of the native so that eventually he might be capable of taking his place as a free man in the new economic and political society which Europeans have introduced into Africa.[70]

He admitted that missionaries had done good spade work but considered the 'gigantic' task as outside their competence. Norman Leys wrote angrily of the contrast between what was spent on African and European education in Kenya,[71] while Charles Roden Buxton regarded the absence of schools in Africa as representing 'a grave dereliction of duty' on the part of the British Government.[72] Other writers, less generally critical of imperial policy, advocated a speeding up of educational programmes and the expenditure of more money on education.[73]

The idea of preserving tribal society, and qualifying educational practice in order to do so, came under direct attack from many people. Norman Leys argued that European civilization, whatever its shortcomings, was quite clearly preferable to that of the Masai, for example, and that the only way to change the Masai was to educate the children.[74] In a letter to the *New Statesman and Nation* in 1932, replying to an earlier letter by C. M. Lawrence justifying the work of anthropology, Leys emphasized the importance of attacking ignorance.

> Neither knowledge nor civilization has, or ever had, a racial frontier. How absurd it is to call the diffusion of western ideas and habits 'Europeanizing' . . . It is our duty to hand on the torch, to share our relative enlightenment, for which we deserve no credit, with the less enlightened, whose ignorance is no fault of theirs. That, and not the development of a hypothetically unique African civilization some . . . anthropologists desire for them, is what . . . Africans themselves desire.[75]

Leys was enthusiastic about the work being done at Achimota and believed it could be done all over Africa.[76] Buxton believed that the African wanted education and recognised that it represented deliverance for him. He saw that education promoted individualism as against the values of communal society, but argued that the answer to the problem thus created was more, and not less, education.[77] A similar rejection of the idea of preserving

African culture by limiting the education available was expressed by Sir James Currie, one time Principal of Gordon College, Khartoum.

> In my view what the native wants is knowledge of a kind that will enable him to take his place in the world's economic struggle on equal terms with the white man . . . [he] has got scant patience with any system which he thinks calculated to strengthen his economic dependence . . . The native would almost rather have no education at all than education by means of a system which he thinks is conceived to preserve him as a picturesque antiquity.[78]

Leonard Barnes so disliked the new rather negative spirit abroad that he referred back with approval to the so-called 'positive policy' of the great evangelists Thomas Fowell Buxton and David Livingstone.[79]

> That the white man has a genuine civilizing mission to perform in Africa is hardly open to question. If it is performed it will be performed by scientists, educationalists, administrators and technicians—in short by the positive policy.[80]

The opinion that the African should be provided as quickly as possible with educational opportunities of all kinds was a view shared by people with widely differing professions and backgrounds. The outstanding example amongst those in the higher echelons of the colonial service was Sir Gordon Guggisberg, governor of the Gold Coast from 1919 to 1927, and largely responsible for the foundation of Achimota School. In his view the chief duty of government

> is nothing more nor less than assisting the Native Races of the country in their progress towards the attainment of those conditions of modern civilization which are best suited to the country and the chief element in this progress is education.[81]

Missionary educationalists who advocated education from the village level to the University included A. G. Fraser and Dr. Robert Laws,[82] who worked in Nyasaland for fifty years. Of those people who contributed regularly to left wing journals or wrote polemics on African questions and who supported rapid modernization of African society, some like Norman Leys and Leonard Barnes had spent long periods in various parts of Africa, while others like C. R. Buxton and Leonard Woolf were active in left wing circles in England. The three academics most clearly interested in questions of education in Africa, W. M. Macmillan, A. Victor Murray and Julian Huxley had all spent some time observing the African situation at first hand. Huxley undertook a tour of African colonies on behalf of the Colonial Office Advisory

Committee on Native Education in 1930 and in 1931 published his observations in *Africa View*. In spite of his commitment to indirect rule, he likened arguments about limiting African educational opportunities to those used by conservatives about the British working classes in the nineteenth century, and affirmed his belief that all educational facilities should be provided in Africa with opportunities for specialized vocational training as well as higher liberal education.[83]

A number of these people made observations about the importance of character training and also of religious teaching as part of the total educative process. Dr. Robert Laws, for example, wrote of education as full development of 'spiritual, moral, mental and physical powers'.[84] However the emphasis here was on the importance of all aspects of the educative process, rather than on character training as an end in itself. Some people recognized that emphasis on character training was sometimes a device to inhibit rather than encourage initiative and independent thought. Professor Murray believed that there could be no value in character training when the atmosphere was one of a specialist operating on a patient,[85] while A. G. Fraser argued that 'we have to expect virtues but not to inculcate them.'[86]

In general it seems clear that the conservative position on education was inspired either by the fear of political instability, even perhaps the desire to maintain the political status quo with existing racial inequalities; or by a growing lack of confidence, apparent particularly among missionaries, partly as a result of the obvious upheavals caused by Western impact, of which education was a considerable part. In both cases the desire to limit the rate of change caused a reaction towards limiting education, not so much in extent, for many advocated mass education at a village level, but in content. It is ironic that the conservatives, so accustomed to speaking in terms of the European civilizing mission in Africa, were now reluctant to make available to Africans the best that their civilization could offer. It was now the turn of the progressives, often critical of imperial intentions and practice in the past, to demonstrate confidence in their own society. They were not uncritical of Western industrial society but they were convinced that Western knowledge should be made available to all mankind. Whereas the arguments of the conservatives often had racist overtones, the progressives were convinced that African backwardness was an accident of history which should be remedied as quickly as possible. They regretted social disorder in Africa in varying degrees but were convinced that rapid change was inevitable. The best solutions to the problems to be encountered by the people of a society in such a state of flux could only be found by people who were educated. More than this some writers had the vision to see that the pursuit of conservative policies in education would inspire the sort of reaction from Africans which was the opposite to that intended. This view was expressed succinctly by one of the most direct and indefatigable critics of imperial policy.

> A vast deal of nonsense is said and written about the supposed evils of 'Europeanizing' and 'detribalization'. What it will come to can be found by asking the question, what are Africans to be encouraged to know? If the answer is that certain knowledge should be withheld from them, then we know that those who give that answer regard Africans as sub-human. But the knowledge and the ideas that have transformed and are transforming our own society cannot be kept from Africans. If we offer them all that we recognize as best in our own lives we may be sure of their gratitude. But if we allow those who regard them as sub-human to restrict their education, vainly in the end to restrict it, to the three R's and manual trades . . . we shall know what to expect if we ask ourselves how we, in these Africans' place, should feel and think in consequence.[87]

There is some evidence that, towards the end of the 1930s the more radical view of education—that it should offer widely the same alternatives as were offered in Britain—was beginning to prevail. The existence of 'a welter of conflicting aims' in African education was observed by the Commissioners who reported on Higher Education in East Africa in 1937.[88] They identified a variety of aims and summarized the view of those who supported and those who rejected Westernization. The report pointed out that Africa had been subject to change long before the arrival of the white man and that, now, the European and African cultures were closely interlocked.

> It is not, therefore, the task of African education to prevent the Europeanization of the Africans. The task, rather, is to interpret to the youth of Africa the higher values of the present world and to assist Africans in the difficult process of adjustment so that they shall be able to live without strain in the composite conditions which have been created.[89]

In this statement questions of environment, and group and individual psychology, took priority over moral questions.

More important, perhaps, than evidence of support for Westernization policies was the gradual growth of support for the idea that Africans themselves should be involved in discussion about educational requirements in Africa. Seven Africans attended a conference on African education, set up by the Seventh

World Conference of the New Education Fellowship in 1936. One
of the ten Europeans present was reported as saying that the
Commission had taken the unusual course of listening while the
Africans explained what they believed was good for Africa. They
heard and discussed six papers read by Africans and were
impressed by their unanimity and moderation.[90] The typically
paternalist division between 'us' and 'them' was beginning to be
eroded.

NOTES

1. *The Report of the East African Commission*, Cmd 2387 (1925), for example,
   stated that the status of trusteeship 'imposes upon the trustee a moral duty
   and a moral attitude'.
2. For an early analysis of the effects of these changes on educational practice
   in Britain see G. A. N. Lowndes, *The Silent Social Revolution*, (London,
   1937).
3. For an analysis of the changes in English educational practice in this period
   see Olive Banks, *Parity and Prestige in English Secondary Education*,
   (London, 1958).
4. The Hadow Reports, (1926, 1931, 1933), The Spens Report, (1939), and
   The Norwood Report, (1941). See Olive Banks, *Parity and Prestige*, and
   John Lello, *The Official View on Education*, (Oxford, 1964).
5. This recognition was reflected in the support for the New Education Fellowship, which preached the importance of education as a means of social
   reconstruction or progress. See, for example, a series of articles called
   'Social Progress through Education' by William Boyd, the first instalment
   of which was published in the *New Era* in March, 1933. William Boyd
   was head of the Department of Education at Glasgow University and
   author of an impressive list of books on education.
6. See C. K. Williams, *Achimota: The Early Years, 1924–1948*, (Accra, 1962),
   for an account of the situation in The Gold Coast before 1920. This period
   is also discussed in *A History of Education in British West Africa*, (London,
   1956) by Colin G. Wise. In C. P. Groves, *The Planting of Christianity in
   Africa*, Part IV (London, 1958), p. 106 there is an account of the first
   governmental intervention in education in parts of East and Central Africa
   before 1920. The situation in Sierra Leone is discussed in D. L. Sumner,
   Education in Sierra Leone, (London, 1963), p. 149 f. The best general
   summary of the whole area is to be found in Lord Hailey, *The African
   Survey*, Ch. XVIII.
7. See E. A. Ayandele, *The Missionary Impact on Modern Nigeria, 1842–1914*,
   (London, 1966), esp. p. 139 f. for a discussion on conflict between indirect
   rule and missionary 'absolutism'.
8. See L. P. Mair, *An African People in the 20th Century*, pp. 1–3.
9. For criticisms of missionary work from people who were also firm supporters
   of indirect rule, see F. D. Lugard, *The Dual Mandate*, Julian Huxley,
   Africa View, and Margery Perham, *Native Administration in Nigeria*.
10. See Julian Huxley, 'Travel and Politics in East Africa', *J.A.S.*, XXX
    (1931), pp. 245–61. Huxley believed that the problem might be solved by

providing the missionary with a more rigorous training, including some knowledge of anthropology.

11. See, for example, J. H. Oldham, 'The Educational Work of Missionary Societies', *Africa*, VII (1934), pp. 47–59 and Margaret Wrong, 'Africa', a chapter in *The Modern Missionary*, edited by J. H. Oldham, (London, 1935).

12. See Lord Hailey, *An African Survey*, p. 1304 f. for a discussion of the difficulties encountered in estimating school populations in Africa. The section on education concludes with a detailed table of expenditure on education in each colony and lists the estimated total school populations. Table X in this section gives the percentages of African children in different school years in 1935 or 1936. In Kenya, for example, 96.8% attended standard I, but only 3% attended standard IV, and 0.2% above standard VI. See also L. P. Mair, *Native Policies in Africa*, for a contemporary coverage of existing educational facilities in African colonies.

13. See J. Merle Davis (Ed.), *Modern Industry and the African*, p. 6, for the view that the missions had earlier had a semi-political role, sometimes acting as agents of Government.

14. The Roman Catholic missions cooperated readily with the State on education in order to secure Catholic 'presence' for religious purposes. See C. P. Groves, *The Planting of Christianity in Africa Part IV*, p. 119–20, and Roland Oliver, *The Missionary Factor in East Africa*, p. 272 f. In 1927 Arthur Hindley, then Rector of the English College in Rome, was appointed to the newly created post of Visitor Apostolic to Catholic Missions in British African colonies. He advocated collaboration with governments in the field of education.

15. In particular the missionaries noted the success of Islam and wrote about it. For example the 1926–27 volume of *World Dominion* contained six articles on questions related to Islam. Less attention was given to the growth of quasi-Christian African churches outside mission control which had begun at this time, and which posed another serious problem for missionary workers. Interest in this phenomenon is of comparatively recent growth. For a bibliography on this subject see R. C. Mitchell and H. W. Turner, *A Comprehensive Bibliography of Modern African Religious Movements*, (Evanston, 1966).

16. For a reprint of the Reports of these Commissions, see L. J. Lewis (Ed.), *Phelps-Stokes Reports on Education in Africa*, (London, 1962).

17. The American Baptist Foreign Missionary Society encouraged the Foreign Missions Conference of North America to set in train research in African educational needs and resources. This body approached the Trustees of the Phelps-Stokes Fund for support for this project. This fund had been established in 1911 by Miss Caroline Phelps-Stokes to educate the negroes of the United States and Africa. The first commission visited East Africa in 1924. Dr. Thomas Jesse Jones and Dr. James Aggrey, members of both commissions, had both been involved in the work of the Hampton school.

18. They criticized the village schools as inadequately equipped, and staffed; the lack of integration between the schools and the communities; the absence of cooperation between missions, governments, and other bodies which should be concerned with education.

19. For an account of the founding of Tuskegee, and the ideas behind this philosophy of education, see Booker T. Washington, *Up From Slavery*, (New York, 1900).

20. It is of interest that A. Victor Murray observed that 'It is a serious limitation of the value of the Phelps-Stokes Commission Reports that their views on

native education are orientated not around the Natives' political position but around American educational theory'. See *The School in the Bush,* p. 361.

21. See L. J. Lewis (Ed.), *Phelps-Stokes Reports,* p. 47–8.
22. In *Africans Learn to be French,* (London, 1935), W. Bryant-Mumford and Major G. St. J. Orde-Browne contrast the British and French views of education. 'The French would hold that there is one universal civilization to which the world is moving, and of which Europe is the leader at the present time . . .'
23. In 1917, Lord Chelmsford appointed a Commission to enquire into the affairs of Calcutta University, with Sir Michael Sadler as Chairman.
24. Sir Valentine Chirol (1852–1929), Director of the Foreign Department of *The Times* from 1899 to 1912. He was involved in the Royal Commission on the Indian Public Services in 1912. He wrote extensively on the Middle East, Far East and India.
25. *Indian Unrest,* (London, 1910), contained much that directly concerned education. He also wrote *India, Old and New,* (London, 1921) and *India,* (London, 1926).
26. One of the longest comparisons of Indian and African problems in the field of education, in books dealing primarily with Africa, appeared in *The Golden Stool* by Edwin W. Smith, while Lugard relied heavily on the views of Sir Valentine Chirol in the section on education in *The Dual Mandate.*
27. See, for example, J. Merle Davis (Ed.), *Modern Industry and the African,* p. 2. 'The growth of Anthropolopy, Ethnology, Sociology and Linguistics has opened avenues into hitherto obscure recesses of the African mind, and has revealed values, concepts, controls, sanctions and motivations that must be reckoned with by the Christian message'.
28. B. Malinowski's work was possibly the most generally influential in this period. He published several books throughout the 1920s and 1930s and involved himself in debate about the application of anthropological findings to colonial problems. In 1934 he gave several addresses to the N.E.F. Conference in South Africa. For a summary of the views he expressed see E. G. Malherbe (Ed.), *Educational Adaptations in a Changing Society,* (Capetown, 1937), pp. 423–426.
29. See Basil A. Fletcher, *Education and Colonial Development,* (London, 1936), p. 18. The value of anthropological knowledge in the field of education is discussed on p. 45 f.
30. In 1934 the International Institute of African Languages and Cultures was at the beginning of its Five Year Plan of Research into social change in Africa. Trained anthropologists and linguists were sent to Africa by this organization to make detailed studies of European influence on tribal groups.
31. It is of interest that Margaret Read made the following statement in *Education and Social Change in Tropical Areas,* (London, 1955), p. 68—'I imagine that if a referendum were to be taken of all living anthropologists on the question "Do you, or do you not, approve of modern education in the territory where you have worked", the results would be a 90 to 95 per cent negative answer.' In answering the anthropologists would be expressing their views 'on the the cumulative effects of such education on the stability and cohesion of the society which they were investigating.'
32. One example, late in this period, was the publication in 1938 in *Africa* of a study by Meyer Fortes on the education of Tale children in the Gold Coast. Fortes began with the two axioms that (i) education in the widest sense is the process by which the cultural heritage is transmitted from

generation to generation, and (ii) that education attempts the moulding of the individual to the social norm. See M. Fortes, 'Social and Psychological Aspects of Education in Taleland', Supplement to *Africa*, XI, (1938). But the subject was under discussion throughout the 1930s. See, for example, J. H. Driberg, 'Indigenous Systems of Education in Africa.' A talk given at the N.E.F. Conference of 1931 and published in W. Rawson (Ed.), *Education in a Changing Commonwealth*, (London, 1931), pp. 92–96. See, also, D. Westermann, *Africa Today and Tomorrow*, p. 98 f.

33. This did seem to be the advice of F. Clarke, at this time Professor of Education at McGill University, Montreal, Canada, but who had spent eighteen years in South Africa as Professor of Education at Capetown. In 'The Double Mind in African Education', *Africa*, 5 (1932), p. 166, he argued that the West was not in a position to be dogmatic about its own educational needs, let alone those of Africa. He believed that Europe was passing through a period of upheavals 'so that the task of this generation is to analyse and watch rather than to embark upon adventures which presuppose a faith no longer vital . . .'

34. See Arthur Mayhew, *Educational Policy in the Colonial Empire*, (London, 1938), p. 13. It is true that Mayhew recognized that some people denied the existence of any universally valid system of values. See *Ibid.*, p. 16.

35. See Basil A. Fletcher, *Education and Colonial Development*. The objectives of colonial education are described on p. 87 f.

36. *Ibid.*, p. 17. 'The new ideas must be presented in such a selective way that only those parts that can be grafted on to the racial past of the people are allowed to be potent for change.'

37. For details of this and other conferences of missionaries see M. Warren, *The Missionary Movement from Britain in Modern History*, (London, 1965).

38. See Edwin W. Smith, *The Golden Stool*, p. 260, for his statement about 'the Christianization of everything that is valuable in the African's past experience and registered in his customs.'

39. The phrase of J. H. Oldham, *The Remaking of Man in Africa*, p. 50.

40. The Jeanes Schools were possibly the most interesting example of this theory put into practice. Several articles concerning the operations of the Jeanes Schools appeared in *Oversea Education* from its first issue in 1929 onwards. Other information about the Jeanes Schools appeared in *Village Education in Africa*, a report of the Jeanes Conference held at Salisbury in Southern Rhodesia, in 1935; E. G. Malherbe (Ed.), *Educational Adaptations in a Changing Environment*, p. 505, and Richard C. Thurnwald, *Black and White in East Africa*, pp. 245–7.

41. This was sometimes an attack on earlier so-called literary education which had prepared clerks for government service—a particular form of vocational training.

42. *Educational Policy in British Tropical Africa*, Cmd 2374, (1925), and *The Education of African Communities* (1935).

43. This committee, representing missionary and secular interests, was set up in 1923 to advise the Colonial Office concerning education policy in Africa. It was reconstituted in 1929 and called the Advisory Committee on Education in the Colonies. In 1933 it set up a sub-committee to make recommendations for future investigation concerning higher education in Africa.

44. Cmd 2374, p. 4

45. A Conference of African Missionaries held at High Leigh in September 1923. Practically all British-African Missionary Societies sent representatives. There were about twenty representatives from American Societies and others

from the Continent. Some members of the Phelps-Stokes Education Commission were present as well as Sir Frederick Lugard. For a summary of the conclusions of this Conference see the Editorial Notes, *Journal of the African Society,* XXIV (1924–25), p. 61, and J. H. Oldham, 'Christian Education in Africa', *Church Missionary Review,* 75 (1924), pp. 305–314.

46. The Le Zoute Conference was an international one, attended by Dr. Jesse Jones, Sir Frederick Lugard and J. H. Oldham. Education was one of the five main themes of discussion and the Conference accepted the recommendations of the Phelps-Stokes Commissions. For a detailed account of the Conference see Edwin W. Smith, *The Christian Mission in Africa,* (London, 1926).

47. Sir Frederick Lugard, 'New Forces in Africa'. A speech delivered to the Le Zoute Conference and recorded in Edwin W. Smith, *The Christian Mission in Africa,* p. 150 f.

48. Edwin W. Smith, *Ibid.,* p. 63.

49. *Ibid.,* p. 62. Edwin Smith referred to the book *The Four Essentials of Education,* (New York, 1926), by Dr. Jesse Jones. These four essentials were (i) health and sanitation; (ii) appreciation and use of the environment; (iii) the household and the home; (iv) recreation (mental, moral and spiritual development).

50. The words of L. P. Mair, 'The Anthropologists' Approach to Native Education', *Oversea Education,* VI, 2 (1935), p. 57.

51. This journal was published for the Secretary of State for the Colonies and contained regular reports of the Proceedings of the Advisory Committee on Education in the Colonies, as well as articles discussing the theory and practice of education in Africa, and in colonies elsewhere.

52. T. G. Benson, 'Some Problems of Education in Africa Today', *Oversea Education,* VII, 1 (1935), pp. 10–14.

53. L. P. Mair, 'The Anthropologists' Approach to Native Education', *Oversea Education,* VI, 2 (1935), pp. 53–60.

54. A. G. Fraser, 'Education and Vocational Training', *Oversea Education,* III, 2 (1935), pp. 71–73.

55. T. G. Benson, 'Some Problems of Education in Africa Today', *Oversea Education,* VII, 1 (1935), pp. 10–14.

56. This was almost certainly true, as it undoubtedly would have been in Britain. It was aggravated by the fact that educated Africans were not permitted to occupy important administrative and technical posts.

57. G. Howard Jones, 'Educational Needs in West Africa', *J.A.S.,* XXVI (1926–27), p. 344.

58. Robert Stokes, *New Imperial Ideals,* p. 178.

59. The Earl of Selbourne, 'The Native Problem on the West Coasts', *J.A.S.,* XXI (1921–22), p. 261. See also, R. C. F. Maugham, *Africa as I have known it,* (London, 1929), p. 310.

60. R. Coupland, *The Empire in Three Days,* p. 169. See similar views expressed by Brig. Gen. Charles P. Fendell, 'East African Troubles', *Empire Review,* LIII (1931), p. 59, 'Civilize him by all means, but suit the civilization to his nature and environment.'

61. F. D. Lugard, *The Dual Mandate,* p. 426. 'The impact of European civilization on tropical races has indeed a tendency to undermine that respect for authority which is the basis of social order'.

62. For articles reflecting this view point, see e.g. G. C. Latham, 'Indirect Rule and Education in East Africa', *Africa,* VII (1934), pp. 423–30 and J. Russell

Orr, 'The Use of the Kinema in the Guidance of Backward Races', *J.A.S.*, XXX (1931), pp. 238–44.

63. See E. G. Dr. Cuthbert Christy, 'White Settlement in Tropical Africa', *J.A.S.*, XXVII (1927–28), p. 340 for an extreme version. 'The three R's are of small use to the peasant'.

64. Sir Frederick Lugard, 'Education in British Tropical Africa', *Edinburgh Review*, 242 (1925), p. 2.

65. Evans Lewin, 'The Black Cloud in Africa', *Foreign Affairs*, 4 (1925–26), p. 642.

66. Sir Horace Byatt, 'Tanganyika', *J.A.S.*, XXIV (1924–25), p. 7.

67. F. D. Lugard, *The Dual Mandate*, p. 428.

68. W. M. Macmillan, 'Position of Native Education in British Africa', *United Empire*, New Series, XXV (1934), pp. 172–3.

69. A. Victor Murray, *The School in the Bush*, p. 117.

70. Leonard Woolf, *Imperialism and Civilization*, p. 89.

71. Norman Leys, *A Last Chance in Kenya*, p. 104.

72. Charles Roden Buxton, 'Missionaries in East Africa', *Contemporary Review*, 135 (1933), p. 442.

73. See, for example, Frank Melland who also wrote under the pseudonym of 'Africanus' in several articles including 'East African Kaleidoscope', *19th Century*, 115 (1934), pp.525–34; 'Native Education in Central Africa', *J.A.S.*, XX (1920–21), pp. 95–100; 'Reconstruction in Central Africa', *J.A.S.*, XIX (1919–20), pp. 92–100. See also H. S. Scott, 'The effects of Education on the African', *J.A.S.*, XXVII (1938), pp. 504–9.

74. Norman Leys, *Kenya*, p. 139.

75. Norman Leys, Letter to the Editor, *N.S. & N.*, 16 Jan. 1932.

76. Norman Leys, 'A College in the Gold Coast', *N.S. & N.*, 22 April, 1933.

77. Charles Roden Buxton, 'Missionaries in East Africa' *Contemporary Review*, 143 (1933), p. 442.

78. Sir James Currie, 'Present Day Difficulties of a Young Officer in the Tropics', *J.A.S.*, XXXII (1933), p. 33.

79. This policy involved the spread of Christianity, commerce and colonization.

80. Leonard Barnes, *The Duty of Empire*, p. 148.

81. Sir F. G. Guggisberg, 'The Goal of the Gold Coast', *J.A.S.*, XXI, (1921–22), p. 87.

82. See Dr. Robert Laws, 'Native Education in Nyasaland', *J.A.S.*, XXVIII (1928–29), pp. 347–67.

83. See Julian Huxley, 'East Africa: Politics and Native Questions', *Contemporary Review*, 138 (1930), pp. 459–69.

84. Dr. Robert Laws, 'Native Education in Nyasaland', *J.A.S.*, XXVIII (1928–29), p. 347.

85. Prof. A. Victor Murray, *A School in the Bush*, p. 210.

86. A. G. Fraser, 'Aims of African Education', *I.R.M.*, XIV (1925), p. 519.

87. Norman Leys, *A Last Chance in Kenya*, p. 77.

88. *Higher Education in East Africa* (The De La Warr Commission), Col. No. 142, (1937).

89. *Ibid.*, p. 10.

90. See *The Anti-Slavery Reporter and Aborigines Friend*, Series V, 26, (1937), p. 194–5.

CHAPTER 8

ADMINISTRATION

Before World War I adminstrative personnel had been sent out to Africa with little preparation and little knowledge of what to expect except that the areas they were expected to administer would usually be vast, and communication with Britain slow and uncertain. In the post-war period the services were spread more evenly, communications improved and more emphasis was placed on the importance of administrative work. With the now growing support for indirect rule ideology it was increasingly argued that the administration of alien people posed problems which could only be solved by people with special skills and knowledge. Above all the administrator needed to know something of the societies over which he would be exercising political control. It was characteristic of this period between the wars that many anthropologists and others made fairly extravagant claims about the application of anthropological knowledge to colonial administrative problems.[1] It was they who could provide vital information about the nature of various African societies and they who could analyse and predict the nature and direction of social change.

The importance of anthropological training for the administrative services was canvassed by a number of people in several journals and books in the 1920s,[2] and in 1925 the idea received support in the Report of the East African Commission.[3] These, and later observations on the same theme, assumed some basic unanimity in British society about the continuance of British administrative presence in Africa. Criticisms of particular policies and of administrative practice might be made, but British presence in Africa was believed to be a necessity and likely to be more efficient with expert help. By the 1930s this advocacy of a marriage between anthropology and administration was receiving wide-spread support, a result partly attributable to the work of the International Institute of African Languages and Cultures, especially through its journal *Africa,* partly to the influence of a great variety of books and journals published in this period.[4]

The belief in the importance of this alliance between administration and anthropology paralleled the new approach to African societies now apparent within the discipline of anthropology. Fairly radical changes had recently occurred within the discipline itself, so that it had ceased to be dilettante and antiquarian. Long periods of fieldwork in societies under examination were now recognized as essential, and major questions of methodology were under debate. In Britain two scholars, A. R. Radcliffe-Browne and B. Malinowski, were important in introducing new approaches to the discipline and raising vital methodological issues. The trend was away from the historical and evolutionist approach, which had emphasized the origins and development of particular societies, and towards the study of the way in which societies functioned.[5] And because it was rapidly becoming clear that soon no societies would be completely outside the pervasive influence of European culture, the functionalists were increasingly forced to concern themselves with the problems of social change.[6] These changes within the discipline opened up debates, still unsettled, concerning questions of methodology, the place of social anthropology in the social sciences,[7] and the extent to which social anthropology was identified with colonial rule.[8]

In the period between the wars there were a few propagandists who saw the colonial administrative service as part of the apparatus for creating an African proletariat in the interests of European capitalism, and who therefore rejected all notions of 'improvement' within the service.[9] But most writers believed that good administration was crucial to the well-being of the African. These paternalists were optimistic that administrative problems could be overcome, and African cultural patterns understood and intelligently changed with the help of the anthropologist. The interesting thing about this period, particularly in the 1930s, is the widespread support for the idea that intelligent study could provide Europeans with the answers about what was in the best interests of the Africans. This paternalist view prevented the European anthropologist seeing that the African might envisage a time when the European had left him to work out his own future, however uncertain. It was in fact the propaganda of Hobson and Lenin that appealed to the educated African nationalist and made it possible for him to believe that he had a part to play in African politics.[10]

The note of self-confidence, even arrogance, of the 'experts' of the 1930s indicated a conviction that there was no real alternative to British paternalism for an indefinite and lengthy period in the future, and that Africans would remain quiescent while Europeans made the decisions about the direction of progress. The commitment of the International Institute to this position is clear in Smith's statement that the Institute

aims not primarily at adding to the world's knowledge of Africa and the Africans, but assisting in the formulation and execution of plans to secure the orderly progress of the Africans by the development, in contact with western civilization, of all that is best in their own culture.[11]

This well-meaning commitment is apparent in articles by many anthropologists and experts in other fields in the 1930s. Lucy Mair was typical of many whose faith in the value of scientific knowledge and its rational application to human problems blinded them to their own limitations.[12] They saw African society as something able to be manipulated by Europeans for the Africans' ultimate good, unaware of the wider political issues, or perhaps choosing to ignore them.

This tendency was reinforced because the idea of a British ruling caste, superbly fitted for the task of bringing peace and good government to primitive and barbarous Africa, survived well into the twentieth century.[13] In the contemporary analysis of the disruptive effects of European influence on Africa, the administration often escaped the accusations so often levelled at the missionary and trader. According to the myth which had grown up about the exploits of the British imperial administration, the people of the colonies were governed much better than they could hope to govern themselves, by men who belonged to the elite of a society which had long accepted the responsibility for governing less fortunate or inferior people. The 'right type of officer', frequently referred to as the product of the English public schools and two great universities,[14] was believed to have the characteristics which could not fail to give him enormous prestige in the eyes of the 'natives', a prestige which he was exhorted to maintain at all costs.[15] A composite picture of this remarkable paragon was provided by Professor Zimmern.

The English gentleman represents a specific and clearly marked type of humanity . . . He has evolved his own special technique of government, the result of long development and much stored up experience . . . For courage, for honour and loyalty, for tolerance, for wisdom and calm judgement, for self-control in emergencies, I doubt whether the world has ever seen his equal . . . The English gentleman has been, in fact, an unrivalled primary teacher of peoples . . .[16]

Zimmern went on to refer to Lord Lugard as the most distinguished living representative of the tradition of British colonial rule. Lugard's own views on the superiority of British administrative officers can be found in several places in his influential book, a superiority which he believed was produced very largely by the English public schools and universities. They produced, he believed,

> an English gentleman with an almost passionate conception of fair play, of protection of the weak and of 'playing the game'. They have taught him personal initiative and resource, and how to command and obey. There is no danger of such men falling a prey to that subtle moral deterioration which the exercise of power over inferior races produces in men of a different type and which finds expression in cruelty.[17]

These views received support in the Fisher Report which asserted the value of public school and university education in producing qualities of fair play and just dealing towards less favoured races.[18] While these training grounds may have inculcated valuable qualities of incorruptibility the fact that this service was also authoritarian and alien to the people being governed was usually totally ignored.

However, criticism was not unknown in the 1920s, and by the 1930s, was comparatively frequent. Criticism of the service itself was sometimes made on the grounds that, for all its incorruptibility, it was intolerant of people who showed 'symptoms of independence'.[19] This comparatively mild criticism was put more trenchantly in the 1930s by Harold Laski, who argued that the administrative service did not welcome innovation, and was positively hostile to the idea of civil liberty. In his view African criticism of British rule was regarded as sedition.[20] This criticism was sometimes linked with the important question of the irresponsible nature of colonial rule, due to the fact that neither the British Parliament nor the British electorate (theoretically responsible for policy in Africa) showed any continuous interest in African affairs. Harold Laski referred to this absence of effective criticism in Britain,[21] while Norman Leys believed the absence of responsible government had led to evils which would not have been possible in a free society. In spite of the theory of trusteeship

> in Kenya, Europeans are masters and Africans servants. The vast majority of Europeans in Africa believe that relationship to be an integral part of the natural order of human society.[22]

He argued that this lack of administrative responsibility, which would have been a reality in a democratic self-governing community, had led to a denial of ordinary rights and liberties to Africans[23] and to attempts by the white settlers in Kenya to promote a permanent racial oligarchy.[24] The criticisms of Leys, and of a number of other well known writers on colonial policy, were not primarily directed at the nature or performance of the administrative personnel, but at the British Government's failure to promote a firm policy on a number of questions crucial to the future of the African in East and Central Africa. The questions of land rights, labour laws, taxation systems, native reserves and general administrative methods, particularly as they applied to Kenya and to Northern and Southern Rhodesia were debated frequently in liberal and socialist journals.[25] The work of the British administrative service was only justified if it carried out a firm interventionist policy in Africa, in the interests of the Africans. These critics feared the subjugation of the Africans by an increasingly vocal white minority which could command influential support in England. But the unrepresentative and paternalist nature of the British administration in Africa was not an important issue even with most radicals in this period. They did not demand immediate self-government for the African colonies but a better performance by the imperial government, which would be reflected in administrative changes. And here there was quite fundamental disagreement about what constituted good administration. This can be most clearly demonstrated by considering the views prevailing at this time about the device of 'indirect rule', first applied in West Africa, but later extended, with varying degrees of thoroughness, to other colonies in East and Central Africa.[26]

It was argued by supporters of Leninist theories of imperialism that indirect rule was simply a device for keeping Africans in a position from which they could be most readily exploited. Other critics of imperial policy believed that the system had its origins in racist beliefs which held Africans incapable of governing through any institutions other than their own inferior ones. A close analysis of various theories advocating indirect rule suggests that its supporters did in fact believe in the unique quality of British political life, the institutions of which could not be transferred successfully to other people. It is clear also that they prized good government far above self government and had a very blurred vision of future political development in Africa. All indirect rule arguments envisaged only very gradual change, the prevention of political disruption which might lead to social chaos, and a future which would take care of itself. Influential support for these views came from the anthropologists. It is paradoxical that, whereas those interested in the application of the physical sciences to African problems suggested radical solutions, those involved in the social sciences tended to emphasize the disruptive and destructive nature of European influence in Africa. They supported the idea of research into African problems, but they tended to be uncritical of paternalist policies. By their emphasis on the danger of rapid social change, they bolstered indirect rule theories.

There were four main arguments used to justify indirect rule in this period. The first was that political change was inevitable and must take place through institutions 'natural' to Africa. According to this theory tribal institutions were somehow fundamentally different from those of western society, either because they were typically 'African', or because they represented an evolutionary stage in the development of institutions of government which Britain had passed through two thousand years before. Where they had broken down they had to be rebuilt so that political evolution could occur along traditional and recognizable lines. A politically immature people should be encouraged to evolve their own methóds of government, their own solutions to political problems. It will be seen that supporters of this view accepted and expected change, but deplored any sudden break in political development. This was sometimes because of straightforward support for social evolutionary theories which implied that 'primitive' institutions could not be successfully replaced by sophisticated ones. But this view also received support from those who believed that all peoples have a peculiar 'genius' which is reflected in their political system. Thus western democratic politics reflected the British qualities of individual initiative, an acceptance of responsibility and a readiness to compromise. Western political systems were unlikely to suit what was frequently referred to as the 'mentality' of the African.

The second strand of indirect rule ideology was the belief that out of the contact of European and African cultures a new synthesis must be built up and this could only be done by preserving what was best in African culture and adding to it the best that Europe could offer. Sometimes the emphasis was on allowing Africans the maximum freedom to make this new synthesis. This interest in the survival of aspects of African culture suggested a tolerance of alien customs as well as a belief that societies should not be uprooted. Change should be gradual and selective.[27] However some of the exponents of this theory displayed quite unwarranted optimism in believing that the best of the two societies could be preserved and integrated, even supposing some general agreement could be reached about what constituted the best. The argument tended to oppose the two societies quite artificially, since some sort of synthesis could be said to exist at any moment in time after the first contact. This theory, too, was conservative and uncertain as to goals.

The third major argument for indirect rule theory was that which made it an educative device to expand and develop the native faculty for government. In this argument political education and development were key ideas. But the process of educating the African to govern himself must take place through those institutions already in existence and understood, institutions which could be modified gradually as European concepts could be introduced.[28] It was believed that from this basis even those in the earliest stage of social evolution could develop. This argument placed no necessary emphasis on the ultimate value of African cultural patterns, and implied, in fact, that much of Western political practice would be incorporated into African systems and gradually effect a political transformation. The exponents of political education through indirect rule spoke of *moulding, expanding, modifying* and *developing* old institutions; of *grafting* ideas on to root stocks; of the adaptation of old institutions to new purposes.[29] This argument sounds progressive but it depended on a real programme of action connected with transforming subsistence economies; it implied a greater outlay than could reasonably be expected from the British exchequer.

The fourth and final strand of indirect rule ideology was more direct and far simpler than all the others. Whereas the other three arguments were characterized by a failure to make explicit the goal of political development, the fourth argument was anti-democratic in its implications, and stated clearly what was intended. Indirect rule was a system which aimed at the growth of a responsible African elite, out of the old tribal elite, which would gradually be taught the duties and responsibilities of rulers of a modern state. It involved an identification between the British administrative elite in Africa, most of whom came from the upper classes of English society and felt they had a duty and right to govern others, and the traditional elite groups in tribal society. These indirect rulers believed that the existing hierarchy in African society should be perpetuated. This theory led to support for the idea of educating chiefs' sons so that they would be better able to take part in modernizing tribal institutions.[30] At the same time they deplored the political activities of those educated Africans who attempted to create pressure groups outside traditional politics.[31]

All these supporters of indirect rule thought in terms of generations of tutelage, of Africans being required to prove

themselves *ready* for self-government, before it could be *granted.*
The Africans were to be *permitted* to develop through their own
institutions, they were to be *encouraged* to manage their own
affairs, while the European acted as guide, guardian, adviser and
helpmate. Finally they were to be *allowed* to govern themselves. It
was J. H. Oldham who succinctly put the Indian reaction to this
sort of paternalism when he argued that there was hardly an Indian
who wanted the British to leave and hardly one for whom it was
not intolerable that the British should stay.

> To know from day to day that decisions regarding the affairs of one's
> country are made by alien rulers, to be conscious of social exclusive-
> ness among the governing race, to incur social slights which seem to cast
> a stigma of inferiority, to run the risk of being exposed on occasion to
> insolence, insult and humiliation which rankle in the memory . . .[32]

these were the considerations which produced a loss of self respect
and an urge for independence.

There were many supporters for one or other of the indirect rule
theories outlined above, among whom were practising Colonial
governors,[33] conservative politicians interested in colonial affairs,[34]
historians[35] and other members of the intelligentsia.[36] Some
supported the idea of indirect rule but were critical of the
practice;[37] some people changed their minds over the twenty year
period.[38] Two great experts on African affairs may be cited in this
context—one writing at the beginning and one at the end of the
period. The difference in attitudes over a period of twenty years is
instructive.

Lord Lugard may be regarded as reflecting views held in the
1920s, but the awe in which he was held as an expert makes it
necessary to regard him as a source, as well as a repository, of
current wisdom on a variety of questions. His book, *The Dual
Mandate in British Tropical Africa,* was first published in 1922 and
contained a wealth of advice and detail on how Africans should be
governed. He justified the practice of indirect rule in this book and
in a variety of different articles published in the period between
1920 and 1940.[39] In his book published in 1922 he devoted
considerable space to various aspects of indirect rule and recorded
some of the objections of which he had been made aware. He set
out what he regarded as the three major divergent opinions about
how native races should be ruled,[40] and indicated his preference
for the

> rule of native chiefs unfettered in their control of their people as
> regards all those matters which are to them the most important attri-
> butes of rule, with scope for initiative and responsibility, but admittedly

—so far as the visible horizon is concerned—subordinate to the control of the protecting Power in certain well-defined directions.

These 'directions' are elaborated on a later page[41] where Lugard set out the limitations imposed on the native chiefs, making clear that they were not permitted to raise or control armed forces, to impose taxation, to legislate, to appropriate land for public purposes, to exercise any control over aliens, or to confirm the choice of a chief (a right reserved to the Governor). The reader is bound to wonder how Lugard could persuade himself that they had been left all those matters which were to them the important attributes of rule. His own account suggested that indirect rule was a device to emasculate the African people politically, while at the same time preserving the forms of indigenous government so that alternative expressions of political opinion could be the more readily stifled.

In 1938 *The African Survey* was published and Lord Hailey subsequently wrote a number of articles which dealt with administrative problems in Africa.[42] He believed that the debate about indirect rule should be reopened. He argued that while it had been regarded at first as a useful administrative device, it had subsequently been treated as a political doctrine and finally a religious dogma. He believed that the African should play a greater part in his own political life and in determining his own future and said that he could envisage a time when tribal institutions 'bore no substantial position as a political factor nor any considerable part in a share of administration'.[43] Hailey pointed out that there had been no solution found as to how to integrate the two systems of indirect rule and the development of parliamentary institutions. He regarded the latter as essential.

> The rapid development of a system of indirect rule, though not necessarily incompatible with the evolution of Parliamentary institutions, can nevertheless take a course which may hamper their introduction.[44]

He made clear that the aim of British policy should be self-government for African colonies with some sort of representative institutions.[45] While he thought that indirect rule may have provided for a period of adjustment,[46] he warned

> that the small educated element in Africa will grow, and will in time contain stronger leaders of African native opinion than will the circle of traditional authorities. If you do not associate the educated element with your own government system . . . you will drive it into a political activity of which the first victims will be the traditional authorities themselves.[47]

Hailey conceded the possibility that representative institutions might be developed which did not follow the British model[48] but he believed that however these institutions developed, every step towards some sort of popular election 'must clearly be a fresh blow to the welfare of the traditional authorities'.[49] Hailey was an advocate of social and economic development which he believed should be accompanied by a growth of political involvement and responsibility among the Africans themselves. The goal was clearly eventual independence. But Hailey made clear that it would be totally unreal to erect a political edifice, similar to that of Great Britain, without attempting a corresponding social revolution which he believed should be engineered and not waited for. In a sense Hailey is the forerunner of those African nationalist leaders of the 1940s and 1950s who wanted to see Africa kicked into the twentieth century. In this he was fundamentally at odds with the indirect rulers.

Just as Lugard had his followers throughout the twenties and thirties, Hailey had his precursors amongst many of the commentators on the theory and practice of indirect rule. Criticisms of this method of government began even before Lugard's book was published. Probably the earliest really trenchant criticism came from a district officer in Nigeria, J. F. J. Fitzpatrick, who wrote a number of articles for British journals in the early twenties.[50] He argued that the system of indirect rule replaced the comparatively more desirable system of 'autocracy, tempered by assassination'. The protection of the autocratic rulers by British bayonets created a feudal system which was inefficient, expensive and corrupt. In his view the administration had been needlessly duplicated and, as far as the native administration was concerned, the population tended to divide into those on the pay-roll and those paying taxes. In order to put an end to this corruption, with which he believed the British were identified, he advocated an increased European administrative staff, with African additions where possible, to undertake all administrative services. Another criticism in the same vein came from Lord Raglan who categorised all chiefs as tyrants or weaklings so that 'the administration is placed in the dilemma of having either continually to upset the decisions of the chiefs or else to connive at injustice'.[51]

These two men were critical of the actual operation of indirect rule, and were writing about the limited success of the system as it operated in Northern Nigeria.[52] Here the worst excesses of the old Fulani rule had ended, but the Emirs had had their authority strengthened by British power and prestige at the expense of older indigenous institutions. It will be recalled that indirect rule was justified because indigenous institutions had some value for Africans and because, in one way or another, they had to be made the basis for change. In Nigeria it seemed that some indigenous institutions had been ignored, while others had been preserved and made more resistant to change.

Criticisms of indirect rule became more frequent after 1930 and were more clearly centred around the two questions of whether or not the system did preserve African institutions, and whether such institutions could be made the basis for gradual political development. Many critics suggested that old institutions were not really being preserved at all. Old sources of political legitimacy had been destroyed inevitably, the more democratic aspects of African societies undermined, and African aristocracies entrenched in positions from which they could now be removed only by the British administration.[53] One critic pointed to the danger of indirect rule bolstering the power of oppressive and incompetent chiefs[54] while R. S. Rattray thought that the people themselves were likely to become estranged within the system because it had produced centralized African autocracies 'disregarding the bases of former African constitutions and states which were essentially decentralized and democratic'.[55] Was it not the case, the critics asked, that African chiefs had become the tools of the British, and were often so regarded by their own people?

In so far as the institutions could be said to have survived they were increasingly anachronistic. The critics believed that political systems should reflect economic and social realities, which meant that there should be a chance for participation in politics for the increasingly large number of Africans who lived outside the tribal milieu. This fundamental criticism shaded into a second one which was to the effect that people learn about politics by being active in politics. Under the system of indirect rule, important groups were denied a chance to participate, while the role of the traditional elite was seriously restricted and distorted by the imposition of an alien super-structure.

It was characteristic of almost all the critics that they spoke of the system as having made change extremely difficult. In fact at times the suggestion was that the system of indirect rule actively prevented change. Professor Macmillan, for example, wrote of the people of the Gold Coast as being too advanced to be 'pushed back into effete tribalism under reactionary chiefs',[56] while many writers connected the anthropologists with the urge to revive 'dead or moribund organizations'.[57]

There were thus three main criticisms of indirect rule. It was an inefficient and corrupt method of governing alien people; it was a vehicle of reaction and not progress; it had the effect of submerging democratic elements in tribal society under an authoritarian framework. These criticisms were commonly connected with whether or not the system was likely to impede or enhance the development of institutions through which Africans would eventually govern themselves. It is clear that Lord Hailey doubted the wisdom of maintaining indirect rule for this reason. It was also true, said the critics, that educated Africans themselves were critical of indirect rule and regarded this method of administration as an imperialist device for preventing development, or as an indication that the British regarded them as inferior people who could not be expected to operate in their superior western institutions. Leonard Barnes, for example, argued that Africans rightly understood that local institutions and traditions were preserved

> less from any sense that these things may be intrinsically worthy of preservation and development than in a profound conviction of their inferiority to British counterparts and therefore to their suitability to backward people.[58]

The system of indirect rule could be interpreted therefore as 'a Machiavellian design to keep the African in his place',[59] and a means of actually preventing development.[60] The educated African was being turned against the British by 'the not wholly unjust doubts about the honesty of our intentions'.[61]

Some of the criticisms of indirect rule imputed to large groups of Europeans, involved in colonial politics, a kind of sinister design to defraud the African. According to one writer the African was beginning to suspect that

> the anthropologist would like nothing better than to see him penned-up and pinned-down in a kind of mental cold storage, preserving for perennial future study the paradox of arrested development; and he has sense enough to perceive that the amateurs of that system of protectorate administration known as indirect rule would be by no means reluctant to compass such a state—at least until they had obtained from the anthropologist sufficient data for their fell fallacious purpose.[62]

Certainly the intention to exploit the Continent for European advantage found expression in the theory of the dual mandate. But the suggestion of a deliberate conspiracy serves to conceal rather than explain the attachment of many writers of that time to the practice of indirect rule. A clearer understanding of the basis of indirect rule theorizing may be gained if it is regarded as representing the genuine view of many well-intentioned people, sufficiently well-educated to be familiar with ideas current in their own society and basically convinced that Britain had some sort of civilizing mission in Africa. Sir Donald Cameron expressed this conviction very clearly.

> Above all, we are using their own indigenous institutions in order to promote higher standards of civilization amongst them. This is the most vital principle in my conception.[63]

The belief that existing institutions made the best basis for change was a Burkean notion. It was part of the British conservative tradition that change should always be introduced slowly, retaining what was valuable in the existing institutions of society. Some British institutions, apparently anachronistic, were seen as an integral part of the historical tradition of that society and therefore not lightly to be thrown aside. The same argument could be applied to the situation in Africa, once the question of British administrative methods became a matter for debate.

The 'indirect rulers' knew, and perhaps even felt a sense of guilt, about the damage done to African societies in the past. They were undoubtedly familiar with current criticism of the way in which the missions had tried to suppress those aspects of African social systems most clearly anathema to Christian beliefs as interpreted through western culture. They were aware of a new growth of cultural relativism and suspected that there was some truth in the argument that Europeans—and the British in particular—had displayed considerable arrogance in the presence of those people with inferior technologies and different cultural patterns. New anthropological knowledge filtered down to the layman suggesting the existence of something unique in each culture which should not lightly be torn asunder.[64] More than this, there existed a conflict between a belief in the advantages of progress as manifested in the application of scientific discoveries to the solution of human problems and a recognition of the loss of a sense of security which the individual tends to suffer in a mass society. The convinced paternalist may often have cast himself in the role of the protector, responsible for praiseworthy attempts to slow down the speed of change and postpone this entry into modern society.

It is an essential part of paternalist thought to see a clear cut distinction between 'us' and 'them'. It was the role of the paternalist to manipulate the situation in such a way that the African could participate in chosen areas. And because the paternalist enjoyed his superior role he may subconsciously have hoped to maintain the gulf between the two groups. In any case, only small areas of the 'superior' culture were available for

African participation. He was not permitted to take what he wanted, to participate where he liked, to have a voice in what the direction of change should be. As a result he often fell back from his precarious hold on western cultural patterns—back into old tribal patterns. The paternalist was thus reinforced in his convictions that it would take many generations before the African would be really civilized.

Finally, part of the explanation for the growth of indirect rule theory at this time may be found in Britain's desire after World War I to demonstrate her superiority as a ruler of backward races,[65] supposedly in need of tutelage before they could stand by themselves. It was argued that whereas Germany and France had imposed direct administrations over their African territories, regarding them always as extensions of metropolitan territory, Britain operated under a system which genuinely envisaged the independence of colonies at some future time.[66] Once her peace-keeping and educative task could be seen to be complete the British administration would be withdrawn, to make way for the accession to power of refurbished indigenous institutions. The British reluctance to allow educated Africans to participate in work at a high administrative level could thus be explained as due to a conviction that political experience should be sought within tribal institutions which would form the nucleus of later institutions of self-government.[67]

The critics of indirect rule shared some of these attitudes. Yet they differed from the supporters of indirect rule on two crucial issues. Whereas, among the 'indirect rulers', there was ample evidence of continuing faith in the British civilizing mission, a mission helped rather than hindered by the satisfaction of 'legitimate' economic interests in Africa, the small group of critics believed there was something fundamentally wrong about the way the colonies had come into British possession and something equally wrong about the purpose for which they were administered. For them the talk of a civilizing mission was cant, used to conceal the intention to exploit African territories. For these critics the key question was how to operate in such a way as to prepare the Africans for independence as soon as possible, so that exploitation would cease. Rapid change was essential, and this the system of indirect rule could not bring about, any more than it could provide experience in institutions which are suitable organs for the political life of a modern state. The Imperial Government had failed to undertake a programme of mass education, it had failed to provide adequate resources to attack disease and poverty, it had allowed British nationals to exploit African resources without encouraging genuine economic growth and development. Above all it had failed to provide experience in government which would have made the transfer of power to Africans a possibility in the not too distant future. These attacks on the Imperial Government tend to obscure the fact that these radicals were paternalists too. But they thought not in terms of a long term civilizing mission but of a modernizing with the explicit goal of independence.

The fact that they had their own brand of paternalism is highlighted by a comparison with Leninist propaganda, published in the *Labour Monthly* at the end of the thirties. This journal had never given a great deal of space to specifically African problems and certainly not to questions of alternative methods of administration, since all methods, they believed, would clearly be aimed to exploit the coloured masses. The growing demands of Germany for a return of her African colonies, and the growing threat of war in the late 1930s, introduced a new note of urgency into the debate about the future of the colonies. In particular the extreme left-wing writers and the Communist Party of Great Britain took advantage of the fact that in so much of the debate of the time the colonies were treated as though they were pawns in a rather disreputable game, to attack imperialism generally and to 'expose' conditions in the colonies.[68] In the quotation which follows, which is part of a statement adopted by the Communist Party of Great Britain and printed in the *Labour Monthly,* all considerations of 'backwardness' or unreadiness for self-government are absent. Africans are people with the problems common to all peoples 'exploited' by the imperialists.

> In the colonies millions of coloured people are denied the vote; they are not consulted about the administration nor about the management of their lives. It is the white settlers or the businessmen who advise the bureaucracy. Government is carried on by ordinance; there is no freedom of speech or of the press; trade union and political organization is either illegal or functions under the daily threat of a persecution for 'sedition'. The peasantry are driven by heavy taxes from their land to work in British owned mines or plantations; and, as workers they are paid a few shillings a month and are forced to live in foul conditions, so that the British capitalist may earn his profits.

Both this article and others warned the colonial independence movements against the dangers of fascism, the worst kind of imperialism, and argued that the colonies should press for complete independence.[69] This was, however, simply a propaganda device, for the Leninist argument was that the colonial masses would have to engage in a revolutionary struggle before the imperialists would grant independence. Out of this struggle against the reactionary forces of imperialism would come viable unified states.

For the radicals who did not envisage the revolutionary struggle, it was difficult to envisage the unity. They saw instability ahead for newly created states in which existed extremes in educational standards and in which ethnic loyalties had been encouraged, under the system of indirect rule, at the expense of national loyalties. On the other hand their interpretation of the situation of Africans, more particularly of East Africans, was not so very different from that of the Leninists. The difference lay in the fact that they were reformist in temperament and genuinely believed that the Europeans still had a role to play in Africa. Norman Leys, for example, believed that an immediate grant of independence to the African colonies was impossible because the spread of genuine education had not gone far enough. The granting of independence would allow power to be usurped by white minorities or by African autocracies, so that the masses would have to face a long struggle for liberty. Immediate independence could not then be envisaged, but there were a variety of proposals put forward so as to prepare the way for such independence at the earliest possible time.

The criticisms and suggestions for change were of three different kinds. The first was an attack on the kind of paternalism which allowed the African no voice in his own affairs. The second concerned the necessity for development, especially in the field of education. The third concerned the immediate extension of political and civil liberties and a close examination of what direction political development should follow.

Objections to the exclusive nature of paternalist policies came from a variety of sources. One particular incident which highlighted the ability of Africans to manage their own affairs was that of the visit to England of a number of Africans to give evidence before the Joint Parliamentary Committee on East Africa. They surprised many people with their grasp of political issues and their ability to put their point of view. The impression made by these African delegates on this occasion caused comment in many articles, including one in the *New Statesman and Nation.*

> Africa has spoken, and whether she achieves anything on this occasion or not, the moment has been vastly dramatic. Something unexpected, something portentous has arisen, marking the end of Darkest Africa and the beginning of a new dispensation. African leaders can now speak for their people: this is the startling fact with which we are con-

fronted today, and it is a fact which must influence all our future policies.[70]

A number of articles during the 1930s dealt with this question of allowing Africans to contribute towards their own political development. Archdeacon Owen advocated greater consultation and the development of the habit of working *with* Africans rather than *for* them.[71] Frank Melland believed that colonial administration was a form of dictatorship, operating with the conflicting aims of preserving old cultures and developing an African version of western culture. He wanted to see the Africans occupying the centre of the stage.[72] Leonard Barnes believed a revolutionary change in attitude would be required so that the Africans could be prepared for independence.

> The life of our colonies today will contribute nothing to the world's stock of civilization until the Briton lays down his authority as alien and arbitrary overlord, divests himself of political ascendancy based on the irrelevancies of race and material power, and returns as simple educationalist, co-operator and missionary in the widest sense.[73]

The second strand in the ideas and criticisms of the radicals was often expressed in articles which contained 'programmes' for development. These programmes suggested basic economic and social reforms, such as the granting of land to all Africans, the alteration of taxation levies to free the poorest, the grant of the franchise to all literates; and in the case of Leonard Barnes, the public ownership of all land, minerals and machines and the prohibition on all lending and borrowing at interest.[74] Leonard Barnes wanted to see the transformation in Africa occur through the creation of socialist states. This insistence on all kinds of developmental projects in order to modernize African societies was quite different from the sort of slow evolution which the theories of indirect rule seemed to envisage. In fact these critics questioned whether there had been any progress at all under indirect rule.

The third strand of their criticism concerned the question of civil liberties which they believed had been curtailed and not extended as tribal cohesion weakened. Norman Leys gave an account of regulations in Kenya which he believed had been erected to control, if not to make impossible, political activities among Africans.[75] Leonard Barnes set out the steps by which the Dominions had gained independence,[76] and pointed out that no African colony had reached the first stage. He believed it was impossible to move towards independence with the harsh sedition and association laws which prevented the growth of a free press and an alert public opinion.

The contrasts between the indirect rulers, the modernizers and the Marxists are quite clear. The Marxists saw the creation of independent states in Africa as the outcome of a revolutionary struggle. They gave no consideration to the particular weaknesses, failures or even possible goals of the British administrative service since it was part of their ideology about imperialism that the administrative services were operating in the interest of the British, or other European, capitalist classes. The African proletariat which had been created by European entry into Africa, would be united in each colony against their oppressors and eventually seize political power.

The indirect rulers were supporters of the idea of the British civilizing mission in Africa, but, in the main, rejected the idea that Africans would ever be able to govern themselves within western parliamentary institutions. In so far as they had a goal, it seemed to be some sort of synthesis between African and European institutions, cleansed of the abuses of pre-European tribal politics and operating according to the new sense of responsibility taught them by the British. The indirect rule theories failed to provide any formula for an ultimate transfer of power to Africans and played down the question of how Africans were to participate in choosing their own governments. Lugard, for example, argued that

> the bases of parliamentary institutions—membership by election in secret ballot for selected political constituencies, and decisions by a majority vote in a debating assembly—are wholly foreign to the tradition and the mentality alike of African and eastern races.[77]

Thus Lugard and many others were led to support the idea that there could never be a government in East Africa, elected by popular franchise, representative of all races. This view led to the advocacy of the development of separate native states, the nucleus of which already existed in the African reserves created by earlier land policies, in which Africans could learn to govern themselves. This system of apartheid, which usually involved political segregation but not economic separation from the white community, was given a variety of names and advocated in several different forms during the 1920s and 1930s.[78] More than any other issue it hampered the consideration by the radical element of the way in which independence could be granted, because a multi-racial society based on political equality seemed totally unacceptable to the Europeans. In his book *A Last Chance in Kenya*[79] Norman Leys stated, with some insight, that if there was bloodshed some day the people responsible may be assumed to be the men who think that 'Africans should be encouraged to develop all that is best in their own civilization', which, in practice, means that they are not allowed to adopt or adapt what they think best in our civilization.

The critics of indirect rule wanted to see economic and social development, as well as increasing African participation in the western institutions of government which had already been planted in African soil and to which the educated African aspired.

So long as the laws which regulate the life and labour of the African are made in the Legislative Council, no developments of local self-government, however excellent in themselves, can compensate for his exclusion from it.[80]

They believed that western concepts of democracy and of responsible government should and could be introduced into Africa and that the synthesis of the two cultures could take care of itself.

NOTES

1. See, for example, L. P. Mair, *An African People in the Twentieth Century*, p. xi. 'If, therefore, we are to envisage the government of native races as a process of scientifically controlled adaptation, it is of the first importance to discover what the results of such change in the past have been.'
2. See, for example, Sir H. H. Johnston, 'Anthropology, the First of the Sciences', *Contemporary Review*, 123 (1921), pp. 185–92; W. C. Willoughby, *The Soul of the Bantu*, Introduction: R. S. Rattray, *Ashanti*, Preface; and J. H. Driberg, *The East African Problem*, p. 79.
3. Cmd 2387. See p. 80 of the Report.
4. See, for example:—
   W. G. A. Ormsby-Gore and L. S. Amery, 'Problems and Development in Africa', *J.A.S.*, XXVIII (1928–29), pp. 325–39.
   Julian Huxley, 'Travel and Politics in East Africa', *J.A.S.*, XXX (1931), pp. 245–61.
   Lord Lugard, 'Education and Race Relations', *J.R.A.S.* XXXIV (1933), pp. 1–11.
   Sir Alan Pim, 'Anthropological Problems of Indirect Rule in Northern Rhodesia', *Man*, 38 (1938), pp. 180–85.
   M. Perham, *Native Administration in Nigeria*, Introduction, p. ix.
   J. H. Oldham, *White and Black in Africa*, p. 41 f.
   D. Westermann, *The African Today and Tomorrow*, pp. 1–9.
5. See Paul A. Robinson, *The Freudian Left*, (1969), pp. 132–39 for an interesting analysis of the two related attitudes represented by functionalism and, in particular, the fact that it implied a position of cultural relativism.
6. See B. Malinowski, 'The Present State of Studies of Culture Contact: Some Comments on an American Approach', *Africa*, 12 (1939), pp. 27–48.
7. See E. E. Evans-Pritchard, *Anthropology and History* (Manchester, 1961). A. L. Kroeber, *An Anthropologist Looks at History* (Berkeley, 1963).

R. A. Lystad, *The African World* (London, 1965).

I. Schapera, 'Should Anthropologists be Historians?', *J.R.A.I.*, 92, Part 1 (1962), pp. 73–85.

8. James R. Hooker, 'The Anthropologists' Frontier—The Last Phase of African Exploitation', *Journal of Modern African Studies*, 1, 4 (1963), pp. 455–9.

J. J. Maquet, 'Objectivity in Anthropology', *Current Anthropology*, 5, 1 (1964), pp. 47–55.

H. G. Barnett, 'Anthropology as an Applied Science', *Human Organization*, 17, 1 (1958), pp. 9–11.

P. C. Onwuachi and A. W. Wolfe, 'The Place of Anthropology in the Future of Africa', *Human Organization*, 25, 2 (1966), pp. 93–95.

9. The *Labour Monthly* was the most obvious source for these opinions.

10. See S. Andreski, *The African Predicament*, (London, 1968), p. 199, 'The ruling graduates have acquired the taste for the socialist phraseology during their studies in Paris and London because the socialists, and above all the communists, were the only Europeans who favoured the cause of African independence before the granting of it became imminent . . .'

11. Edwin W. Smith, 'The Story of the Institute . . .', p. 27.

12. See, for example, her articles:—
'Native Land Tenure in East Africa', *Africa*, 4 (1931), pp. 314–29.
'A Science of Colonial Government', *Contemporary Review*, 136 (1934), pp. 80–87.
'The Study of Culture Contact as a Practical Problem', *Africa*, 7 (1934), pp. 415–22.

13. For example, see Edwin W. Smith, 'Northern Rhodesia', *Empire Review*, XXXIX (1924), pp. 436–444; Captain V. A. Cazalet, M.P., 'My Visit to the Gold Coast', *Empire Review*, XLVIII (1928), pp. 52–8, and R. C. F. Maugham, 'British Trusteeship in Africa', *Empire Review*, LIV (1931), pp. 33–6.

14. For details of the relationship between the Colonial Service and Cambridge and Oxford, see Robert Heussler, *Yesterday's Rulers*.

15. According to Lugard there was 'no room for those who, however high their motives, are content to place themselves on the same level as the uncivilized races. They lower the prestige by which alone the white races can hope to govern and guide'. *The Dual Mandate*, p. 59.

16. A. Zimmern, *The Third British Empire*, (London, 1926), pp. 102–3.

17. F. D. Lugard, *The Dual Mandate*, p. 132.

18. *A Report of the Committee on the System of Appointments in the Colonial Office and the Colonial Services*, Cmd 3554, (1930). See p. 23 f of this report for an account of the predominance of Oxford and Cambridge as recruiting grounds.

19. The view of A. Victor Murray, *A School in the Bush*, p. 233.

20. See H. J. Laski, 'The Colonial Civil Service', *Political Quarterly*, XI (1938), pp. 541–51.

21. *Ibid.*, p. 549.

22. Norman Leys, *A Last Chance in Kenya*, p. 102.

23. *Ibid.*, p. 149.

24. Norman Leys, 'The Problem of Kenya', *Socialist Review*, XXI (1923), pp. 205–212.

25. The major critics of imperial policy included Norman Leys, John H. Harris, W. M. Macmillan and Lord Olivier.

26. Some of the most interesting accounts of how indirect rule operated may be found in books about Nigeria, including:—
C. L. Temple, *Native Races and Their Rulers*, (Capetown, 1918), A. C. G. Hastings, *Nigerian Days*, (London, 1925), W. R. Crocker, *Nigeria. A Critique of British Colonial Administration*, Joyce Cary, *Mister Johnson*, (London, 1939), and John Smith, *Colonial Cadet in Nigeria*, (Durham, N.C., 1968).
For an analysis of the ideology of indirect rule see the study of R. C. Pratt in Low, D.A. and Pratt, R.C., *Buganda and British Overrule: Two Studies*. See also, R. S. Rattray, 'Present Tendencies in African Colonial Government', *J.R.A.S.*, 33 (1934), pp. 22–36, for an account of the origins of indirect rule.

27. For the interesting view that rapid change promotes greater stability see M. Mead, *New Lives for Old*, (London, 1956), esp. Ch. 18. 'Partial change . . . can be seen as a bridge between old and new . . . but rather as the condition within which discordant and discrepant institutions and practices develop and proliferate with corresponding discrepancies and discordancies in the lives of those that live within them.'

28. See, for example, L. P. Mair, *Native Policies in Africa*, p. 269. 'Indirect rule is an attempt to preserve what can still be preserved of indigenous institutions in a situation in which the radical modification of many of them is assumed as necessary and desirable.'

29. W. G. A. Ormsby-Gore and L. S. Amery, 'Problems and Development in Africa', p. 328. '. . . in government we endeavour, whenever we can, to make use of existing authorities, existing institutions, and to enlist on our side the intuitive sentiments and traditions which support them. Our whole principle is that of grafting our ideas and our civilization on to the root stocks which we know can grow in the soil . . .',

30. The question of continuity between traditional elites and modern elites is discussed in P. C. Lloyd, *The New Elites of Tropical Africa*, (London, 1964), especially p. 13 f. The various case studies in this book indicate how difficult it is to generalize about this question. However it seems clear that in the colonial period few Western educated Africans were completely alienated from their own societies or detribalized. It also seems clear that most Western educated Africans resented being excluded from national, as opposed to tribal, politics.

31. For example, the activities of the West African Congress were condemned. So, too, were those of the Kikuyu Central Association.

32. J. H. Oldham, *Christianity and the Race Problem*, p. 138.

33. For example, Sir Hugh Clifford, Sir Donald Cameron, Sir Horace Byatt, Sir William Gowers, Sir Edward Grigg.

34. For example, L. S. Amery, and W. G. A. Ormsby-Gore.

35. For example, Margery Perham and Sir Reginald Coupland.

36. For example, Professor Julian Huxley and A. Victor Murray.

37. See, for example, M. Perham, *Native Administration in Nigeria*, p. 192, for criticism of the way the system had been applied.

38. See, for example, R. S. Rattray, in 'Present Tendencies . . .', p. 22 f, for the view that 'indirect rule' was desirable in an ideal form but that it had been corrupted in the process of applying it. As a result the participatory democracy, which he believed had existed in pre-European times, had been destroyed and African institutions were not being used for purposes of education.

39. Some of these were:—
'Growth of Empire', 'The White Man's Task in Africa', 'Education and Race Relations', and 'Some Colonial Problems of Today'. See Bibliography.

40. *The Dual Mandate*, pp. 194–5.

41. *Ibid.*, p. 205.

42. See Bibliography for a list of these articles.

43. Lord Hailey, 'Some Problems Dealt with in the African Survey', p. 197.

44. *Ibid.*, p. 200.

45. Lord Hailey, *The African Survey*, p. 1639.

46. Lord Hailey, 'African and Indian Government', *United Empire*, 30 (1939), pp. xi–xvi.

47. *Ibid.*, p. xiv.

48. He regarded local legislatures already established in Africa as simply agents of the imperial government.

49. *Ibid.*, p. xiv.

50. See Bibliography.

51. Lord Raglan, 'Crime and Punishment in Tropical Africa', *19th Century and After*, 93 (1923), pp. 575–82.

52. The views of J. F. J. Fitzpatrick and Lord Raglan were noted by the members of the Anti-Slavery Society, which sent a letter to the Under Secretary of State for the Colonies, enquiring as to the truth of their allegations. See *The Anti-Slavery and Aborigines Friend*, 15, 1 (1925).

53. See, for example, J. H. Driberg, 'Khama's Country', *N.S. & N.* 6 Jan., 1934. 'The salutary checks on autocracy which all native constitutions imposed have been largely abrogated under indirect rule', and W. M. Macmillan reviewing Patrick Balfour's *Lords of the Equator: An African Journey, N.S. & N.*, 13 Nov., 1937, 'Mr. Balfour stresses the real danger that indirect rule may build up a privileged African bureaucracy, alienating the educated class, and bolstering up chiefs against people'.

54. Norman Leys, *A Last Chance in Kenya*, p. 70.

55. Capt. R. S. Rattray, 'Present Tendencies in African Colonial Government', p. 22.

56. Professor W. M. Macmillan, 'The Importance of the Educated African', *J.R.A.S.*, XXXIII (1934), p. 141.

57. For example, G. C. B. Cotterell, 'Squeers at the Colonial Office', *English Review*, 58 (1934), p. 455, and W. M. Macmillan in a review of two books in *N.S. & N.*, 26 Sept., 1936. The books were *Native Policies in Africa* by L. P. Mair and *Ten Africans* by M. Perham. Macmillan attacked Lucy Mair for wanting to see a 'healthy tribal life' rather than the hopeful development of backward people.

58. See Leonard Barnes, *The Duty of Empire*, p. 284.

59. See Frank Melland, 'The Anthropologist in Africa', *Fortnightly*, 136 (1934), p. 228. This is Melland's view of how the educated African interpreted indirect rule.

60. Frank Melland, 'East African Kaleidoscope', pp. 525–34.

61. W. M. Macmillan, 'The Importance of the Educated African', *J.R.A.S.*, XXXIII (1934), p. 137. See also Tracy Philips, 'The New Africa, Part I', *19th Century and After*, 122 (1937), p. 568, and E. J. Arnett, 'French and British Administration in West Africa', *J.R.A.S.*, XXXII (1933), p. 240.

62. C. C. B. Cotterell, 'Squeers at the Colonial Office', *English Review*, 58 (1934), p. 454.

63. Sir Donald Cameron, 'Native Administration in Tanganyika and Nigeria', *J.R.A.S.*, XXXVI (1937), Supplement, p. 9.

64. *Ibid.,* p. 6. 'Where native society is organized . . . have we, indeed, any right to set out to destroy that society, all that it means in the hearts and minds of the people; their customs and their traditions; the very foundations on which the whole of their existence has been built . . .'

65. See Sir Donald Cameron, 'Native Administration . . .', p. 4, for a comment on how bad was the German system of administration through Akidas in Tanganyika.

66. Although Lord Hailey was critical of 'indirect rule', he argued in 'Nationalism in Africa', *United Empire,* 28 (1937), pp. 82–92, that other colonizing nations educated Africans to direct their interests towards the metropolitan power and identify with it—the aim of such a policy was unquestioned and permanent control of native areas. Britain, on the other hand, encouraged each unit to operate separately.

67. Both Lugard and Perham deplored the interest of the educated Africans in Legislative Council activities and in politics outside tribal institutions.

68. See 'The Colonies and War', *Labour Monthly,* 21 (1939), pp. 751–758. A statement adopted by the Central Committee of the C.P.G.B.

69. See Reginald Bridgeman, 'Colonies and War: Today's Big Issue', *Labour Monthly,* 20 (1938), pp. 44–53. 'It must of course be understood that their choice will not be limited to a decision between British, French or German rule, but that they will also have the right of voting for national independence, free from any sort of foreign tutelage or control, should they desire to do so. Such consultations will take a long time, but there is no reason why they should not be immediately begun.'

70. Unsigned article in *N.S. & N.,* 16 May, 1931.

71. Archdeacon Owen, 'Some thoughts on Native Development in East Africa', *J.A.S.* XXX (1931), pp. 225–37.

72. Frank Melland, 'Our Colonial Complacency', *19th Century,* 118 (1935), pp. 151–62.

73. See Leonard Barnes, *The Duty of Empire,* p. 288.

74. *Ibid.,* p. 290.

75. Norman Leys, *A Last Chance in Kenya,* p. 89.

76. Leonard Barnes, *Empire or Democracy?* The steps were:—
    (1) Autonomy in internal affairs.
    (2) Fiscal autonomy.
    (3) Autonomy in military defence.
    (4) Autonomy in Foreign relations.

77. Lord Lugard, 'Native Policy in East Africa', *Foreign Affairs,* 9 (1930–31), p. 69.

78. Much of the propaganda on this issue referred to South African experience. Smuts thought 'separation' imperative and believed South African experience was relevant to colonial problems. See J. C. Smuts, *Africa and Some World Problems* (Oxford, 1930), especially pp. 92–94.

79. *A Last Chance in Kenya,* p. 116.

80. Drummond Shiels, 'The East African Report', *Political Quarterly,* III (1932), p. 86.

CONCLUSION

The period between the wars was characterized by almost universal support for the idea that it was necessary for Britain to stay in Africa, either indefinitely or until particular reforms had been achieved. The doctrine of trusteeship, developed after World War I, promoted the idea that a consideration of African interests had to be made central to Britain's African policy. As a result of the new enthusiasm for trusteeship, liberal arguments about leaving Africa to its own devices, and conservative interest in 'imperial estates' were left behind, as both groups developed a new language about British 'responsibility' and African 'progress'. Conservatives now eagerly promoted the idea of the dual mandate, while liberals sought to define what they regarded as the necessary conditions for carrying out a policy of trusteeship.

For the conservatives this change involved little more than a shift of emphasis. The survival of beliefs in racial superiority made British control over African territories seem both inevitable and desirable. In particular there survived that Social Darwinian strand which claimed that those who had demonstrated their superiority had a right as well as a duty to exercise political control over inferior people. British genius was manifested, it was claimed, in the conduct of political affairs, both in the domestic sphere and in the administration of 'native' peoples. Darwinian and racist beliefs were bolstered by a kind of lay appreciation of social evolutionary theory which seemed to justify political control over people thought to be still in their political infancy. The strongest statements of social evolutionary beliefs undoubtedly came from those who, like Lugard, were approaching retiring age. But even those who were familiar with later anthropological theory would have found nothing to undermine conservative faith. For according to the new functional theory societies were natural systems each part of which served a vital part in the society as a whole. The preservation of as much as possible of the total system was desirable in the interest of political stability and human well-being.

But conservative opinion did not remain unaffected by the new mood of reform which assailed the liberals and radicals more strongly. Conservatives constantly used the omnibus term 'trusteeship' to evoke the idea that African interests were in fact central to British policy. More important the theory of the dual mandate, the only real innovation in conservative ideology, was believed by many to demonstrate that the pursuit of British interests was not in fact inimical to those of the African.

The position of people of more liberal views was confused and uncertain in this period. Earlier liberal objections to imperial adventures were no longer relevant and traditional attachment to laisser-faire policies had to be abandoned in the context of Britain's African policies. The evidence provided by the humanitarian liberals and the persuasive writing of Hobson had convinced them that Britain had to accept her trusteeship responsibilities to prevent exploitation in Africa. More than this, there had to be a positive policy of intervention in the interest of the Africans. It was, above all, the liberal writers who preached the need for morality in British dealings with Africa and the importance of creating stable societies in the African colonies. They emphasized the need for a moral and social transformation of the African people, rather than any kind of economic or political revolution. The State should provide a shield against exploitation while the work of civilizing and Christianizing was carried out.

Here lay the real difference between liberal and radical writers for the latter believed that colonial rule should be brought to an end just as soon as a systematic attack could be made on disease, malnutrition, poverty and ignorance. They were not so much interested in proselytizing in the field of ideas as in providing basic education services of the broadest kind so that Africans would find themselves equipped to participate fully in all aspects of community life. At the same time the radicals attacked the old conservative myths about the Empire and began erecting a theory about how decolonization should occur. Their writings often reflected a suspicion that the institutions of the State had operated in the past in the interests of private capital. But their belief in social engineering, rather than revolution, as a solution to urgent problems, compelled them to advocate reform and planning in the colonial field, on the assumption that political power in Britain would eventually pass to people who shared their views.

Only a few writers of more extreme radical opinion, who shared Marxist-Leninist views about economic exploitation in Africa in the past, elaborated programmes designed to bring an end to the economic dominance of European capital in Africa. In retrospect it seems clear that many of the radical programmes ignored the close relationship between welfare state policies and economic growth and prosperity in Western societies. They failed to see how crucial the economic relationship between Europe and Africa would be. Thus they neglected the question of the future economic basis of African society and the problems which future states would face in maintaining welfare programmes.

The Marxist-Leninists, the only group whose arguments did not carry paternalist overtones, made economic considerations basic to their arguments. They advocated and expected a political revolution which would develop as a result of the changes in the economic basis of society consequent on operations in Africa of European capital. The contribution of the Marxist-Leninists was twofold. They provided a new revolutionary ideology, developed by Lenin to apply to the colonial situation, thereby, as with so many revolutionary predictions, helping to create the conditions and the situations which their doctrine claimed to be inevitable. But, more than this, they began that process of polarization between extreme left and right which was to gain momentum after the Second World War as the doctrine spread to the colonial people themselves.

But during the 1920s and 1930s in England such polarization existed only in embryo. There is evidence that in this period the reformist groups, which included many people with mildly humanitarian views, as well as those of quite vehement radical opinion, had achieved something of a propaganda victory. These groups relied on appeals to political morality and enlightened self-interest. By the late 1930s, they had a large following committed to reform in British colonial policy, expressed most frequently in terms of education and social development.

After 1940 some attempt was made to begin such a programme of reform but in the long run there was to be too little time and too few resources to make a significant impact. More important for the future of the newly independent states two decades later, the more radical suggestions in the field of economic change were never seriously considered. The basic economic situation in each colony remained largely untouched, while piece-meal reforms in education and health attempted to keep pace with population increases. At the same time each colony was hastily fitted out with a new set of political institutions which were intended to provide the framework for political activity after independence. These reforms were begun by the Conservative Government in 1940 and it was a Conservative Government which completed the programme of decolonization in Africa in the 1950s and 1960s.

The Marxist-Leninists had failed to envisage Britain's readiness to relinquish political control which, in most colonies, passed fairly peacefully into African hands. They had under-estimated the influence of ideas in British politics and reckoned without the effects of the Second World War.

But by their attack on the views of both conservatives and reformers they exposed the condescension and implied racism common to paternalist arguments. Not for them the 'cant' about race and civilization common to conservative writing. Not for them the private bearing of public guilt common to the liberals, nor the new secular missionary zeal apparent in the ideas of the radicals. By applying Marxist stereotypes to the African situation they identified the African masses as a proletariat, just like any other proletariat, disregarding skin colour and cultural standards. In doing so they accorded them a kind of equality, which had previously been denied them, suggesting that they did not need to be treated as a special case. The clear cut Marxist ideology offered the colonial people both an explanation and a programme for change which did not reduce their stature.

But the British actors in the drama of post-war Africa did not follow the script prepared for them by the Marxist-Leninists. They had been cast in the role of agents of progress because they were part of the inevitable historical process whereby barbarian people were to be kicked into the twentieth century. In correct Marxist terms it was believed that Western economic control over African resources would produce a climate of opinion which would create political unity in the colonies, and thus the basis for political revolution. Only then could the economy be reconstructed in the interests of the African people.

By 1940 British policy makers had accepted the need to promote development in Africa. The changing attitudes in Britain were almost certainly related to the fact that the economic recession was over in Britain and that the experience of the depression had led to a heightened awareness of the importance of economic development. They were now prepared to undertake the kind of programmes which might have proved effective if they had been begun fifty years earlier. But events in both Europe and Africa compelled them to abandon their emphasis on the primacy of social and economic change, the mid-twentieth century version of the 'civilizing mission', and concentrate on preparations for political independence. The victory of the liberals and radicals came too late.

The preparations for independence meant allowing Africans to participate in the area of national politics from which they had been excluded in the inter-war years. Small beginnings were made in development and welfare but, whatever the hopes of good intentions of the British, the Africans were finally left with few resources and few skills to solve the almost insoluble problems left after fifty or more years of colonial rule. These problems included malnutrition, disease and ignorance as before. They included the existence of tribal and ethnic animosity based on past conflict and present fear of domination, in states arbitrarily created by European powers. They involved the question of how to achieve support for the central government of local rulers, accustomed under indirect rule to a share of political power. They included the problem of promoting economic development in societies where there was little or no indigenous capital, and where all major economic operations were controlled by Western interests.

The paternalist claim to be able to promote desirable political, economic and social development seems to be denied by the evidence in Africa. Certainly there is no way in which it can be demonstrated that more prosperous and stable African societies would have developed without the intervention of European powers in the nineteenth century. But the political turbulence of the post-independence era, and the widening gap between the standards of African and European societies, invites cynicism about the more extravagant of the paternalist claims. More than this, paternalist doctrine has always implied some claim to superiority. According to some criteria this claim may be demonstrably true. But while many colonial people have been anxious to close the economic and social gap between the two kinds of society, they have increasingly shown resentment at the exercise of political power by Western nations. Until 1940 Africans were effectively insulated from other models of social change but the impact of the Second World War hastened their involvement in global politics. The events of the post-war period have resulted in a healthy spread of cynicism about altruism in politics. As a result colonial powers must now spend a disproportionate amount of their resources maintaining political stability or prepare to replace themselves as rapidly as possible.

BIBLIOGRAPHY

PRIMARY SOURCES—books and articles

ALLEN, Roland, 'Islam and Christianity in the Sudan', *International Review of Missions*, IX (1920), pp. 531–43.
'The Need for Non-Professional Missionaries', *World Dominion*, VI, 2 (1928), pp. 195–201.
'The Work of Non-Professional Missionaries', *World Dominion*, VI, 3 (1928), pp. 298–303.
AMERY, L. S., *Empire and Prosperity*. London: Faber, 1930.
The Forward View. London: Geoffrey Bles, 1935.
'Economic Development of the Empire', *United Empire*, New Series, XVI (1925), pp. 143–155.
'Anglo-French Colonial Cooperation', *National Review*, 89 (1927), pp. 700–708.
'The Church and the Empire', *The East and the West*, 25 (1927), pp. 223–29.
'Problems and Development in Africa', *Journal of the African Society*, XXVIII (1928–29), pp. 325–39. (In collaboration with W. G. A. Ormsby-Gore.)
'Ideals of the British Commonwealth', *United Empire*, New Series, XXVI (1935), pp. 506–9.
'The problem of the Cession of Mandated Territories in Relation to the World Situation', *International Affairs*, XVI, 1 (1937) pp. 1–16.
'Claims to Colonies', *Journal of the Royal African Society*, XXXVI (1937), Supplement pp. 3–46.
'The German Colonial Claim', *National Review*, 108 (1937), pp. 730–38.
'The African Mandates and Their Future', *United Empire*, New Series, XXVIII (1937), pp. 204–11. (In collaboration with Sir Arnold Wilson.)
ANDREWS, C. F., 'The Indians in Kenya', *The East and the West*, 21 (1923), pp. 216–233.
'India, Africa and Europe', *The East and the West*, 22 (1924), pp. 35–47.
'India and Africa', *Church Overseas*, 1 (1928), pp. 303–7.
'The Indians in Zanzibar and East Africa', *Contemporary Review*, 147 (1935), pp. 684–691.
ANDREWS, R. F., 'Hitler and Colonies', *Labour Monthly*, 21 (1939), pp. 145–51.
ANGELL, Norman, *If Britain is to Live*. London: Nisbet, 1923.
This Have and Have Not Business. London: Hamish Hamilton, 1936.
'Colonies, Defence and Peace', *United Empire*, New Series, XXVII (1936), pp. 248–59.
ARNETT, E. J., 'French and British Administration in West Africa', *Journal of the Royal African Society*, XXXII (1933), pp. 240–51.
'West Africa in Review', *Journal of the Royal African Society*, XXXIV (1935), pp. 60–71.

BAKER, G. C., 'An Experiment in Applied Anthropology', *Africa*, 8 (1935), pp. 304–14.

'The Issue in Tanganyika', *Quarterly Review*, 269 (1937), pp. 119–131.

BAKER, Richard St. Barbe, 'The Awakening of Tropical Africa', *English Review*, 39 (1924), pp. 739–46.

'The Men of the Trees', *Contemporary Review*, 139 (1931), pp. 57–65.

BARNES, Leonard, *Caliban in Africa*. London: Gollancz, 1930.

The New Boer War. London: Hogarth Press, 1932.

The Duty of Empire. London: Gollancz, 1935.

Zulu Paraclete: A Sentimental Record. London: Peter Davies, 1935.

The Future of the Colonies, Day to Day Pamphlet No. 32, London: Hogarth, 1936.

Skeleton of the Empire. Fact Pamphlet No. 3 edited by Raymond Postgate, London, 1937.

Empire or Democracy? London: Gollancz, 1939.

'Tshekedi—and After', *Nineteenth Century and After*, 114 (1933), pp. 573–82.

'The Humanitarian Spirit', *Nineteenth Century and After*, 114 (1933), pp. 201–14.

'The Crisis in Bechuanaland', *Journal of the Royal African Society*, XXXII (1933), pp. 342–9.

'The Empire as Sacred Trust: the Problems of Africa', *Political Quarterly*, IX (1938), pp. 503–15.

BEER, G. L., *African Questions at the Peace Conference*. New York: Macmillan, 1923.

BELL, G., 'Neglecting our Estate', *United Empire*, New Series, XIV (1923), pp. 178–9.

'Nigeria: Then and Now', *United Empire*, New Series, XVI (1925), pp. 208–13.

BENSON, T. G., 'Some Problems of Education in Africa Today', *Oversea Education*, VII, 1 (1935), pp. 10–14.

'The Jeanes School and the Education of the East African Native', *Journal of the Royal African Society*, XXXV (1936), pp. 418–31.

BENSON, W., 'The African Labourer in 1929', *Nineteenth Century and After*, 108 (1930), pp. 62–73.

African Labour in 1930', *Journal of the African Society*, XXX (1931), pp. 142–7.

'Closer Union in Africa', *Journal of the African Society*, XXX (1931), pp. 337–42.

'The Study of African Development', *Journal of the African Society*, XXXI (1932), pp. 148–152.

BENTWICH, Norman, *The Mandates System*. London: Longmans, 1930.

'Ten Years of International Mandates', *Political Quarterly*, 11 (1931), pp. 564–76.

'Colonies and Mandates', *Contemporary Review*, 149 (1936), pp. 43–51.

BOURDILLON, Sir Bernard, 'Native Production in the African Colonies and Protectorates', *United Empire*, New Series, XXVIII (1937), pp. 145–9.

'Guiding the Native Towards Home Rule', *The Listener*, 20 June, 1937.

BRADLEY, Kenneth, 'The Riddle of the African', *Empire Review*, LXV (1937), pp. 26–30.

BRAILSFORD, H. N., 'Africa Faces Fascism', *N.S. and N.*, 18 Feb., 1939.

BRIDGEMAN, R., 'The World Struggle Against Imperialism', *Labour Monthly*, (1929), pp. 417–24.

'Colonies and War: Today's Big Issue', *Labour Monthly*, 20 (1938), pp. 44–53.

BUELL, R. L., *The Native Problem in Africa*. London: Cass, 1967. (First published New York: Macmillan, 1928.)

BURNS, Sir Alan, *History of Nigeria*. London: Allen & Unwin, 1956. (First published London: Allen & Unwin, 1929.)

BURNS, Emile, 'The World Congress of the League Against Imperialism', *Labour Monthly*, 11 (1929), pp. 559–63.

BUXTON, C. R., *Exploitation of the Coloured Man*. London: Anti-Slavery and Aborigines Protection Society, 1925.
The Race Problem in Africa. London: Hogarth, 1931. (A reprint of the Merttens Lecture for 1931.)
'Missionaries in East Africa', *Contemporary Review*, 143 (1933), pp. 438–46.
'Some African Friends', *Spectator*, 28 Dec., 1934.
'The Dissatisfied Powers and the World's Resources', *Contemporary Review*, 148 (1935), pp. 539–545.
'Is Norman Angell Right?', *Contemporary Review*, 150 (1936), pp. 148–155.
'The Government of Crown Colonies: the Development of Self-Government', *Political Quarterly*, IX (1938), pp. 516–28.

BYRNE, J., 'Sierra Leone: Trade and Communications', *Journal of The African Society*, 29 (1928–30), pp. 1–6.

BYATT, Sir Horace, 'Tanganyika', *Journal of the African Society*, XXIV (1924–25), pp. 1–9.

CADBURY, L. J., 'Cocoa Colony. The Romance of the Gold Coast', *Geographical Magazine*, 3 (1937), pp. 153–168.

CAMERON, D. C. (later Sir Donald), *Principles of Native Administration and Their Application*, Nigeria: Miscellaneous Official Publications, 1935.
My Tanganyika Service and Some Nigeria, London: Allen & Unwin, 1939.
'Position and Prospects in Tanganyika', *Journal of the African Society*, XXIV (1926–27), pp. 315–22.
'Native Administration in Tanganyika and Nigeria', *Journal of the African Society*, XXXVI (1937), Supplement 29.
A Review of Hailey's *African Survey*, *Spectator*, 11 Nov., 1938.

CARY, Joyce, *Mister Johnson*. London: Michael Joseph, 1939.

CATLIN, George, 'Colonial Policy from a New View', *Fortnightly Review*, 145 (1936), pp. 458–64.
A Review of Hailey's *African Survey*, *Fortnightly Review*, 145 (1939), p. 113.

CAVENDISH-BENTINCK, F., 'Indians and the Kenya Highlands', *National Review*, 114 (1940), pp. 51–8.

CAZALET, Captain V. A., 'My Visit to the Gold Coast', *Empire Review*, XLVIII (1928), pp. 52–8.

CHANCELLOR, Sir John, 'Southern Rhodesia and its Problems', *The Journal of the African Society*, XXVI (1926–27), pp. 1–9.
'Progress and Development in Southern Rhodesia', *The Journal of the African Society*, XXVIII (1928–29), pp. 149–54.

CHIRGWIN, A. M., 'The New Idea of Empire and Where it Came From', *London Quarterly Review*, 142–144 (1924–25), pp. 68–78.
'Bechuanaland: Its Poverty and Prospects', *Empire Review*, LIX (1934), pp. 158–63.

'Is there Slavery in Bechuanaland?', *Empire Review*, LXIV (1936), pp. 40–44.

CHIROL, Sir Valentine, *Indian Unrest*. London: Macmillan, 1910.
India, Old and New. London: Macmillan, 1921.
India. London: Ernest Benn, 1926.

CHRISTY, R. Cuthbert, 'White Settlement in Tropical Africa', *Journal of the African Society*, XXVII (1927–28), pp. 338–41.

CHURCH, A. G., *East Africa: A New Dominion*. London: Witherby, 1927.

CLARKE, F., *Education and Social Change*. London: Sheldon Press, 1940.
'The Double Mind in African Education', *Africa*, 5 (1932), pp. 158–68.

CLARKE, J. D., *OMU, an African Experiment in Education*. London: Longmans, 1937.
'Aim and Adaptation in Education', *Oversea Education*, V, 4 (1934), pp. 164–167.

CLIFFORD, Sir Hugh, *German Colonies*. A Plea for the native races. London: John Murray, 1918.
The Gold Coast Regiment. London: John Murray, 1920.
'United Nigeria', *Journal of the African Society*, XXI (1921–22), pp. 1–14.
'Murder and Magic', *Blackwood's Magazine*, 213 (1923), p. 820 and 214 (1924), p. 48.

COLVIN, Ian, 'The Order of the Round Table', *National Review*, 79 (1922), pp. 783–787.

COMMUNIST PARTY OF GREAT BRITAIN, 'Colonies and War', *Labour Monthly*, 21 (1939), pp. 751–58.
'Colonies and Fascism', *Labour Monthly*, 21 (1939), pp. 465–475.

COOKSON, Captain C. E., 'Experimenting with Africa', *National Review*, 106 (1936), pp. 51-56.

CORYNDON, Sir Robert, 'Uganda', *United Empire*, New Series, XI (1920), pp. 291–305.
'Problems of Eastern Africa', *Journal of the African Society*, XXI (1921–22), pp. 177–186.

COTTERELL, G. C. B., 'Squeers at the Colonial Office', *English Review*, 58 (1934), pp. 453–63.
'The Native Interpreter', *Crown Colonist*, 6 (1936), p. 406.

COUPLAND, Sir Reginald, *Kirk on the Zambesi*. Oxford: Clarendon, 1928.
The British Anti-Slavery Movement. London: Cass, 1966. (First published London: Thornton Butterworth, 1933.)
The Empire in These Days. London: Macmillan, 1935.
The Exploitation of East Africa. London: Faber, 1939.
'The Native Problem in Africa' (A Review of Buell's book), *International Review of Missions*, XVIII (1929), pp. 381–9.
'The Hailey Survey', *Africa*, 12 (1939), pp. 1–10.

CRANWORTH, 1st Baron (GURDON, Bertram Francis). *Kenya Chronicles*. London: Macmillan, 1939.
'Kenya Colony and Her Critics', *Empire Review*, XLII (1925), pp. 327–35.
'Kenya Colony', *United Empire*, New Series, XVII (1926), pp. 260–272.

CREECH JONES, A., 'The Colonies in the War', *Political Quarterly*, XI (1940), pp. 384–395.
'Labour in the Colonies', *New Fabian Research Bureau Quarterly*, 18 (1938), pp. 4–10.

CRIPPS, A. Shearly, *An Africa for Africans.* London: Longmans, 1927.
'An Africa for Africans', *International Review of Missions,* X ₁1921),
pp. 99–109.
'Dispossession of the Africans', *The East and the West,* 20 (1922),
pp. 211–26.
'A New Native Affairs Act in Southern Rhodesia', *Contemporary Review,*
132 (1927), pp. 721–26.
'Areas for Africans', *The East and the West,* 25 (1927), pp. 146–52.
CROCKER, W. R., *Nigeria. A Critique of British Colonial Administration.*
London, Allen & Unwin, 1936.
'Colonial Administration. Criticism of the Present System', *Crown
Colonist,* 6 (1936), p. 157.
CULWICK, A. T. and G. M., 'Culture Contact on the Fringe of Civilization',
Africa, 8 (1935), pp. 163–70.
'What the Wabena Think of Indirect Rule', *Journal of the Royal African
Society,* XXXVI (1937), pp. 176–93.
CUNLIFFE-LISTER, Sir Philip, 'Great Britain and Africa', *Journal of the
African Society,* XXXI (1932), pp. 225–33.
CURRIE, Sir James, 'Indirect Rule and Education in Africa', *United Empire,*
New Series, XXIII (1932), pp. 613–14.
'Present Day Difficulties of a Young Officer in the Tropics', *Journal of
the Royal African Society,* XXXII (1933), pp. 31–36.
'Educational Experiment in the Anglo-Egyptian Sudan, Parts I and II',
Journal of the Royal African Society, XXXIII (1934), pp. 361–71 and
XXXIV (1935), pp. 41–59.
DAVIS, J. Merle (Ed.), *Modern Industry and the African.* London: Cass 1967.
(First published London: Macmillan, 1933).
'The Cinema and Missions in Africa', *International Review of Missions,*
XXV (1936), pp. 378–83.
DELMEGE, J. de G., 'Native Policies in White Africa', *Nineteenth Century and
After,* 106 (1929), pp. 163–75.
'Indirect Rule in East Africa', *Empire Review,* LI (1930), pp. 216–220.
'The Omwoleko of Buganda', *Empire Review,* LV (1932), pp. 120–2.
DOUGALL, J. W. C., *Missionary Education in Kenya and Uganda.* London:
I.M.C., 1936.
'Characteristics of African Thought', *Africa,* 5 (1932), pp. 249–65. (Also
published as I.I.A.L.C. memorandum 10, London O.U.P., 1932.)
'The Relation of Church and School in Africa', *International Review of
Missions,* XXVI (1937), pp. 204–14.
'The Development of the Education of the African in Relation to Western
Contact', *Africa,* 11 (1938), pp. 312–24.
'The Case for and against Mission Schools', *Journal of the Royal African
Society',* XXXVIII (1939), pp. 91–108.
DRIBERG, J. H., *The Savage as He Really is.* London: Routledge, 1929.
The East African Problem. London: Williams and Norgate, 1930.
At Home with the Savage. London: Routledge, 1932.
'Primitive Law in Eastern Africa', *Africa,* 1 (1928), pp. 63–72.
'Articulate Africa', *New Statesman,* 16 May, 1931.
'Black and White Law', *New Statesman,* 29 April, 1933.
'Khama's Country', *New Statesman,* 6 January, 1934.
DUNDAS, Captain L. M., 'The African Native', *Empire Review,* LI (1930),
pp. 450–55.

DUTT, Palme, 'The British Empire', *Labour Monthly*, 5 (1923), pp. 206–215.

ELLIOT, Major Walter, 'The Parliamentary Visit to Nigeria', *Journal of the African Society*, XXVII (1927–28), pp. 205–18.
  'Impressions of a Tourist in West Africa', *Empire Review*, XLVIII (1928), pp. 169–76.

EMBREE, E. R., 'The objectives of Colonial Education', *Political Quarterly*, V (1934), pp. 221–35.

EVANS, Ifor L., *British in Tropical Africa: an Historical Outline*. Cambridge University Press, 1919.
  'Establishment of British Rule in Africa', *Listener*, 14 Feb., 1934.
  'Economic Expansion of British Rule in Africa', *Listener*, 21 Feb., 1934.

FENDALL, Brig. Gen. C. P., 'Kenya Problems', *English Review*, 41 (1925), pp. 158–62.
  'East African Troubles', *Empire Review*, LIII (1931), pp. 53–9.

FITZPATRICK, J. F. J., 'Nigeria's Curse—The Native Administration', *National Review*, 84 (1924–25), pp. 617–24.
  'Christian Missions in Nigeria', *Nineteenth Century and After*, 98 (1925), pp. 550–59.
  'On the Niger', *National Review*, 85 (1925), pp. 235–45.
  'When the District Commissioner goes Tax Gathering', *World Today*, 45 (1925), pp. 390–97.
  'Eyewash in Nigeria', *World Today*, 47 (1925–26), pp. 301–8.
  'District Commissioner Shows the Flag', *World Today*, 48 (1926), pp. 169–76.
  'Justice in the Bush', *World Today*, 49 (1926–27), pp. 339–44.
  'Off to the White Man's Grave', *New Statesman*, 12 May, 1928.
  'Back to Bows and Arrows', *New Statesman*, 12 Oct., 1929.

FLETCHER, Basil A., *Education and Colonial Development*. London: Methuen, 1936.

FORTES, Meyer, 'Culture contact as a Dynamic Process—An Investigation of the Northern Territory of the Gold Coast', *Africa*, 9 (1936), pp. 24–55.
  'Social and Psychological Aspects of Education in Taleland', *Africa*, 11 (1938), Supplement, 64 pp.
  'The Scope of Social Anthropology', *Oversea Education*, X, 3 (1939), pp. 125–130.

FRANKEL, S. H., *Capital Investment in Africa*. London: O.U.P., 1938.

FRANKLYN, J., 'Racial Decay Among Savages', *Contemporary Review*, 146 (1934), pp. 730–736.

FRASER, A. G., *The Future of the Negro*. London: S.C.M., 1929. *Africa and Peace*. London: O.U.P., 1936. (In collaboration with Sir Gordon Guggisberg.)
  'Aims of African Education', *International Review of Missions*, XIV (1925), pp. 514–22.
  'Sir Frederick Gordon Guggisberg'', *Oversea Education*, 1, 4 (1930), pp. 117–118.
  'Educational and Vocational Training', *Oversea Education*, 111, 2 (1932), pp. 67–70.
  'Education and Responsibility', *International Review of Missions*, XXIII (1934), pp. 172–88.

FRASER, Donald, *African Idylls*. London: Seeley Service, 1923.
  The Autobiography of an African. London: Seeley Service, 1924.
  The New Africa. London: Edinburgh House, 1927.

'The Church and Games in Africa', *International Review of Missions,* X (1921), pp. 110–117.

'The Evangelistic Approach to the African', *International Review of Missions,* XV (1926), pp. 438–49.

'The Building of the Church in Africa', *Church Missionary Review,* 77 (1926), pp. 117–123.

FURSE, Lt. Gen. Sir W. T., 'The Imperial Institute', *Empire Review,* XLVIII (1928), pp. 265–70.

GEARY, W. N. M., *Nigeria Under British Rule.* London: Cass, 1966. First published London: Methuen, 1927.

GERIG, Benjamin, *The Open Door and the Mandates System.* London: Allen & Unwin, 1930.

GORDON, H. L., 'The Mental Capacity of the African', *Journal of the Royal African Society,* XXXIII (1934), pp. 226–42.

GORE-BROWNE, Lt. Col. Stewart, 'The Federated States of Rhodesia', *Journal of the Royal African Society,* XXXVI (1937), pp. 2–7.

'The Relations of Black and White in Tropical Africa', *Journal of the Royal African Society,* XXXIV (1935), pp. 378–86.

'Northern Rhodesia, Southern Rhodesia and Nyasaland', *Empire Review,* LXVII (1938), pp. 344–7.

GOWERS, Sir William, 'Uganda and its Future', *Journal of the African Society,* XXVI (1926–27), pp. 85–92.

'Some Thoughts on Uganda', *Journal of the African Society,* XXIX (1929–30), pp. 467–70.

'Uganda and Indirect Rule', *United Empire,* New Series, XXIV (1933), pp. 101–103.

GRAHAM, G., 'The Demand for Colonies', *Labour Monthly,* 18 (1936), pp. 364–73.

GREAVES, I. C., *Modern Production Among Backward Peoples.* London: Allen & Unwin, 1935.

GREGORY, J. W., The *Menace of Colour.* London: Seeley Service, 1925.

'The Future of East Africa', *Edinburgh Review,* 242 (1925), pp. 20–31.

GRIGG, E. W. M., (Sir Edward), *The Greatest Experiment in History.* London: Humphrey Milford, 1924.

The Constitutional Problem of Kenya. Cust Foundation Lecture, Nottingham University College, 1933.

'British Policy in Kenya', *Journal of the African Society,* XXVI (1926–27), pp. 193–208.

'Our Own People in East Africa', *Church Missionary Review,* 78 (1927), pp. 250–55.

'The East Africa Report', *Empire Review,* LIV (1931), pp. 370–7.

'The Problem of Government in East Africa', *United Empire,* New Series, XXII (1931), pp. 127–36.

'Closer Union in East Africa', *National Review,* 97 (1931), pp. 351–6.

'Land Policy and Economic Development in Kenya', *Journal of the African Society,* XXXI (1932), pp. 1–14.

'Problems of Development in Tropical Africa', *United Empire,* New Series, XXIV (1933), pp. 473–4.

'Black and White in East Africa', *Listener,* 14 March, 1934. (A discussion with J. H. Oldham.)

GRIMBEL, A., 'Administrators and Anthropologists', *United Empire,* New Series, XII (1921), pp. 765–9.

GUEST, Dr. L. H., *The New British Empire*. London: John Murray, 1929.
The Labour Party and the Empire. London: Labour Publishing Co., 1926. 'West Africa', *United Empire*, New Series, XXX (1939), pp. lxiv–lxvii.
'Impressions of Africa', *Crown Colonist*, 9 (1939), pp. 235 and 238.

GUGGISBERG, Sir Gordon, *The Future of the Negro*. London: S.C.M., 1929. (In collaboration with A. G. Fraser.)
'The Goal of the Gold Coast', *Journal of the African Society*, XXI (1921–22), pp. 81–91.
'Policies and Problems in an African Colony', *National Review*, 90 (1927–29), pp. 218–30.

GUNN, Hugh (Ed.), *The British Empire: A Survey*. 12 vols. London: Collins, 1924.
'Missionaries and the Empire', in *Makers of the Empire*, Vol. 8 of *The British Empire. A Survey* (see above).
'Christian Missions in Africa', *United Empire*, New Series, XVII (1926), pp. 434–6.
'The Definition of the British Empire of 1926', *National Review*, 94 (1929–30), pp. 710–14.
'The Prince of Wales' Tour', *United Empire*, New Series, XXI (1930), pp. 303–6.

HAILEY, Sir William Malcolm, *An African Survey*. London: O.U.P. 1957. (First published in London by the Committee of the African Research Survey, 1938. For contemporary comment on the survey from many writers see 'Lord Hailey's Survey', *Africa*, 38 (1939), Supplement, pp. 1–84.)
'Nationalism in Africa', *Journal of the Royal African Society*, XXXVI (1937), pp. 134–47.
'Scrutiny of Africa I and II', *Listener*, 10 Nov., 1938, and 24 Nov., 1938.
'Some Problems dealt with in the African Survey', *International Affairs*, XVIII (1939), pp.194–210.
'Present Trends in Colonial Policy', *Listener*, 10 Aug., 1939
'African and Indian government', *United Empire*, New Series, XXX (1939), pp. xi–xvi.

HALL, Sir Daniel, *The Improvement of Native Agriculture in Relation to Population and Public Health*. London: O.U.P. 1936. (The University of London Heath Clark Lectures, 1935.)
'The Native Question in Kenya', *Nineteenth Century and After*, 107 (1930), pp. 70–80.

HAMILTON, Sir Robert, 'The International Institute of African Languages and Cultures', *Journal of the African Society*, XXXI (1932), pp. 371–4.
'Criminal Justice in East Africa', *Journal of the Royal African Society*, XXXII (1935), pp. 7–26.

HAMMOND, S. A., 'Biology and African Education', *International Review of Missions*, XVII, (1928), pp. 495–504.
'Fact and Feeling in Colonial Education', *Oversea Education*, VII, 1 (1939), pp. 4–9.

HARRIS, Sir Alexander, 'The Problem of the Mandated Territories', *Quarterly Review*, 267 (1936), pp. 250–66.
'These Colonial Claims', *National Review*, 112 (1939), pp. 317–20.

HARRIS, J. H., (Later Sir John) *Africa: Slave or Free?* London S. C. M. 1919.
The Chartered Millions. London: Swarthmore Press, 1920.
Slavery or 'Sacred Trust'? London: Williams and Norgate, 1926.
A Century of Emancipation. London: Dent, 1933.

'The Challenge of the Mandates', *Contemporary Review*, 119 (1921), pp. 462–70.

'Back to Slavery?', *Contemporary Review*, 120 (1921), pp. 190–197.

'The Colonial Mandates', *Contemporary Review*, 122 (1922), pp. 604–11.

'Christian Church and the Colour Bar', *Contemporary Review*, 123 (1923), pp. 706–713.

'The Mandatory System', *New Statesman*, 13 Oct., 1923.

'British Justice and Native Races', *Contemporary Review*, 126 (1924), pp. 443–48.

'The Mandatory System after Five Years' Working', *Contemporary Review*, 127 (1925), pp. 171–178.

'The Black Man's Burden Today: The Real Issue', *Nation and Atheneum'*, 36 (1925), pp. 879–80.

'Freeing the Slaves', *Contemporary Review*, 128 (1925), pp. 743–750.

'Backward Races: An International Charter', *New Statesman*, 2 Oct., 1926.

'The Challenge to Trusteeship', *Contemporary Review*, 133 (1928), pp. 201–207.

'New Colonial Issues', *New Statesman*, 18 Feb., 1928.

'The Challenge of Kenya', *Contemporary Review*, 138 (1930), pp. 598–604.

'A World "Native" Policy', *Spectator*, 28 June, 1930.

'Liberian Slavery: The Essentials', *Contemporary Review*, 139 (1931), pp. 303–309.

'Slavery: World Abolition', *Contemporary Review*, 142 (1932) pp. 308–314.

'The Challenge of the Protectorates', *Contemporary Review*, 145 (1934), pp. 672–78.

'Proposed Transfer of Native Protectorates', *Listener*, 18 July, 1934.

'Slavery: A World Review', *Contemporary Review*, 150 (1936), pp. 164–171.

'Britain's Greatest African Problem', *Contemporary Review*, 150 (1936), pp. 699–706.

'The Protectorate Dilemma', *Contemporary Review*, 152 (1937), pp. 538–45.

'The African Survey', *Contemporary Review*, 155 (1939), pp. 140–45.

'Native Labour: Success after Thirty Years', *Contemporary Review*, 156 (1939), pp. 296–303.

'Empire's Racial Peril', *National Review*, 113 (1939), pp. 33–40.

'Colonies and Peace Aims', *Contemporary Review*, 157 (1940), pp. 670–77.

HASTINGS, A. C. G., *Nigerian Days*. London: Lane, 1925.

'The Real Nigeria', *National Review*, 89 (1927), pp. 764–74.

HEWINS, W. A. S., *Apologia of an Imperialist (2 vols.)*. London: Constable, 1929.

HICHENS, William, 'Black Magic in Eastern Africa', *Empire Review*, LI (1930), pp. 30–40.

'The Rise of the Black People', *Fortnightly Review*, 135 (1931), pp. 229–44.

'Waylaying the Witch Doctor', *Fortnightly Review*, 135 (1931), pp. 93–99.

HINDEN, Rita, 'Colonial Blind Alley', *Fabian Quarterly*, 28 (1940), pp. 20–25.

HOBLEY, C. W., *Bantu Beliefs and Magic.* London: Witherby, 1938. (First published London: Witherby, 1922. Revised and enlarged for the 1938 edition.)
Kenya, from Chartered Company to Crown Colony. London: Witherby, 1929.
'Some Native Problems in Eastern Africa', *Journal of the African Society,* XXII (1922–23), pp.189–202.
'The Utilization of Native Effort in the Development of East Africa', *Contemporary Review,* 125 (1924), pp. 331–37.

HOBSON, J. A., *Imperialism: A Study,* London: Allen and Unwin, 1938. (First published London: James Nisbet & Co., 1902.)
Towards International Government. London: Allen & Unwin, 1915.
'The Open Door', in C. R. Buxton, (Ed.), *Towards a Lasting Settlement.* London: Allen & Unwin, 1915.
Problems of the New World. London: Allen & Unwin, 1921.

HOLE, H. M., *The Making of Rhodesia.* London: Macmillan, 1926.
Old Rhodesian Days. London: Macmillan, 1928.
'*Natives of Southern Rhodesia*', *United Empire,* New Series, XX (1929), pp. 505–9.
'Native Customs in Rhodesia', *Empire Review,* XLIX (1929), pp.152–156.
'Pioneer Days in Southern Rhodesia', *Journal of the Royal African Society.* XXXV (1936), pp. 37–47.

HOOPER, H. D., *Leading Strings: Native Development and Missionary Education in Kenya Colony.* London: C.M.S., 1921.
Africa in the Making. London: U.C.M.E., 1922.
'The Expression of Christian Life in Primitive African Society', *International Review of Missions,* XIII (1924), pp. 67–73.
'A Synthesis in Missionary Field Work', *Church Missionary Review,* 76 (1925), pp. 334–342.
'Le Zoute—an Impression', *Church Missionary Review,* 77 (1926), pp. 329–339.

HUNTER, Monica, 'The Effects of Contact with Europeans in the Status of Pondo Women', *Africa,* 6 (1933), pp. 251–276.
'Methods of Study of Culture Contact', *Africa,* 7 (1934), pp. 335–50.
'An African Christian Morality', *Africa,* 10 (1937), pp. 265–92.

HUSSEY, E. R. J., 'Village Education in Africa', *Journal of the Royal African Society,* XXXVI (1937), pp. 56–61.
'Higher Education in East Africa', *Journal of the Royal African Society,* XXXVI (1937), Supplement pp. 3–19.
Some Aspects of Education in Tropical Africa. London: O.U.P., 1936. (University of London Institute of Education Studies and Reports IX. In collaboration with H. S. Scott and J. J. Willis.)
Europe and West Africa. London: O.U.P., 1940 (in collaboration with W. M. Macmillan and C. K. Meek).

HUXLEY, Elspeth, *White Man's Country: Lord Delamere and the Making of Kenya.* (2 vols.). London: Chatto & Windus, 1935.

HUXLEY, Julian, *African View.* New York: Harper, 1931.
We Europeans: A survey of Racial Problems. London: Jonathan Cape, 1935. (In collaboration with A. C. Haddon.)
'Principles of Indirect Rule in African Administration', *Nineteenth Century and After,* 108 (1930), pp. 753–9.

'East Africa: Politics and Native Questions', *Contemporary Review*, 138 (1930), pp. 459–69.

'Land, Population and General Smuts', *Nineteenth Century and After*, 108 (1930), pp. 226–35.

'Travel and Politics in East Africa', *Journal of the African Society*, XXX (1931), pp. 245–61.

'Why is the White Man in Africa?', *Fortnightly Review*, 137 (1932), pp. 60–69.

'Biology and Empire Education', *United Empire*, New Series, XXIV (1933), pp. 226–7.

'The Future of Colonies', *Fortnightly Review*, 154 (1940), pp. 120–30.

INTERNATIONAL INSTITUTE OF AFRICAN LANGUAGES AND CULTURES, 'Five Year Plan of Research', *Africa*, 5 (1932), pp. 1–13.

JESSE, William, 'How is Kenya Treated?', *National Review*, 100 (1933), pp. 393–7.

'Natives in East Africa', *National Review*, 103 (1934), pp. 733–40.

'East African Justice', *Empire Review*, LXI (1935), pp. 139–44.

'If Germany Recovered Tanganyika', *Empire Review*, LXVI (1937), pp. 101–15.

'Kenya and Jewish Refugees', *Empire Review*, LXVIII (1938), pp. 305–10.

'Higher Education of the African', *Empire Review*, LXX (1939), pp. 96–99.

JOELSON, F. S. (Ed.), *Eastern Africa Today and Tomorrow*, London: East Africa, 1934.

The Tanganyika Territory. London: Fisher Unwin, 1920.

Germany's Claim to Colonies. London: Hurst and Blackett, 1939.

'Germany and Tanganyika', *National Review*, 100 (1933), pp. 617–20.

JOHNSTON, H. H. Sir, *The Story of My Life*. London: Chatto & Windus, 1923.

'Address on Retirement from the Presidency of the African Society', *Journal of the African Society*, XX (1920–21), p. 83.

'Anthropology: the first of the Sciences', *Contemporary Review*, 119 (1921), pp. 185–92.

'Race Problems in the New Africa', *Foreign Affairs*, 2 (1923–24), pp. 598–612.

JOLLIE, Mrs. Tawse (Ethel Colquhoun), *The Real Rhodesia*. London: Hutchinson, 1924.

'The Passing of Empire', *National Review*, 78 (1921–22). pp. 810–17.

'Britain's Youngest Colony', *National Review*, 82 (1923–24), pp. 447–57.

'Empire and Life', *National Review*, 89 (1927), pp. 139–146.

'Try Southern Rhodesia', *National Review*, 98 (1932), pp. 87–94.

JONES, G. Howard, 'Educational Needs in West Africa', *Journal of the African Society*, XXVI (1926–27), pp. 341–67.

JONES, H. G., *Uganda in Transformation, 1876–1926*. London: C.M.S. 1927.

JONES, Thomas Jesse, *Education in Africa: A Study of West, South and Equatorial Africa*. 1921.

Education in East Africa. 1925.

See L. J. Lewis (Ed.), *Phelps Stokes Reports on Education in Africa*. London: O.U.P. 1962.

Four Essentials of Education. New York: Scribner, 1926.

'New Forces in Africa', Speech at Le Zoute Conference recorded in Edwin W. Smith, *The Christian Mission in Africa*, London: I.M.C., 1926.

KEITH, Sir Arthur, *Darwinism and What it Implies*. London: Watts, 1928.
The Place of Prejudice in Modern Civilization. London: Ethnos, 1931.
'The Evolution of the Human Races', *Journal of the Royal Anthropological Institute*, 58 (1928), pp. 305–321.

KERR, Philip (Lord Lothian), 'From Empire to Commonwealth', *Foreign Affairs*, 1 (1922–23), pp. 83–98.
'Lord Milner', *Nation and Atheneum*, 36 (1925), pp. 227–8.

KIDD, Benjamin, *Control of the Tropics*. New York: Macmillan, 1898.

LAGDEN, Sir Geoffrey, *Native Races of the Empire*. Vol. 9 of *The British Empire. A Survey*, edited by Hugh Gunn. London: Collins, 1924.

LASKI, Harold J., 'The Colonial Civil Service', *Political Quarterly*, IX (1938), pp. 541–551.

LATHAM, G. C., 'The African and Education', *United Empire*, New Series, XXV (1934), pp. 405–6.
'Indirect Rule and Education in East Africa', *Africa* 7 (1934), pp. 423–30.

LAWS, Dr. Robert, *Reminiscences of Livingstonia*. Edinburgh: Oliver and Boyd, 1934.
'Native Education in Nyasaland', *Journal of the African Society*, XXVIII (1928–29), pp. 347–67.

LEAKEY, L. S. B., *Kenya Contrasts and Problems*. London: Methuen, 1936.
White African. London: Hodder & Stoughton, 1937.

LEGGET, Sir Humphrey, 'The Economic Problem of British Tropical Africa', *United Empire*, New Series, XIII (1922), pp. 436–40.
'Commercial Possibilities in British East Africa', *United Empire*, New Series, XIV (1923), pp. 181–2.
'Economics and Administration in British East Africa', *United Empire*, New Series, XIX (1928), pp. 91–7.

LENIN, Vladimir Il'ich, *Selected works*. London: Lawrence and Wishart, 1936–39. Vol. 5, 'Imperialism and Imperialist War, 1914–17'.

LEPPER, G. H., 'Nyasaland's Transport Problem', *English Review*, 39 (1924), pp. 450–8.
'Germany and her Former Colonies', *United Empire*, New Series, XVII (1926), pp. 663–5.
'East African Development and what it means for us', *English Review*, 42 (1926), pp. 481–90.
'Germany and Colonial Mandates', *English Review*, 43 (1926), pp. 63–7.
'The Two East Africas', *United Empire*, New Series, XVIII (1927), pp. 502–3.
'East Africa at the Crossroads', *English Review*, 46 (1928), pp. 168–75.

LEVEY, Lt.-Col. J. H., 'Gold Coast Development', *United Empire*, New Series, XVII (1926), pp. 432–4.

LEVY-BRUHL, Lucien, *Primitive Mentality*. London: Allen & Unwin, 1923.
The 'Soul' of the Primitive. London: Allen & Unwin, 1928.

LEWIN, Percy Evans, *Africa*. Oxford: Clarendon Press, 1924.
'The Black Cloud in Africa', *Foreign Affairs*, 4 (1925–26), pp. 637–47.

LEYS, Norman, *Kenya*. London: Hogarth Press, 1925. (First Edition, 1924).
A Last Chance in Kenya. London: Hogarth Press, 1931.
The Colour Bar in East Africa. London: Hogarth Press, 1941.
'The Tropics and the League of Nations', *Socialist Review*, XVIII, 96 (1921), pp. 68–78.
'The Problem of Kenya', *Socialist Review*, XXI, No. 116 (1923), pp. 205–212.

'The History of Kenya Colony', *Socialist Review*, XXII, 120 (1923), pp. 129–133.

'The Problem of Empire', *Socialist Review*, XXXI, May (1928), pp. 22–27.

'Africa Again', *New Statesman*, 27 Sept., 1930.

'Kenya and the Gold Coast—a Contrast', *N.S. and N.*, 15 April, 1933.

'A College in the Gold Coast', *N.S. and N.*, 22 April, 1933.

'The Report of the Kenya Land Commission', *N.S. and N.*, 28 July, 1934.

'An Incident in Imperial History', *N.S. and N.*, 4 Jan., 1936.

'Christianity and Labour Conditions in East Africa', *International Review of Missions*, 9 (1920), pp. 544–51. (Leys used the pseudonym Fulani bin Fulani in this journal.)

LINFIELD, F. C., 'Empire Development', *Contemporary Review*, 129 (1926), pp. 300–324.

LITTLE, J. S., 'Lost Opportunities, their results and their lessons', *United Empire*, New Series, XII (1921), pp. 492–5.

'Urgent Problems of Empire', *United Empire*, New Series, XII (1921), pp. 770–72.

'False Analogies', *United Empire*, New Series, XIII (1922), pp. 71–73.

'Our Imperial Heritage', *United Empire*, New Series, XIII (1922), pp. 178–80.

'Empires, old and new', *United Empire*, New Series, XVI (1925), pp. 94–104.

LITTLE, Sir Ernest Graham-, 'The British Empire and Backward Races', *Empire Review*, 66 (1937), pp. 269–75.

LUCAS, Sir Charles, *The Partition and Colonization of Africa*. London: O.U.P., 1922. (A reprint of lectures given to a study circle of teachers of the London County Council, at the Royal Colonial Institute in 1921.)

The Story of the Empire. London: Collins & Sons, 1926.

'The Meaning of the Empire to the Labour Democracy', *United Empire*, New Series, XI (1920), pp. 110–21.

'Balance of Power within the Empire', *United Empire*, New Series, XIII (1922), pp. 17–26.

'Tropical Dependencies', *Edinburgh Review*, 235 (1922), pp. 263–282.

LUGARD, F. D., *The Dual Mandate in British Tropical Africa*. Edinburgh: William Blackwood & Sons (4th Edition), 1929. (First published in 1922.)

'Dependencies of the British Empire and the Responsibilities they involve', *Foundation Address to Birkbeck College*: London, 1928.

'Crown Colonies and the British War Debt', *Nineteenth Century and After*, 88 (1920), pp. 239–55.

'Colour Problem', *Edinburgh Review*, 233 (1921), pp. 267–283.

'Growth of Empire', *United Empire*, New Series, XIII (1922), pp. 737–51.

'The Mandate System', *Edinburgh Review*, 238 (1923), pp. 398–408.

'Education in British Tropical Africa', *Edinburgh Review*, 242 (1925), pp. 1–19.

'Progress in Africa', (A speech at the Le Zoute Conference). See Edwin W. Smith, *The Christian Mission in Africa* (1926).

'Slavery, Forced Labour and the League', *Nineteenth Century and After*, 99 (1926), pp. 76–85.

'The White Man's Task in Tropical Africa', *Foreign Affairs*, 5 (1926), pp. 57–68.

'Problems of Equatorial Africa', *International Affairs*, VI (1927), pp. 214–225.

'Responsibilities of Rule in Africa', *United Empire*, New Series, XVIII (1927), pp. 161–3.

'The International Institute of African Languages and Cultures', *Africa*, 1 (1928), pp. 1–12.

'The Human Side of African Development', *United Empire*, New Series, XIX (1928), pp. 415–8.

'Native Policy in East Africa', *Foreign Affairs*, IX (1930), pp. 65–78.

'Child Welfare in Africa', *Spectator*, 18 April, 1931.

'Education and Race Relations', *Journal of the Royal African Society*, XXXII (1933), pp. 1–11.

'Slavery and the League', *Spectator*, 21 July, 1933.

'Slavery in all its Forms', *Africa*, 6 (1933), pp. 1–14.

'Africa and the Powers', *Journal of the Royal African Society*, XXXV (1936), pp. 4–17. (Reprinted from two articles in *The Times*.)

'The Claims to Colonies', *Journal of the Royal African Society*, XXXV (1936), pp. 115–122. (Reprinted from *The Times*.)

'Some Colonial Problems of Today', *United Empire*, New Series, XXVII (1936), pp. 661–72.

'The Basis of the Claim for Colonies', *International Affairs*, XV (1936), pp. 3–17.

'British Policy in Nigeria', *Africa*, 10 (1937), pp. 377–400.

'Fifty Years of Colonies', *Spectator*, 11 June, 1937.

'Our Title to Colonies', *Spectator*, 11 Aug., 1939.

MACKINDER, Sir Halford, 'The English Tradition and Lord Milner's Credo', *United Empire*, New Series, XVI (1925), pp. 724–35.

'The Empire and the World', *United Empire*, New Series, XXV (1934), pp. 519–522.

MACMILLAN, W. M., *Warning from the West Indies: A Tract for Africa and the Empire*, London: Faber, 1936.

Africa Emergent. London: Faber, 1938.

Europe and West Africa. London: O.U.P., 1940. (In collaboration with E. R. J. Hussey and C. K. Meek.)

'The South African Protectorates', *New Statesman*, 2 June, 1924.

'Southern Rhodesia and the Development of Africa', *Journal of the African Society*, XXXII (1933), pp. 294–8.

'The Real Moral of the Tshekedi Case', *N.S. and N.*, 23 Sept., 1933.

'The Development of Africa', *Political Quarterly*, 111 (1932), pp. 552–69.

'Position of Native Education in British Africa', *United Empire*, New Series, XXV (1934), pp. 172–3.

'The Importance of the Educated African', *Journal of the Royal African Society*, XXXIII (1934), pp. 137–42.

'Colour and the Commonwealth', *N.S. and N.*, 1 June, 1935.

'Neglected Outposts of Africa', *N.S. and N.*, 6 May, 1939.

'The Real Colonial Question', *Fortnightly Review*, 154 (1940), 548–57.

'What about the Colonies?', *N.S. and N.*, 10 Feb., 1940.

McPHEE, Allan, *The Economic Revolution in British West Africa*. London: Routledge, 1926.

MAIR, Lucy P., *An African People in the Twentieth Century*. London: Routledge, 1934.

Native Policies in Africa. London: Routledge, 1936.

'Native Land Tenure in East Africa', *Africa*, 4 (1931), pp. 314–29.

'Colonial Administration as a Science', *Journal of the Royal African Society*, XXXII (1933), pp. 366–371.

'The Study of Culture Contact as a Practical Problem', *Africa*, 7 (1934), pp. 415–22.

'A Science of Colonial Government', *Contemporary Review*, 145 (1934), pp. 80–87.

'The Growth of Economic Individualism in African Society', *Journal of the Royal African Society*, XXXIII (1934), pp. 261–73.

'The Anthropologists' approach to Native Education', *Oversea Education*, VI, 2 (1935), pp. 53–60.

'Chieftainship in Modern Africa', *Africa*, 9 (1936), pp. 305–16.

MALINOWSKI, B., *The Dynamics of Culture Change: an enquiry into Race Relations in Africa* (edited by P. M. Kaberry). Newhaven: Yale University, 1945.

'Practical Anthropology', *Africa*, 2 (1929), pp. 22–38.

'The Rationalization of Anthropology and Administration', *Africa*, 3 (1930), pp. 405–30.

'Native Africa in a Nutshell', *N.S. and N.*, 14 March, 1931.

'Native Education and Culture Contact', *International Review of Missions*, XXV (1936), pp. 480–515.

'The Present State of Studies in Culture Contact: Some Comments on an American Approach', *Africa*, 12 (1939), pp. 27–48.

MATHEWS, Basil, *Clash of Colour*. A Study in the Problem of Race. London: United Council for Missionary Education, 1925.

Consider Africa. London: Edinburgh Press, 1935.

'Missions and the League', *Church Missionary Review*, 76 (1925), pp. 137–144.

MAUGHAM, R. C. F., *Africa as I have Known It*. London: Murray, 1929.

Nyasaland in the Nineties. London: Lincoln Williams, 1935.

'Salesmanship in Africa', *Empire Review*, XLIX (1929), pp. 225–231.

'British Trusteeship in Africa', *Empire Review*, LIV (1931), pp. 33–6.

'Amalgamation of the Two Rhodesias', *United Empire*, New Series, XXX (1939), pp. 1164–5.

MAXWELL, Sir James, 'Some Aspects of Native Policy in Northern Rhodesia', *Journal of the African Society*, XXIX (1929–30), pp. 471–7.

MAYHEW, Arthur T., *Educational Policy in the Colonial Empire*. London: Longmans, 1938.

'A Comparative Survey of Educational Aims and Methods in British India and British Tropical Africa', *Africa*, 6 (1933), pp. 172–86.

'Some Impressions of an International Conference on Education', *Oversea Education*, VIII, 2 (1937), pp. 57–68.

'Recent Educational Progress in England: What can we Learn from it?', *Oversea Education*, IX, 3 (1938), pp. 113–119.

'Aims and Methods of Indigenous Education in Primitive Societies', *Oversea Education*, X, 2 (1939), pp. 68–74.

MEEK, C. K., *Europe and West Africa*. London: O.U.P., 1940. (In collaboration with W. M. Macmillan and E. R. J. Hussey.)

MELLAND, F. H., *African Dilemma*. London: Religious Tract Society, 1931. (In collaboration with T. Cullen-Young.)

In Witch Bound Africa. London: Cass, 1967. (First published London: Seeley Service, 1923.)

'The Future of West Africa', *English Review*, 46 (1928), pp. 441–4.

'Closer Union in East Africa', *Fortnightly Review*, 129 (1928), pp. 747–59.

'Eastern Africa—Our Opportunity', *Fortnightly Review*, 131 (1929), pp. 500–07.

'Northern Rhodesia: A New Field for Settlement', *Empire Review*, 50 (1929), pp. 116–21.

'Northern Rhodesia: Retrospect and Prospect', *Journal of the African Society*, XXIX (1929–30), pp. 490–8.

'The Great Opportunity', *Journal of the African Society*, XXX (1931), pp. 262–271.

'The Native Resources of Africa', *Journal of the African Society*, XXXI (1932), pp. 113–32.

'Modern Industry and the African', *Listener*, 13 Dec., 1933.

'East African Kaleidoscope', *Nineteenth Century and After*, 115 (1934), pp. 525–34.

'Non-Professional Missionaries', *World Dominion*, XII, 4 (1934), pp. 337–344.

'The Anthropologist in Africa', *Fortnightly Review*, 142 (1934), pp. 224–32.

'The Misjudged Witch Doctor', *Listener*, 3 Jan., 1934.

'Our Colonial Complacency', *Nineteenth Century and After*, 118 (1935), pp. 151–62.

'And Now—Africa', *English Review*, 62 (1936), pp. 32–40.

'Civilizing Africa', *Spectator*, 20 March, 1936.

'Against the White Man's Law', *Listener*, 3 November, 1937.

'Nationalism and Internationalism in Africa', *Empire Review*, LXV (1937), pp. 370–375.

'The Unknown African', *Listener*, 13 April, 1938.

'Africa and the League of Nations', *Journal of the African Society*, XIX (1919–1920), pp. 317–19.

'Reconstruction in Central Africa', *Journal of the African Society*, XIX (1919–1920), pp. 92–100.

'Native Education in Central Africa', *Journal of the African Society*, XX (1920–1921), pp. 95–100.

'The Guild System for African Races', *Journal of the African Society*, XXI (1921–22), pp. 31–34.

'Shall we Betray our Trust?', *National Review*, 107 (1936), pp. 593–600.

(Melland used the pseudonym Africanus, for the last five articles listed.)

MIGEOD, F. W. H., *Through British Cameroons*. London: Heath Cranton, 1925.

'A View of the Colony of Sierra Leone', *Journal of the African Society*, XXV (1925–26), pp. 1–9.

MITCHELL, P. E., 'The Anthropologist and the Practical Man', *Africa*, 3 (1930), pp. 217–223.

MOREL, E. D., *The Black Man's Burden*. Manchester: National Labour Press, 1920.

'Two African Policies', *Contemporary Review*, 124 (1923), pp. 310–20.

MUMFORD, W. Bryant, *Africans Learn to be French*, London: Evans Bros., 1935. (In collaboration with Major G. St. J. Orde-Browne.)

'Some Growing Points in African Higher Education', *Year Book of Education*, London: Evans Bros. (1936).

'Native Schools in Central Africa', *Journal of the African Society*, XXVI (1926–27), pp. 237–44.

'Education and Social Adjustment of Primitive Peoples of Africa to European Culture', *Africa*, 2 (1929), pp. 138–61.

'East Africa. Some Problems in Native Economic Development and a possible Solution in Co-operative Societies', *Africa*, 6 (1933), pp. 27–37.

'Racial Comparison and Intelligence Testing', *Journal of the Royal African Society*, XXXVII (1938), pp. 46–57. (In collaboration with C. E. Smith.)

'Education in British African Dependencies', *Journal of the Royal African Society*, XXXVI (1937), pp. 17–32. (In collaboration with B. N. Parker.)

'The Problem of Mass Education in Africa', *Africa*, 11 (1938) ,pp. 187–207.

MURRAY, A. Victor, *A School in the Bush*. London: Longmans Green, 1938. (First published in 1929. The 1938 edition includes the article 'Education under Indirect Rule' first published in the *Journal of the Royal African Society*, in 1935.)

'Christianity and Rural Civilization', *International Review of Missions*, XIX (1930), pp. 388–97.

'A Missionary Education Policy for Southern Nigeria', *International Review of Missions*, XXI (1932), pp. 516–31.

'Education under Indirect Rule', *Journal of the African Society*, XXXIV (1935), pp. 227–68.

NEW EDUCATION FELLOWSHIP, *Education in a Changing Commonwealth*. London: N. E. F. 1931 (edited by W. Rawson).

Educational Adaptations in a Changing Society. Capetown: N. E. F. 1937 (edited by E. G. Malherbe).

NEW FABIAN RESEARCH BUREAU, 'The Protection of Colonial Peoples', Fabian Research Series No. 10, 1933.

OLDHAM, J. H., *Christianity and the Race Problem*. London: S. C. M. 1924.

White and Black in Africa. London: Longmans Green, 1930. (A critical Examination of the Rhodes Lecture of General Smuts, published in *Africa and Some World Problems*.)

The Remaking of Man in Africa. London O.U.P., 1931. (In collaboration with B. D. Gibson.)

'The Relation of Christian Missions to the New Forces that are reshaping African Life', A speech at the Le Zoute Conference, recorded in Edwin W. Smith, *The Christian Mission in Africa* (1926).

'Nationality and Missions', *International Review of Missions*, IX (1920), pp. 372–83.

'Christian Missions and African Labour', *International Review of Missions*, X (1921), pp. 183–95.

'Christian Education in Africa', *Church Missionary Review*, 75 (1924), pp. 305–314.

'Educational Policy of the British Government in Africa', *International Review of Missions*, XIV (1925), pp. 421–7.

'Christian Opportunity in Africa: Some Reflections on the Phelps-Stokes Commission', *International Review of Missions*, XIV (1925), pp. 173–87.

'Population and Health in Africa', *International Review of Missions*, XV (1926), pp. 402–17.

'Christian Missions in Africa as seen at the International Conference at Le Zoute', *International Review of Missions*, XVI (1927), pp. 24–35.

'Report of the Commission on the Closer Union of the Eastern and Central African Dependencies', *International Affairs*, VIII (1929), pp. 227–257.

'Development in the Relations between Black and White in Africa, 1911–31', *Journal of the African Society*, XXXII (1933), pp. 160–70.

'Black and White in East Africa', (A discussion with Sir Edward Grigg) *Listener*, 14 March, 1934.

'The Educational Work of Missionary Societies', *Africa*, 7 (1934), pp. 47–59.

OLIVER, R. A. C., 'The Adaptation of Intelligence Tests to Tropical Africa—I and II', *Oversea Education*, IV, 4 (1933), pp. 186–191 and V, 1 (1933), pp. 8–12.
'Comparisons of Cultural Achievement', *Oversea Education*, V, 3 (1934), pp. 107–111.
'Mental Tests in the Study of the African', *Africa*, 7 (1934), pp. 40–46.

OLIVIER, Sir Sidney, *White Capital and Coloured Labour*. London: Hogarth Press, 1929. (First published in 1906 but rewritten for the 1929 edition.)
The Anatomy of African Misery. London: Hogarth Press, 1927.
'Are we going to deal justly in Africa?', *Contemporary Review*, 118 (1920), pp. 198–206.
'Colour Prejudice', *Contemporary Review*, 124 (1923), pp. 448–57.
'Native Land Rights in Rhodesia', *Contemporary Review*, 130 (1926), pp.145–51.
'The Conversion of Kenya', *New Statesman*, 27 Nov., 1926.
'Segregation in Southern Rhodesia', *New Statesman*, 26 June, 1926.
'The Five Years of South Africa', *Contemporary Review*, 132 (1927), pp. 144–51.
'Wisdom From British East', *New Statesman*, 18 June, 1927.
'The European Problem in Africa', *Contemporary Review*, 134 (1928), pp. 454–60.
'The British Trust in Africa', *Contemporary Review*, 136 (1929), pp. 273–81.
'The Meaning of Imperial Trusteeship', *Contemporary Review*, 136 (1929), pp. 303–12.
'An Imperial Comedy', *New Statesman*, 26 Jan., 1929.
'Settled Policy in East Africa', *Contemporary Review*, 140 (1931), pp. 694–701.
'A Glimpse of Justice in Africa', *Contemporary Review*, 141 (1932), pp. 569–74.
'The Kaffir and the Cow Complex', *Fortnightly Review*, 139 (1933), pp. 601–7.
'Development Policy in the Colonies', *Crown Colonist*, 4 (1934), p. 108.
'The Key to the Colour Question', *Contemporary Review*, 148 (1935), pp. 665–73.
'Colonial Administration', *Crown Colonist*, 6 (1936), p. 253.

ORDE-BROWNE, G. St. J., *The Vanishing Tribes of Kenya*. London: Seeley Service, 1925.
The African Labourer. London: O.U.P., 1933.
Africans Learn to be French. London: Evans Bros., 1935. (In collaboration with W. B. Mumford.)
'Native Labour in Tanganyika', *Journal of the African Society*, XXVI (1926–27), pp. 112–16.
'African Labour and International Relations', *Journal of the African Society*, XXXI (1932), pp. 394–401.
'British Justice and the African (I and II)', *Journal of the Royal African Society*, XXXII (1933), pp. 148–59, and 280–293.
'The African Prisoner', *Contemporary Review*, 151 (1937), pp. 577–82).

ORMSBY-GORE, W. G. A. (later Lord Harlech), 'The Work of the West African Commission', *Journal of the African Society*, 24 (1924–25), pp. 165–177.

'My Recent Travels in East Africa', *United Empire,* New Series, XVI (1925), pp. 357–64.

'British West Africa', *United Empire,* New Series, XVIII (1927), pp. 28–41.

'Problems and Development in Africa', *Journal of the African Society,* XXVIII (1928–29), pp. 325–39. (In collaboration with L. S. Amery.)

'The Meaning of Indirect Rule', *Journal of the African Society,* XXXIV (1935), pp. 283–286.

'Educational Problems of the Colonial Empire', *Journal of the Royal African Society,* XXXVI (1937), pp. 162–9.

ORR, Sir Charles, 'The Founder of Nigeria', *Listener,* 5 Aug., 1936.

'The Northern Provinces of Nigeria', *Journal of the Royal African Society,* XXXVI (1937), pp. 8–16.

ORR, J. Russell, 'The Use of the Kinema in the Guidance of Backward Races', *Journal of the African Society,* XXX (1931), pp. 238–44.

OWEN, W. E., Archdeacon of Kavirondo, 'Empire and Church in Uganda and Kenya', *Edinburgh Review,* 245 (1927), pp. 43–57.

'The Relationship of Missionary and African in East Africa', *Church Missionary Review,* 78 (1927), pp. 21–30.

'Forced Labour in East Africa', *Church Overseas,* 4 (1931), pp. 216–25.

'Some Thoughts on Native Development in East Africa', *Journal of the African Society,* XXX (1931), pp. 225–37.

PADMORE, George, *The Life and Struggles of Negro Toilers.* London: Red International of Labour Unions, 1931.

How Britain Rules Africa. London: Wishart, 1936.

Africa and World Peace. London: Secker & Warburg, 1937.

'Forced Labour in Africa', *Labour Monthly,* 13 (1931), pp. 237–47.

'British Finance Capital in West Africa', *Labour Monthly,* 13 (1931), pp. 105–16.

'Labour Imperialism in East Africa', *Labour Monthly,* 13 (1931), pp. 308–314 and pp. 366–373.

'"Left" Imperialism and the Negro Toilers', *Labour Monthly,* 14 (1932), pp. 313–19.

PALMER, Sir Richmond, 'Some observations on Captain R. S. Rattray's paper "Present Tendencies of African Colonial government" ', *Journal of the Royal African Society,* XXXIII (1934), pp. 37–48.

PERHAM, Margery, *The Protectorates of South Africa: the question of their transfer to the Union.* London: O.U.P., 1935. (In collaboration with L. Curtis.)

Ten Africans. London: Faber, 1936.

Native Administration in Nigeria. London: O.U.P., 1937.

'Indirect Rule', *Crown Colonist,* 4 (1934), p. 249 and p. 253.

'The System of Native Administration in Tanganyika', *Africa,* 4 (1931), pp. 302–12.

'The Census of Nigeria', *Africa,* 5 (1933), pp. 415–30.

'Teaching the Native African to Govern Himself', *Listener,* 28 Feb., 1934..

'A Restatement of Indirect Rule in Africa', *Africa,* 7 (1934), pp. 321–34.

'Future Relations of Black and White in Africa', *Listener,* 28 March, 1934.

'Some Problems of Indirect Rule in Africa', *Journal of the Royal African Society,* XXXIV (1935). Supplement. This article is reprinted in *Colonial Sequence 1930–1949.*

'The Basuto and their Country', *Geographical Magazine*, 1, 2 (1935), pp. 117–125.

'Educating Africa', *Spectator*, 11 Nov., 1938.

'War and the Colonies', *Spectator*, 6 Oct., 1939.

PETO, G. K., 'Kenya and Madagascar: a Comparison and a Moral', *Empire Review*, LII (1930), pp. 31–8.

PHILIPPS, Captain J. E. T., 'The Tide of Colour I; Pan Africa and Anti-White', *Journal of the African Society*, XXI (1921–22). pp. 129–135, and 'The Tide of Colour II: Anti-White or Not', *Journal of the African Society*, XXI (1921–22), pp. 309–315.

PHILIPPS, Tracy, 'The New Africa: I. The Need for New Forms of Government for Africans', *Nineteenth Century and After*, 122 (1937), pp. 568–95.

'The New Africa: II. A New Statute for Colonies and a New Status for Africans. A Plan', *Nineteenth Century and After*, 123 (1938), pp. 351–61.

PIM, Sir Alan, *The Financial and Economic History of the African Tropical Territories*. Oxford: Clarendon Press, 1940.

'The Question of the South African Protectorates', *International Affairs*, XIII (1934), pp. 668–682.

'British Protectorates and Territories', *United Empire*, New Series, XXV (1934), pp. 266–79.

'The South African Protectorates', *United Empire*, New Series, XXVI (1935), pp. 514–5.

'Anthropological Problems of Indirect Rule in Northern Rhodesia', *Man*, 38 (1938), pp. 180–185.

RAGLAN, Lord, 'Crime and Punishment in Tropical Africa', *Nineteenth Century and After*, 93 (1923), pp. 575–82.

RATHBONE, H., 'The Problem of African Independence', *Labour Monthly*, 18 (1936), pp. 161–172 and pp. 237–249.

RATTRAY, R. S., *Ashanti*. Oxford: Clarendon, 1956 (First published in 1923).

'Present Tendencies of African Colonial Government', *Journal of the Royal African Society*, XXXIII (1934), pp. 22–36.

'The Making of Nigeria', *Fortnightly Review*, 143 (1935), pp. 443–54.

READ, Margaret, *Native Standards of Living and African Culture Changes*. International Institute of African Languages and Cultures, Memorandum 16. London: O.U.P., 1938.

RICHARDS, Audrey I., *Land, Labour and Diet in Northern Rhodesia*: an Economic Study of the Bemba Tribe. London: O.U.P., 1939.

'Anthropological Problems in North-Eastern Rhodesia', *Africa*, 5 (1932), pp. 121–44.

'From Bush to Mine', *Geographical Magazine*, 1, 6 (1935), pp. 463–76.

'Tribal Government in Transition. The Bemba of Northern Rhodesia', *Journal of the Royal African Society*, XXXIV (1935), Supplement, pp. 1–26.

ROBERTSON, Wilfred, 'Gone Native', *Fortnightly Review*, 134 (1933), pp. 695–9.

'European Civilization and African Reactions', *National Review*, 101 (1933), pp. 358–64.

'African Drug Addicts', *Empire Review*, LX (1934), pp. 89–92.

'The Bantu and the Prison System', *Empire Review*, LIX (1934), pp. 103–7.

ROOME, W. J. W., *A Great Emancipation*. A Missionary Survey of Nyasaland, Central Africa. London: World Dominion Press, 1926.
Can Africa be Won? London: Black, 1927.
Tramping Through Africa. London: Black, 1930.
ROSCOE, John, *Twenty-five Years in East Africa*. London: Cambridge Univ. Press, 1921.
'Uganda and Some of its Problems', *Journal of the African Society*, XXII (1922–23), pp. 96–108, and 218–225.
ROSS, William McGregor, *Kenya from Within*. London: Allen & Unwin, 1927.
'A Comb-out in Kenya', *New Statesman*, 25 April, 1925.
'On the Prince's Trail in Kenya', *United Empire*, New Series, XIX (1928), pp. 450–55.
'East Africa Now', *Church Overseas*, 2 (1929), pp. 206–15.
ROUND TABLE, 'The Imperial Conference', *Round Table*, XI (1920–21), pp. 735–758.
'The Indian Problem in East Africa', *Round Table*, XII (1921–22), pp. 338-361.
'The Colour Question in Politics', *Round Table*, XIII (1922–23), pp. 38–70.
'Kenya', *Round Table*, XIII (1922–23), pp. 507–529.
'Lord Milner', *Round Table*, XV (1924–25), pp. 427–30.
'Southern Rhodesia and Responsible Government', *Round Table*, XVI (1925–26), pp. 757–769.
'Achimota', *Round Table*, XVI (1925–26), pp. 78–93.
'The New Problem of Africa', *Round Table*, XVII (1927–28), pp. 447–472.
'The African Labour Problem', *Round Table*, XVIII (1927–28), pp. 498–521.
'East Africa: The Report of the Commission', *Round Table*, XIX (1928–29), pp. 479–518.
'The British Commonwealth, Freedom and the Seas', *Round Table*, XIX (1928–29), pp. 229–254.
'Great Britain and France in Northern Africa', *Round Table*, XIX (1928–29), pp. 717–738.
'An Experiment in African Education in Kenya', *Round Table*, XX (1929–30), pp. 558–572.
'Foreign Law in the British Empire', *Round Table*, XXIII (1932–33), pp. 362–382.
'The Protectorates and the Union', *Round Table*, XXIV (1933–34), pp. 785–801.
'The Future of Colonial Trusteeship', *Round Table*, XXIV (1933–34), pp. 732–745.
'The South African Protectorates', *Round Table*, XXV (1934–35), pp. 318–323.
'Kenya: The Settler's Case', *Round Table*, XXVI (1935–36), pp. 82–97.
'Rudyard Kipling', *Round Table*, XXVI (1935–36), pp. 330–334.
'Dust Bowls of the Empire', *Round Table*, XXIX (1938–39), pp. 338–351.
'Problems of British West Africa', *Round Table*, XXIX (1938–39), pp. 291–308.
ROYAL EMPIRE SOCIETY, *The Crucial Problem of Imperial Development*. London: Longmans, 1938.
ROYAL INSTITUTE OF INTERNATIONAL AFFAIRS, *Raw Materials and Colonies*. London: O.U.P., 1936.

The Colonial Problem. London: O.U.P., 1937.
The British Empire. London: O.U.P., 1937.
Germany's Claim to Colonies. London: R.I.I.A., 1939.
ROY, M. N., 'Socialism and the Empire', *Labour Monthly*, 10 (1928), pp. 85–94.
'The Future of the Empire', *Labour Monthly*, 10 (1928), pp. 663–74.
RUST, William, 'The Economic Crisis of British Imperialism', *Labour Monthly*, 12 (1930), pp. 404–12.
SCHAPERA, I., 'Labour Migrations from the Bechuanaland Reserves', *Journal of the Royal African Society*, XXXII (1933), pp. 386–97 and 33 (1934), pp. 49–58.
'Field Methods in the Study of Modern Culture Contacts', *Africa*, 8 (1935), pp. 315–28.
SCOTT, Lord Francis, 'The A.B.C. of Kenya', *National Review*, 81 (1923), pp. 937–944.
'Tanganyika: The Urgent Question', *National Review*, 107 (1936), pp. 33–36.
'Kenya', *National Review*, 109 (1937), pp. 321–26.
SCOTT, H. S., 'European Settlement and Native Development in Kenya', *Journal of the Royal African Society*, XXXV (1936), pp. 178–90.
'Education in East Africa', *United Empire*, New Series, XXVIII (1937), pp. 101–2.
'Education and Nutrition in the Colonies', *Africa*, 10 (1937), pp. 458–471.
'The Effect of Education on the African', *Journal of the African Society*, XXXVII (1938), pp. 504–9.
'The Development of the Education of the African in relation to Western Contact', *The Year Book of Education*, London: Evans Bros., 1938.
SCURR, John, 'The Fundamental Motive of British Foreign Policy', *Socialist Review*, XXVI 141, (1925), pp. 5–24.
'Labour and the Empire', *Socialist Review*, XXIV No. 130 (1924), pp. 6–16.
SELBORNE, Earl of, 'The Native Problem on the West Coast', *Journal of the African Society*, 21 (1921–22), pp. 261 ff.
SELIGMAN, C. G., *Races of Africa*. London, O.U.P., 1957. (First published in 1930.)
SHIELS, Dr. Drummond, 'The East Africa Report', *Political Quarterly*, 111 (1932), pp. 71–87.
'The Colonial Empire', *United Empire*, New Series, XXVIII (1937), pp. 526–8.
SLATER, Sir Ransford, 'The Gold Coast of Today', *Journal of the African Society*, XXVII (1927–28), pp. 321–8.
'The Gold Coast: Some Facts and Figures', *Journal of the African Society*, XXIX (1929–30), pp. 343–9.
'Changing Problems of the Gold Coast', *Journal of the African Society*, XXIX (1930), pp. 461–6.
SMITH, Edwin W., *The Golden Stool: Some Aspects of the Conflict of Cultures in Africa*. London: Holborn Publishing House, 1926.
The Christian Mission in Africa. London: International Missionary Council, 1926.
The Way of the White Fields in Rhodesia. London: World Dominion Press, 1928.
Aggrey of Africa: A Study in Black and White. London: S.C.M. 1929.
African Beliefs and Christian Faith. London: United Society for Christian Literature, 1936.

The Secret of the African. London: S.C.M. 1929.
'The Sublimation of Bantu Life and Thought', *International Review of Missions,* XI (1922), pp. 83–95.
'An Unbroken Fellowship', *Church Missionary Review,* 75 (1924), pp. 18–26.
'Social Anthropology and Missionary Work', *International Review of Missions,* XIII (1924), pp. 518–31.
'The Disintegration of African Society', *The East and the West,* 22 (1924), pp. 143–160.
'Northern Rhodesia', *Empire Review,* XXXIX (1924), pp. 436–444.
'These Fifty Years in Africa, 1875–1925', *Church Missionary Review,* 76 (1925), pp. 296–308.
'The Story of the Institute: A Survey of Seven Years', *Africa,* 7 (1934), pp. 1–27.
'Africa: What do we know of it?', *Journal of the Royal Anthropological Institute,* 65 (1935), pp. 1–81.
'Land in Kenya', *Journal of the Royal African Society,* XXV (1936), pp. 246–50.
'The South African Protectorates', *Journal of the Royal African Society,* XXXVII (1938), pp. 199–205.
SMUTS, Jan Christian, *Africa and Some World Problems,* including the Rhodes Memorial lectures delivered at Michaelmas term, 1929, Oxford: Clarendon Press, 1930. (Two of the chapters of this book were published separately as articles in the *Journal of the African Society.* They were published as 'Native Policy in Africa', *Journal of the African Society,* XXIX (1929–30), pp. 248–68, and 'African Settlement', *J.A.S.,* XXIX (1929–30), pp. 109–31.)
SPECTOR, Maurice, 'The Empire Labour Conference', *Labour Monthly,* 7 (1925), pp. 548–52.
STODDARD, Lothrop, *The Rising Tide of Colour Against White World Supremacy.* London: Chapman & Hall, 1920.
The Revolt Against Civilization. London: Chapman & Hall, 1922.
STOKES, Robert, *New Imperial Ideals.* London: Murray, 1930.
STONE, Brig. Gen. F. G., 'The Kenya Conferences', *Nineteenth Century and After,* 93 (1923), pp. 767–75.
'The Kenya Decision', *Nineteenth Century and After,* 94 (1923), pp. 430–36.
'Indians in the Empire', *Fortnightly Review,* 121 (1924), pp. 820–31.
STRICKLAND, C. F., *Cooperation for Africa.* London: O.U.P., 1933.
'Cooperation for Africa', *Africa,* 6 (1933), pp. 15–26.
'The Cooperative Movement in Africa', *Journal of the Royal African Society,* XXXIV (1935), Supplement pp. 3–15.
TEMPLE, C. L., *Native Races and Their Rulers.* London: Cass, 1967. (First published Capetown: Argus Co., 1918.)
THOMSON, Sir Graeme, 'Some Problems of Administration and Development in Nigeria', *Journal of the African Society,* XXVI (1926–27), pp. 305–14.
THURNWALD, Richard, *Economics in Primitive Communities.* London: O.U.P., 1933.
Black and White in East Africa. London: Routledge, 1935.
'The Social Problems of Africa', *Africa,* 2 (1929), pp. 130–37.
'Social Systems of Africa', *Africa,* 2 (1929), pp. 221–43, and pp. 352–80.
'The Missionary's concern in Sociology and Psychology', *Africa,* 4 (1931), pp. 418–433.

'The African in Transition. Some Comparisons with Melanesia', *Africa*, 11 (1938), pp. 174–86.

WESTERMANN, D., *The African Today and Tomorrow*. New York: O.U.P., 1934.

Africa and Christianity. London: O.U.P., 1937.

'The Place and Function of the Vernacular in African Education', *International Review of Missions*, XIV (1925), pp. 25–36.

'Value of the Africans' Past', *International Review of Missions*, XV (1926), pp. 418–37.

'The Missionary as Anthropological Field Worker', *Africa*, 4 (1931), pp. 164–176.

'The Standardization of African Languages', *Oversea Education*, VI, No. 1 (1934), pp. 1–7.

'The Work of the International Institute of African Languages and Cultures', *International Review of Missions*, XXVI (1937), pp. 493–9.

WIGGLESWORTH, Alfred, 'Regeneration of Africa', *United Empire*, New Series, XIV (1923), pp. 535–8.

'What I Found in East Africa', *United Empire*, New Series, XXI (1930), pp. 594–8.

'Signposts of Tropical Development', *Journal of the Royal African Society*, XXXV (1936), pp. 169–177.

WILLOUGHBY, W. C., *Race Problems in the New Africa*. Oxford: Clarendon Press, 1923.

The Soul of the Bantu. London: S.C.M., 1928.

'Building the African Church', *International Review of Missions*, XV (1926), pp. 450–66.

WILSON, Godfrey, *The Study of African Society*. Livingstone: Rhodes Livingstone Papers, No. 2, 1939. (In collaboration with Monica Hunter.)

WOOLF, Leonard, *Empire and Commerce in Africa*. London: Allen & Unwin, 1920.

Economic Imperialism. Lord Swarthmore International Handbooks, 1920.

Imperialism and Civilization. London: Hogarth, 1928.

'Economic Imperialism and the Sacred Trust', *Labour Monthly*, 1 (1921), pp. 51–61.

WORTHINGTON, E. B., *Science in Africa*. New York: O.U.P., 1938.

WRONG, Margaret, *The Land and Life of Africa*. London: Edinburgh House, 1935.

'Africa', in *The Modern Missionary*, ed. J. H. Oldham (London, 1935), pp. 66–80.

'Education in Africa', *Listener*, 7 March, 1934.

'Education in Africa', *United Empire*, New Series, XXV (1934), pp. 435–6.

WYNDHAM, H. A., (4th Baron Leconfield) *Problems of Imperial Trusteeship*, Vol. I, *Native Education*, London: O.U.P., 1933.

'The Colour Problem in Africa', *International Affairs*, IV (1924), pp. 174–188.

'The African Problem', *Church Overseas*, 5 (1932), pp. 3–14.

YOUNG, T. Cullen, *African Ways and Wisdom*. London: United Society for Christian Literature, 1937.

African Dilemma. London: Religious Tract Society, 1937. (In collaboration with Frank Melland.)

Contemporary Ancestors: A Beginner's Anthropology for district officers and missionaries in Africa. London: R.T.S. n.d.

'The Communal Bond in Bantu Africa', *International Review of Missions*, XXII (1933), pp. 105–14.

'Bush Schools and Evangelism', *World Dominion*, XIII, 4 (1935), pp. 407–13.

'How Far can African Ceremonial be Incorporated in the Christian System?', *Africa*, 8 (1935), pp. 210–17.

'East African Tax Method Revision', *Journal of the Royal African Society*, XXXV (1936), pp. 381–85.

'The "Native" Newspaper', *Africa*, 11 (1938), pp. 63–72.

YOUNG, Sir Hilton, 'East African Opportunity', *United Empire*, New Series XX (1929), pp. 689–90.

ZIMMERN, Alfred, *The Third British Empire*. London: O.U.P., 1934. (First published in 1926.)

'The Crucial Test of the League', *Contemporary Review*, 148 (1935), pp. 513–20.

PRIMARY SOURCES—
Commission Reports and Policy Statements

Memorandum relating to Indians in Kenya; 1923. Cmd 1922, XVIII, 141.

Memorandum by the Advisory Committee on Native Education in the British Tropical African Dependencies; 1924–25. Cmd 2374, XXI, 27.

Report of the East African Commission; 1925. Cmd 2387, IX, 855.

Summary of Proceedings of the Colonial Office Conference; 1927. Cmd 2883, VII, 751.

Report of the Commission on Closer Union of the Dependencies in Eastern and Central Africa; 1928–29. Cmd 3234, 353.

Report by Sir Samuel Wilson, G.C.M.G., on his visit to East Africa, 1929; 1929–30. Cmd 3378, VIII, 551.

Report of a Committee on the System of Appointments in the Colonial Office and the Colonial Services; 1929–30. Cmd 3554, VIII, 677.

Statement on the Conclusions of H.M. Government in the U.K. as regards Closer Union in East Africa; 1929–30. Cmd 3574, XXIII, 85.

Memorandum on Native Policy; 1929–30. Cmd 3573, XXIII, 105.

Report of the Joint Committee on Closer Union in East Africa, Vol. 1 Report; 1930–31. HC156, VII, 1.

Report by Mr. A. W. Pim on the Financial and Economic Situation in Swaziland; 1931–32. Cmd 4114, VII, 291.

Report by Sir S. Armitage Smith on a Financial Mission to Tanganyika; 1931–32. Cmd 4182, VII, 443.

Report by Mr. A. W. Pim on the Financial and Economic Position of the Bechuanaland Protectorate; 1932–33. Cmd 4368, X, 279.

Report by Mr. A. W. Pim on the Financial and Economic Position of Basutoland; 1934–35. Cmd 4907, VII, 353.

Report of the Commission of Enquiry into the Administration of Justice in Kenya, Uganda and the Tanganyika Territory on criminal matters; 1933–34. Cmd 4623, IX, 653.

Report of the Commission of Enquiry on the Disturbances in the Copper Belt of Northern Rhodesia, Oct., 1935; 1934–35. Cmd 5009, VII, 587.

Report of a Royal Commission òn Rhodesia—Nyasaland; 1938–39. Cmd 5949, XV, 211.

Statement of Policy on Colonial Development and Welfare; 1939–40. Cmd 6175, X, 25.

SECONDARY SOURCES—
books and articles

AJAYI, J. F. Ade, *Christian Missions in Nigeria, 1841–1891.* London: Longmans, 1965.

ALMOND, Gabriel A. and Coleman, James S., *The Politics of the Developing Areas.* Princeton University Press, 1960.

ANDRESKI, S., *The African Predicament: A Study in the Pathology of Modernization.* London: Michael Joseph, 1968.

APTER, D. E. (ed.), *Ideology and Discontent.* London: Macmillan, 1964.
The Politics of Modernization. Chicago University Press, 1965.

ASAD, Talal (ed.), *Anthropology and the Colonial Encounter.* London: Ithaca Press, 1973.

AYANDELE, E. A., *The Missionary Impact on Modern Nigeria, 1842–1919: A political and social analysis.* London; Longmans, 1966.

BALANDIER, Georges, *Ambiguous Africa.* (Translated from the French by Helen Weaver.) London: Chatto and Windus, 1966.

BANKS, Olive, *Parity and Prestige in English Secondary Education: A Study in Educational Sociology.* London: Routledge, 1955.

BANTON, M. (ed.), *Darwinism and the Study of Society.* London: Tavistock, 1961.
'Race as a Social Category', *Race,* 8 (1966), pp. 1–15.
Race Relations. London: Tavistock, 1967.

BARNES, H. E., *An Introduction to the History of Sociology.* Chicago University Press, 1948.
Historical Sociology: Its Origins and Development. New York Philosophical Library, 1948.

BARNES, Leonard, *African Renaissance.* London: Gollancz, 1969.

BARNETT, H. G., 'Anthropology as an Applied Science', *Human Organization,* XVII, 1 (1958), pp. 9–11.

BARZUN, Jacques, *Race: A Study in Superstition.* London: Methuen, 1938.

BAUER, P. T., 'The Economics of Resentment: Colonialism and Underdevelopment', *Journal of Contemporary History,* 4, 1 (1969), pp. 51–71.

BEARCE, George D., *British Attitudes towards India, 1784–1858.* London: O.U.P., 1961.

BEATTIE, J. H. M., 'Ethnographic and Sociological Research in East Africa: A Review', *Africa,* 26 (1956), pp. 265–275.

BEETHAM, T. A., *Christianity and the New Africa.* London: Pall Mall, 1967.

BELL, Sir H. Hesketh, *Glimpses of a Governor's Life, from diaries, letters and memoranda.* London: Sampson Low and Co., 1946.

BENNET, George, 'Paramountcy to Partnership: J. H. Oldham and Africa', *Africa,* 30 (1960), pp. 356–60.

BERLIN, Isaiah, 'Political Ideas in the Twentieth Century', in Henry S. Kariel, *Sources in Twentieth Century Political Thought.* New York: Free Press of Glencoe, 1964.

BING, Geoffrey, *Reap the Whirlwind: An Account of Kwame Nkrumah's Ghana from 1950–1966.* London: MacGibbon and Kee, 1968.

BLYTHE, Ronald, *The Age of Illusion: England in the Twenties and Thirties 1919–1940.* London: Hamish Hamilton, 1963.

BOLT, Christine, *Victorian Attitudes to Race.* London: Routledge and Kegan Paul, 1971.

BOWLE, John, *Politics and Opinion in the Nineteenth Century.* London: Jonathan Cape, 1966.

BOYD, W. C., *Genetics and the Races of Man.* Oxford: Blackwell, 1950.

BRACE, C. Loring and MONTAGU, M. F. Ashley, *Man's Evolution*. New York: Macmillan, 1965.

BRAILSFORD, H. N., 'The Life Work of J. A. Hobson', L. T. Hobhouse Memorial Trust Fund Lecture No. 17 (1947).

BROKENSHA, David, *Applied Anthropology in English-Speaking Africa*. Lexington: Society for Applied Anthropology, 1966.

BROWN, I. C., *Understanding Other Cultures*. New Jersey: Prentice Hall, 1963.

BROWN, J. Murray, *Kenyatta*. London: Allen and Unwin, 1972.

BROWN, Paula, 'From Anarchy to Satrapy', *American Anthropologist*, 65 (1963), pp. 1–15.

BURROW, J. W., 'Evolution and Anthropology in the 1860s: the Anthropological Society of London, 1863–71', *Victorian Studies*, VII (1963), pp. 137–54.
Evolution and Society: A Study in Victorian Social Theory. Cambridge University Press, 1966.

CAIRNS, H. A. C., *Prelude to Imperialism: British reactions to Central African Society 1840–1890*. London: Routledge, 1965.

CHRISTENSEN, J. B., 'African Political Systems: Indirect Rule and Democratic Processes', *Phylon*, 15 (1954), pp. 69–83.

COHEN, Sir Andrew, *British Policy in Changing Africa*. London: Routledge, 1959.

COLE, Margaret, *The Story of Fabian Socialism*. California: Stanford University Press, 1961.
'The Fabian Society', *Political Quarterly*, XV (1944), pp. 245–256.

COMAS, Juan, '"Scientific" Racism Again?', *Current Anthropology*, 2 (1961), p. 303.

CONRAD, Jack, *The Many Worlds of Man*. London: Macmillan, 1967.

COUNT, E. W., 'The Evolution of the Race Idea in Modern Western Culture during the Period of the pre-Darwinian 19th Century', *Transactions of the New York Academy of Sciences*, Second Series, 8 (1946), pp. 139–165.

COURT, W. H. B., 'The Communist Doctrines of Empire' in W. K. Hancock *Survey of British Commonwealth Affairs*. London: O.U.P., 1940, Vol. 2, Part 1.

CREECH JONES, Arthur (Ed.), *New Fabian Colonial Essays*. London: Hogarth Press, 1959.

CROCKER, W. R., *On Governing Colonies*. London: Allen & Unwin, 1947.
Self Government for the Colonies. London: Allen & Unwin, 1949.

CROWDER, Michael, 'Indirect Rule, French and British Style', *Africa*, 34 (1964), pp. 197–205 (reprinted in *Collected Essays*, Cass, 1977).
West Africa under Colonial Rule. London: Hutchinson, 1968.

CURTIN, P. D., 'The British Empire and Commonwealth in Recent Historiography', *American Historical Review*, LXV (1959), pp. 72–91.
'The White Man's Grave: Image and Reality, 1780–1850', *Journal of British Studies*, 1 (1961), pp. 94–110.
African History. American Historical Association Publication No. 56, 1964.
The Image of Africa: British Ideas and Action 1780–1850. Madison: University of Wisconsin Press, 1964.

DANGERFIELD, George, *The Strange Death of Liberal England*. London: Macgibbon and Kee (Reprint), 1966.

DAVIDSON, Basil, 'Africa Today', Review of International Affairs, (Belgrade), XVIII (1967), pp. 414-15.

DAVIS, Kingsley, 'The Myth of Functional Analysis as a Special Method in Sociology and Anthropology', American Sociological Review, 24, 6 (1959), pp. 757-772.

DE BUNSEN, Victoria, Charles Roden Buxton: A Memoir. London: Allen & Unwin, 1948.

DORE, R. P., 'Function and Cause', American Sociological Review, 26, 6 (1961), pp. 843-853.

DOWSE, Robert E., Left in the Centre. The Independent Labour Party 1893-1940. London: Longmans, 1966.

DUTT, R. P., 'Our First Quarter of a Century', Labour Monthly, 28 (1946), pp. 193-194.

EISENSTADT, S. N., 'Primitive Political Systems: a Preliminary Comparative Analysis', American Anthropologist, 61 (1959), pp. 200-220.

EVANS-PRITCHARD, E. E., 'Social Anthropology Past and Present', Man, 50 (1950), pp. 118-124.
Social Anthropology. London: Cohen and West, 1951.
Anthropology and History. Manchester University Press, 1961.

FIELDHOUSE, D. K. and KOEBNER, R., 'Imperialism: An Historiographical Revision', Economic History Review, Second Series, XIV (1961), pp. 187-209.

FIELDHOUSE, D. K. (Compiler), The Theory of Capitalist Imperialism. London: Longmans, 1967.

FIRTH, Raymond, 'The Future of Social Anthropology', Man, 44 (1944), pp. 19-22.
'The Study of Values by Social Anthropologists', Man, 53 (1953), pp. 146-153.
Man and Culture: An Evaluation of the Work of Bronislaw Malinowski. London: Routledge and Kegan Paul, 1957.

FOLSOM, A., The Royal Empire Society, formerly the Royal Colonial Institute: formative years. London: Allen & Unwin, 1933.

FORDE, Daryll, 'Applied Anthropology in Government: British Africa' in A. L. Kroeber (Ed.), Anthropology Today, University of Chicago Press, 1953.
'Anthropology and the Development of African Studies', Africa, 37 (1967), pp. 389-404.

FORTES, M. and EVANS-PRITCHARD, E. E., African Political Systems. London: O.U.P., 1955.

FREEMAN, J. D., 'Anthropology, Psychiatry and the Doctrine of Cultural Relativism', Man, 65 (1965), pp. 65-7.

FRIEDLAND, W. H. and ROSBERG, Carl G., African Socialism. California: Stanford University Press, 1964.

FURSE, Sir Ralph, Aucuparius: Recollections of a Recruiting Officer. London: O.U.P., 1962.

GEERTZ, Clifford, (Ed.), Old Societies and New States: the Quest for Modernity in Asia and Africa. New York: Free Press of Glencoe, 1963.

GELLNER, Ernest, 'Nature and Society in Social Anthropology', Philosophy of Science, XXX (1963), pp. 236-253.

GEORGE, Katherine, 'The Civilized West looks at Primitive Africa 1400-1800; a study in ethnocentrism', Isis, 49 (1958), pp. 62-72.

GIFFORD, Prosser and LOUIS, W. K. (Eds.), Britain and Germany in Africa. Newhaven: Yale University Press, 1967.

GINSBERG, M., 'The Conception of Stages in Social Evolution', *Man*, 32 (1932), pp. 87–91.

GLUCKMAN, M. (Ed.), *Closed Systems and Open Minds: the Limits of Naivety in Social Anthropology*. Edinburgh: Oliver and Boyd, 1963.

GOODALL, N., *A History of the London Missionary Society 1895–1945*. London: O.U.P., 1954.

GREGORY, Robert G., *Sidney Webb and East Africa: Labour's Experiment with the Doctrine of Native Paramountcy*. Berkeley: University of California Press, 1962.

GRIERSON, E., *The Imperial Dream: The British Commonwealth and Empire 1775–1969*. London: Collins, 1972.

GROVES, C. P., *The Planting of Christianity in Africa* (Vol. 4). London: Lutterworth Press, 1958.

GUTKIND, Peter C. W., 'The African Urban Milieu: A force in rapid change', *Civilizations*, XII (1962), pp. 167–191.

HADDON, A. C., *History of Anthropology* (2nd Edition). London: Watts and Co., 1934.

HAGBURG-WRIGHT, G., 'The Evolution of the Periodical', *Nineteenth Century and After*, 101 (1927), pp. 320–29.

HAILEY, Sir William Malcolm, *Britain and Her Dependencies*, London: Longmans Pamphlets on the British Commonwealth, 1945.

HALL, H. D., *Mandates, Dependencies and Trusteeships*. London: Stevens and Sons, 1948.

HALLET, Robin, 'The European Approach to the Interior of Africa in the Eighteenth Century', *Journal of African History*, IV (1963), pp. 191–206.

HANCOCK, W. K., *Survey of British Commonwealth Affairs*. London: O.U.P., 1937.
Argument for Empire. London: Harmondsworth Penguin Books, 1943.

HANKINS, Frank H., *The Racial Basis of Civilization*. New York: Alfred Knopf, 1926.

HARLOW, Vincent, *The Historian and British Colonial History*. Oxford: Clarendon Press, 1951.

HARRIS, Marvin, *The Rise of Anthropological Theory*. Columbia University Press, 1968.

HAZLEWOOD, A. (Ed.), *African Integration and Disintegration*. London: O.U.P., 1967.

HENSHAW, Stanley K., 'Applied Anthropology and Sociology in Tropical Africa', *Human Organization*, XXII, 4 (1963–64), pp. 263–295.

HEUSSLER, Robert, *Yesterday's Rulers. The Making of the British Colonial Service*. London: O.U.P., 1963.
The British in Northern Nigeria. London: O.U.P., 1968.

HEWAT, E. G. K., *Vision and Achievement 1796–1956. A History of the Foreign Missions United in the Church of Scotland*. London: Nelson, 1960.

HEWITT, G., *The Problem of Success. A History of the Church Missionary Society, 1910–1942*. London: S.C.M., 1971.

HOOKER, J. R., 'The Anthropologists' Frontier: The Last Phase of African Exploitation', *Journal of Modern African Studies*, 1, 4 (1963), pp. 455–9.
Black Revolutionary: George Padmore's Path from Communism to pan-Africanism. London: Pall Mall Press, 1967.

HOOTEN, E. A., *Up from the Ape*. London: Allen and Unwin, 1931.

HORTON, W. R. G., 'Social Science, Logical or Psychological Impossibility', *Man*, 61 (1961), pp. 11–15.

HOVDE, B. J., 'Socialistic Theories of Imperialism Prior to the Great War', Journal of Political Economy, XXXVI (1928), pp. 569–591.

HOWE, Susan, Novels of Empire. New York: Columbia University Press, 1949.

HYAMS, Edward, The New Statesman. The history of the first fifty years 1913–1963. London: Longmans, 1963.

JARYC, Marc, 'Studies of 1935–42 on the History of the Periodic Press', Journal of Modern History, 15 (1943), pp. 127–41.

JEFFRIES, Sir Charles (Ed.), A Review of Colonial Research 1940–1960. London: H.M.S.O., 1964.

JOHNSTON, A., 'Sir Harry Johnston', Journal of the African Society, 27 (1927–28), pp. 1–6.

JULY, Robert W., The Origins of Modern African Thought. London: Faber, 1968.

KEITH, Sir Arthur, A New Theory of Human Evolution. London: Watts and Co., 1948.

KEMP, T., Theories of Imperialism. London: Dennis Dobson, 1967.

KENDLE, J. E., Colonial and Imperial Conferences. London: Longmans, 1967.

KILLAM, G. D., Africa in English Fiction, 1874–1939. Ibadan University Press, 1968.

KING-HALL, Stephen, Chatham House. London: O.U.P., 1937.

KIRK-GREENE, A. H. M. (Ed.), Lugard and the Amalgamation of Nigeria. (A republication of the 1920 Report, Cmd 468.) London: Cass, 1968.

KIRKMAN, N. P., Unscrambling an Empire: A Critique of British Colonial Policy 1956–1966. London: Chatto & Windus, 1966.

KNAPLAND, Paul, 'Sir Arthur Gordon and Fiji: Some Gordon-Gladstone Letters', Historical Studies, 8, (1958), pp. 281–296.

KOEBNER, R. and SCHMIDT, H. D., Imperialism: the Story and Significance of a Political Word, 1840–1960. Cambridge University Press, 1964.

KROEBER, A. L., Anthropology. New York: Harcourt, Brace & Co., 1948.
An Anthropologist Looks at History. Berkeley: University of California Press, 1963.

KROGMAN, M., 'What do we know about Race?', Scientific Monthly, 57 (1943), pp. 97–104.

LEE, J. M., Colonial Development and Good Government. London: O.U.P., 1967.

LELLO, John, The Official View on Education. Oxford: Pergamon Press, 1964.

LEWIS, L. J. (Ed.), Phelps Stokes Reports on Education in Africa. London: O.U.P., 1962.

LIENHARDT, Godfrey, 'On the Concept of Objectivity in Social Anthropology'; Journal of the Royal Anthropological Institute, 94, Part 1 (1964), pp. 1–10.

LLOYD, P. C., The New Elites in Tropical Africa. London: O.U.P., 1964.

LOUIS, W. R., and STENGERS, J., E. D. Morel's History of the Congo Reform Movement. Oxford: Clarendon Press, 1968.

LOW, D. A. and PRATT, R. C., Buganda and British Over-rule. Two Studies. London: O.U.P., 1960.

LOW, D. A., 'Studying the Transformation of Africa', Comparative Studies in Society and History, 7 (1964–65), pp. 21–36.

LOWNDES, G. A. N., The Silent Social Revolution. London: O.U.P., 1957.

LYSTAD, Robert A. (Ed.), The African World. A Survey of Social Research. London: Pall Mall, 1965.
'The State of Private Research on Africa', African Studies Bulletin, 8, 1 (1965), pp. 29–42.

McBRIAR, A. M., *Fabian Socialism and English Politics, 1884–1918.* Cambridge University Press, 1962.

McCALL, Daniel, F., *Africa in Time Perspective.* New York: O.U.P., 1969.

MacGAFFEY, Wyatt, 'Concepts of Race in the Historiography of North East Africa', *Journal of African History,* 7, 1 (1966), pp. 1–17.

MacMILLAN, Harold, *Winds of Change, 1914–1939.* London: Macmillan, 1966.

MacMILLAN, W. M., *The Road to Self Rule.* London: Faber, 1959.

MAHOOD, M. M., *Joyce Cary's Africa.* London: Methuen, 1964.

MAIR, L. P., 'The Role of the Anthropologist in Non-Autonomous Territories' in C. M. MacInnes (Ed.), *Principles and Methods of Colonial Administration.* London: Parthenon Press, 1950.
'The Social Sciences in Africa South of the Sahara: the British Contribution', *Human Organization,* 19 (1960), pp. 98–106.

MAQUET, Jacques J., 'Objectivity in Anthropology', *Current Anthropology,* 5 (1964), pp. 47–55.

MARCUS, John T., 'Time and the Sense of History: West and East'. *Comparative Studies in Society and History,* 3 (1960), pp. 123–39.

MARTIN, Kingsley, *Father Figures. A first volume of autobiography, 1897–1931.* London: Hutchinson, 1966.

MAZRUI, Ali M., 'The English Language and Political Consciousness in British Colonial Africa', *Journal of Modern African Studies,* 4, 3 (1966), pp. 295–311.
Towards a Pax Africana: a Study of ideology and ambition. London: Weidenfeld & Nicolson, 1968.

MEAD, Margaret, *New Lives for Old: Cultural Transformation on Manus, 1928–1953.* London: Gollancz, 1956.

MITCHELL, Sir Philip, *African Afterthoughts.* London: Hutchinson, 1954.

MITCHELL, R. C. and TURNER, H. W., *A Comprehensive Bibliography of Modern African Religious Movements.* Evanston: North Western University Press, 1966.

MONTAGU, M. F. Ashley (Ed.), *The Concept of Race.* New York: Free Press, 1964.

MORRIS, James, *Pax Britannica.* London: Faber, 1968.

MOURANT, A. E., 'The Use in Anthropology of Blood Groups and Other Genetical Characters', *Journal of African History,* 3 (1962), pp. 291–6.

NEILL, Stephen, *A History of Christian Missions.* Pelican History of the Church, Part 6. London: Harmondsworth, 1964.

NESTURKH, M., *The Races of Mankind.* (Translated from the Russian by George Hanna.) Moscow: Foreign Languages Publishing House, n.d.

NICOLSON, I. F., *The Administration of Nigeria, 1900–1960: Men, Methods and myths.* Oxford: Clarendon Press, 1969.

NIMOCKS, W., *Milner's Young Men: The Kindergarten in Edwardian Imperial Affairs.* Durham: Duke University Press, 1968.

NKRUMAH, Kwame, *Towards Colonial Freedom.* Bulletin on African Affairs Vol. 2, No. 59. Accra: Bureau of African Affairs, n.d. Probably originally published in 1947.
Neo-Colonialism: the Last Stage of Imperialism. London: Nelson, 1965.

OBEYESEKERE, G., 'Methodological and Philosophical Relativism', *Man,* New Series, 1 (1966), pp. 368–74.

OLIVER, Roland, *The Missionary Factor in East Africa.* London: Longmans, 1952.
Sir Harry Johnston and the Scramble for Africa. London: Chatto and Windus, 1957.

OLIVIER, M. (Ed.), *Sidney Olivier. Letters and Selected Writings*. London; Allen & Unwin, 1948.

ONWUACHI, P. C. and WOLFE, A. W., 'The Place of Anthropology in the Future of Africa', *Human Organization*, 25, 2 (1966), pp. 93–95.

PELLING, Henry, *The British Communist Party: A Historical Profile*. London: Black, 1958.

A Short History of the Labour Party. London: Macmillan, 1961.

PENNIMAN, T. K., *A Hundred Years of Anthropology*. London: Duckworth, 1965. First published 1935.

PERHAM, Margery, 'Lord Lugard: A Preliminary Evaluation', *Africa*, 20 (1950), pp. 228–239.

The Life of Frederick Dealtry Lugard, 2 vols. London: Collins, 1956, 1960.

The Colonial Reckoning. London: Collins, 1963.

Colonial Sequence, 1930–1949. London: Methuen, 1967.

PERRATON, H. D., 'British Attitudes towards East and West Africa, 1880–1914', *Race*, 8 (1967), pp. 223–246.

PORTER, Bernard, *Critics of Empire: British Radical Attitudes to Colonialism in Africa, 1895–1914*. London: Macmillan, 1968.

POTTER, P. B., 'Origin of the System of Mandates', *American Political Science Review*, 16 (1922), pp. 563–83.

PRIESTLEY, M., *West African Trade and Coast Society*. London: O.U.P., 1969.

RADCLIFFE-BROWN, A. R., 'A Note on Functional Anthropology', *Man*, 46 (1946), pp. 38–41.

'The Comparative Method in Social Anthropology', *Journal of the Royal Anthropological Institute*, 81 (1952), pp. 15–22.

Structure and Function in Primitive Society. New York: Free Press of Glencoe, 1952.

Method in Social Anthropology: Selected Essays. Chicago University Press, 1958.

READ, Margaret, *Africans and Their Schools*. London: Longmans, 1953.

Education and Social Change in Tropical Areas. London: Nelson, 1955.

REDFIELD, Robert, 'Societies and Cultures as Natural Systems', *Journal of the Royal Anthropological Institute*, 85, Part 1 (1955), pp. 19–32.

ROBERTS, Fraser, 'The Contribution of Genetics to Physical Anthropology', *Journal of the Royal Anthropological Institute*, 88, Part 2 (1958), pp. 115–29.

ROBINSON, K. E. and MADDEN, F. (Eds.), *Essays in Imperial Government*. Oxford: Blackwell, 1963.

ROBINSON, K. E., *The Dilemmas of Trusteeship*. London: O.U.P., 1965.

ROBINSON, Paul A., *The Freudian Left*. New York: Harper and Rowe, 1969.

ROBINSON, Ronald and GALLAGHER, John, *Africa and the Victorians*. London: Macmillan, 1961.

ROE, J. M., *A History of the British and Foreign Bible Society, 1905–1954*. London: British and Foreign Bible Society, 1965.

ROUND TABLE, 'A Hundred Millions for the Colonies. The Task of the Colonial Development Corporation', *Round Table*, XXXVII (1946–47), pp. 356–361.

SCHAPERA, I., 'Should Anthropologists be Historians?', *Journal of the Royal Anthropological Institute*, 92, Part 2 (1962), pp. 143–154.

SEMMEL, Bernard, *Imperialism and Social Reform. English Social Imperial Thought 1895–1914*. London: Allen and Unwin, 1960.

SMITH, John, *Colonial Cadet in Nigeria*. Durham: Duke University Press, 1968.

SMITH, M. G., 'History and Social Anthropology', *Journal of the Royal Anthropological Institute*, 92, Part 1 (1962), pp. 73–85.

SPIRO, H. J., (Ed.), *Patterns of African Development*. New Jersey: Prentice-Hall, 1967.

STAHL, K. M., *The Metropolitan Organization of British Colonial Trade: Four Regional Studies*. London: Faber, 1957.

STRACHEY, A., *St. Loe Strachey: His Life and His Paper (the Spectator)*. London: Gollancz, 1930.

STRACHEY, John, *The End of Empire*. London: Gollancz, 1959.

SUMNER, D. L., *Education in Sierra Leone*. London(?): Government of Sierra Leone, 1963.

SUTHERLAND, L. C., 'William Miller Macmillan: an Appreciation', in K. Kirkwood (Ed.), *St. Antony's Papers Number 21*. London: O.U.P., 1969.

SYMONDS, Richard, *The British and Their Successors. A Study of the Development of the Government Services in the New States*. London: Faber, 1966.

THOMPSON, E. T. (Ed.), *Race Relations and the Race Problem*. Durham: Duke University Press, 1959.

THOMPSON, H. P., *Into All Lands: The History of the Society for Propagation of the Gospel in Foreign Parts, 1701–1750*. London: Society for Propagation of Christian Knowledge, 1951.

THORNTON, A. P., *The Imperial Idea and its Enemies: A Study in British Power*. London: Macmillan, 1959.
Doctrines of Imperialism. New York: John Wiley and Sons, 1965.

TRIBE, D., 'In the Beginning', *Twentieth Century*, 175, No.1034 (1967), pp. 4–6.

U.N.E.S.C.O., *The Race Question in Modern Science*. Paris: UNESCO, 1956.

USBORNE, Richard, *Clubland Heroes*. London: Constable, 1953.

WARD, W. E. F., *Fraser of Trinity and Achimota*. Accra: Ghana Universities Press, 1965.

WARREN, M., *The Missionary Movement from Britain in Modern History*. London: S.C.M., 1965.

WASHBURN, S. L., 'The Study of Race', *American Anthropologist*, 65 (1963), pp. 521–31.

WASHINGTON, Booker T., *Up from Slavery*. New York: Doubleday, 1900.

WATT, D. C., *Personalities and Politics: Studies in the Formation of British Foreign Policy in the Twentieth Century*. London: Longmans, 1965.

WAUGH, Arthur, 'The Biography of a Periodical', *The Fortnightly Review*, 132, (1929), pp. 512–24.

WEBB, Sydney and Beatrice, *Decay of Capitalist Civilization*. London: Allen & Unwin, 1923.

WEBSTER, J. B., *The African Churches Among the Yoruba*. Oxford: Clarendon Press, 1964.

WHITE, L. A., *The Evolution of Culture*. New York: McGraw Hill, 1959.

WILLIAMS, C. K., *Achimota: The Early Years, 1924–1948*. Accra: Longmans, 1962.

WILSON, Charles, *A History of Unilever: A Study in Economic Growth and Social Change*. Vol.1; London: Cassell, 1954.

WILSON, Trevor, *The Downfall of the Liberal Party, 1914–1935*. London: Collins, 1966.

WINKLER, Henry R., *The League of Nations Movement in Great Britain, 1914–1919*. New Jersey: Rutgens University Press, 1952.

WINKS, Robin W., *The Historiography of the British Empire—Commonwealth*. Durham: Duke University Press, 1966.

WISE, Colin, *A History of Education in British West Africa*. London: Longmans, 1956.
WOOLF, Leonard, *Downhill all the Way*. London: Hogarth Press, 1967.
WORSLEY, Peter, 'The Analysis of Rebellion and Revolution in Modern British Social Anthropology', *Science and Society*, 25 (1961), pp. 26–37.
The Third World. London: Weidenfeld and Nicolson, 1964.
WRAITH, R. A., *Guggisberg*. London: O.U.P., 1967.
YOUNGER, Kenneth, *The Public Service in New States*. London: O.U.P., 1960.

SECONDARY SOURCES—Unpublished Theses

BECKMAN, Bjorn, 'Colonial Traditionalism: Ideology and Action in British Tropical Africa 1920–1945', *Ph.D. thesis*, Department of Political Science, University of Stockholm, 1966.
BRETT, E. A., 'Development Policy in East Africa Between the Wars: A Study of the Political Influences involved in the Making of British Policy, 1919–1939'. *Ph.D. Thesis*, University of London, 1966.
HAMMOND, D., 'The Image of Africa in British Literature of the Twentieth Century', *Ph.D. thesis*, Columbia University, 1966.
HENDERSON, Ian, 'The Attitude and Policy of the Main Sections of the British Labour Movement to Imperial Issues, 1899–1924'. *B. Litt. thesis*, Oxford, 1964.
JABLOW, A., 'The Development of the Image of Africa in British Popular Literature, 1530–1910'. *Ph.D. thesis*, Columbia University, 1963.
TUCKER, M., 'A Survey of the Representative Modern Novel in English about Africa', *Ph.D. thesis*, New York, 1963.

INDEX

Achimota School, 121, 122
Advisory Committee on Education in the Colonies, 38
Africa (journal), 12, 30, 31, 81
Africa and some World Problems, 19
Africa Emergent, 98–9
African Dilemma, 10
African Society, 28–9; journal of, 28–31, 33, 68
African Survey, An, see under Hailey, Lord
African View, 18
African World, 34
Amani Institute, 101
Amery, L. S., 14, 32, 48–9, 94
Andrews, Charles F., 18
anthropological theories, 13, 30–31, 121, 131–2, 154
Anti-Slavery and Aborigines' Protection Society, 37, 95
Anti-Slavery Reporter and Aborigines' Friend, 37
apartheid, system of, 148

Barnes, Leonard, 16, 122; and racial differences, 86, 142; critic of imperialism, 52–3, 72, 96, 97–8, 104, 147
Beer, George Louis, 19
Berlin Conference (1885), 95, 121
Bourdillon, Sir Bernard, 95
Brailsford, H. L., 16
Bridgeman, A. H., 33
Brockway, A. Fenner, 17
Buell, Raymond, 19
Buxton, Charles Roden, 15, 16, 121, 122
Buxton, Lord, 28–9

Cameron, Sir Donald, 6, 50, 85, 143
capital investment, 91, 97–9

Carnegie Corporation, 102
Cary, Joyce, 8
Chatham House, 102
Chirgwin, A. M., 11
Chirol, Sir Valentine, 18, 113
Christianization, 71–2, 111–12
Church, Major Archibald G., 82, 95, 101
Church Missionary Review, 33
Church Overseas (journal), 33–4
Clifford, Sir Hugh, 50
Colonial Development and Welfare Act (1940), 93, 104
Colonial Institute, Education Circle, 32
Colonial Office Advisory Committee on Education in British Tropical Africa, 8, 18, 116, 122–3
Colonial Problem, The, 100
communism, 17, 37, 56, 61, 145; *see also* Leninism; Marxism
Contemporary Review, 36
Cotterell, G. C. B., 8
Couper, Reginald, 17
Coupland, Sir Reginald, 67, 118
Creech-Jones, A., 17
Cripps, Arthur Shearly, 11
Crocker, W. R., 8
Crown Colonist (journal), 34
culture, and race, 80, 84, 136
Currie, Sir James, 8, 122

Davis, John Merle, 19
Dominions Royal Commission (1812), 92
Dougall, Rev. J. W. C., 11, 83
Driberg, J. H., 13, 83
Dual Mandate in British Tropical Africa, 138
dual mandate theory, 46, 54, 103–104, 155
Dutt, Palme, 17, 37, 55

East Africa, Joint Parliamentary Committee on, 146
East African Commission Report (1925), 101, 131
East and the West, 33
Edinburgh Review, 36
Empire Review, 32–3, 81
English Review, 36
Evans, Ifor, 67

Fabian Colonial Bureau, 37
Fabian Quarterly, 37
Fabian Society, 17, 37
Fisher Report, 134
Fitzpatrick, J. F. J., 8, 140
Foreign Affairs (journal), 36
Fortnightly Review, 36
Frankel, Prof. S. H., 100, 102
Fraser, A. G., 11, 77, 122, 123
Fraser, Very Reverend Donald, 11, 95
Future of the Negro, The, 11

Genetics, theory of, 78–9
German colonies, 3, 39, 103, 145
Gowers, Sir William, 85
Grigg, Sir Edward, 6, 32
Guggisberg, Sir Gordon, 7, 11, 50, 77, 85, 122

Haddon, A. C., 79
Haden-Guest, Dr., 15
Hailey, Lord, 7–8, 18, 20, 32; An African Survey, 7, 19, 38, 99–100, 102–103, 139–40; political activities, 14, 76, 98, 142
Hampton School, 113, 117
Harris, Sir John H., 15, 51, 71
Higher Education, Commission on (1937), 124
Hinden, Rita, 17
Hobley, C. W., 9
Hobson, J. A., 16, 46, 52, 54, 56–7, 132
Hole, H. M., 9
Hooper, Handley D., 11
Hussey, E. R. J., 9
Huxley, Julian, 18, 79, 95, 102, 122–3

Imperial Commerce and Affairs (journal), 34

Imperial Institute, 101
Imperial Review, 34
Imperialism and Civilization, 97
Indian Unrest, 113
indirect rule theory, 8, 13, 136–49
International Affairs (journal), 36
International Institute of African Languages and Cultures, 6, 12, 30–31, 83, 102, 131, 133
International Missionary Council, 34
International Review of Missions, 34
interventionist policies, 61–2, 90

Jesse, William, 18
Joelson, F. S., 77
Johnston, Sir Harry H., 4, 28
Jones, G. Howard, 118
Jones, Dr. Thomas Jesse, 19, 117
Jooten, E. A., 78

Keith, Sir Andrew, 79
Kenyatta, Jomo, 17, 37
Kerr, Philip, 48

Labour Monthly, 36, 37, 56, 67, 145
Laski, Harold, 134
Last Chance in Kenya, A, 148–9
Laws, Dr. Robert, 11, 122, 123
League of Nations, 3, 45, 61; see also Permanent Mandates Commission
Lenin, (Leninism), 54–6, 67, 132, 135, 145, 155–7
Lévy-Bruhl, Lucien, 83
Leys, Dr. Norman, 9, 14; and education, 121, 122, 146; and Kenyan regulations, 147; and racial differences, 68, 86; critic of imperialism, 16, 52–3, 64, 96, 97, 134–5, 148–9
Linfield, F. C., 93
Lothian, Lord, 102
Lucas, Sir Charles, 17, 49–50, 84
Lugard, Sir Frederick, 4–5, 14, 31, 32, 134; An African Survey, 102; and dual mandate, 19, 47, 48, 53; and education, 117, 119; and indirect rule theory, 138–9, 148; and racial differences, 81, 82; and social evolution, 64

MacMillan, Prof. W. M., 16–17, 104; and education, 120, 122; and racial differences, 86, 141; critic of imperialism, 35, 98–9

Mair, Lucy, 13, 133
Malinowki, Bronislaw, 6, 13, 132
mandate system, 3, 15, 45
Marxism, 4, 46, 56–7, 61, 73, 148, 155–7
Mathews, Basil, 11
Maugham, R. C. F., 9, 33
Mayhew, Arthur, 18, 115
Meek, C. K., 13, 51
Melland, Frank H., 9–10, 147
Mendel, Gregor, 78
mentality, 'African', 83–4
Milner's Kindergarten, 35
miscegenation, 81–2
missionary activities, 10, 71–2; education, 111–12; see also Christianization
Missionary Conferences (1923 & 1926), 117
missionary journals, 33–4
Mitchell, Sir Philip, 6–7
Morel, E. D., 15, 52, 97
Mumford, Dr. W. Bryant, 9
Murray, Prof. A. Victor, 18, 120, 122, 123

Nation and Atheneum, 36
National Review, 36, 50
nationalist leadership, 56
Native Problem in Africa, The, 19
New Education Fellowship Conference (1936), 125
New Fabian Research Bureau, 37; Quarterly, 37
New Statesman, 36
New Statesman and Nation, 36, 146
Nigeria, indirect rule in, 140–41
Nineteenth Century and after (journal), 36

Oldham, J. H., 11–12, 34, 102; and biological determinism, 64–5, 81; political activities, 14, 71–2, 76, 138
Oliver, R. A. C., 80–81
Olivier, Lord, 15
Open Door Principle, 46
Orde-Browne, G. St. J., 9
Ormsby-Gore, W. G. A., 14, 32
Oversea Education (journal), 38, 81, 117
Owen, W. E., 10–11, 147

Padmore, George, 17, 37

Peace Conference settlement, 15
Perham, Margery, 18, 48, 65
Permanent Mandates Commission, 3, 5, 7, 46, 47
Phelps-Stokes Commission, 112–13
Pim, Sir Alan, 18
Political Quarterly, 36–7
primitive, definition of, 62
Pritchard, E. Evans, 13
protectionist attitudes, 92

race, and culture, 80, 84, 136
race classifications, 78
Radcliffe-Brown, A. R., 13, 132
Raglan, Lord, 140
Rattray, R. S., 13, 51, 141
research projects, 101–102
Richards, Audrey, 13
Roscoe, John, 12
Ross, William McGregor, 9
Round Table (journal), 14, 34–5, 50
Royal Colonial Institute, see Royal Empire Society
Royal Empire Society, 31–2, 100
Royal Institute of International Affairs, 36, 100

Scott, H. S., 8–9
Selborne, Earl of, 118
Seligman, C. G., 79–80
Shiels, Dr. Drummond, 15
slave trade, 91
Smith, Edwin W., 12, 31, 117
social anthropology, 62–5
Social-Darwinism, 52–4, 61, 82, 154
social evolution theories, 62–6, 154
Socialist Review, 36, 37
Spectator, 36
Stoddard, Lothrop, 82
Stokes, Robert, 66
Strickland, C. F., 18
Sykes, Sir Frederick, 7

Tariff Commission (1903), 92
Temple, Sir Charles, 5
The Empire in Africa: Labour's Policy, 16
tribal society and institutions, 67–70, 136, 137, 144
trusteeship, 3, 15, 61, 92, 154 and Chap. 3
Tuskegee School, 113, 117

United Empire (journal), 31–2

Vischer, Hanns, 31

Westermann, Diedrich, 12–13, 30
Willoughby, W. C., 11
Wilson, Godfrey, 13
Wilson, Woodrow, 3
Woolf, Leonard, 16, 52, 73, 97, 121,
    122

World Dominion (journal), 34
Worthington, E. B., 102
Wyndham, Hugh, 70–71

Young, T. Cullen, 10, 12

Zimmern, Prof., 133–4

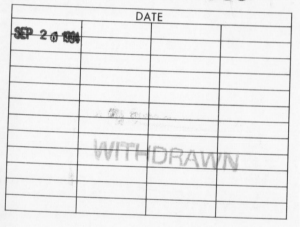

DATE			
SEP 2 0 1994			